PARABLES OF THE MESSIAH

Parables of the Messiah

JOHN CARTER

THE CHRISTADELPHIAN
404 SHAFTMOOR LANE
BIRMINGHAM B28 8SZ

2005

First published 1947
Reprinted 1965
1975
1981
1991
2005

ISBN 0 85189 060 1

Reproduced from copy supplied.
THE CROMWELL PRESS
TROWBRIDGE
WILTSHIRE
ENGLAND
BA14 0XB

PREFACE

THE word parable by derivation means a placing of one thing beside another, from which has arisen the idea of comparison, although this idea is not essentially involved in the meaning of the word. Precise definition of the word is not easy, as may be seen by comparing the attempts that have been made to define it, and by the differences of opinion whether certain sayings should be classified as parables, or as some other figure of speech. The Shorter Oxford Dictionary gives the following meaning: "A comparison, a similitude; any saying or narration in which something is expressed in terms of something else; an allegory, an apologue. Also, any kind of enigmatical or dark saying".

From a particularly Biblical point of view Bengel's definition is good, but not quite adequate: "A parable is a form of speech which by means of a fictitious narration, which yet resembles the truth, and is taken from matters belonging to the usages of ordinary life, represents truths which are less known or of a moral nature".

In the following pages eighty sayings and stories of Jesus have been considered. Some of these might be excluded by a too rigid definition of the word "parable", but we think all are either proper parables, or sayings containing the germ of a parable and therefore capable of being expanded into one. As figures of speech used by Jesus we think readers will approve their inclusion.

The title PARABLES OF THE MESSIAH has been chosen not only because the parables were spoken by Jesus, the Messiah, but because we believe that only by a Messianic interpretation being given to many of them do we reach the meaning Jesus intended. The parables were spoken by the King to people interested in the Kingdom of God. They were a challenge to men to think. The figures Jesus used in his parables were generally connected with Old Testament language concerning the Messiah, failure to discern which hinders recognition of what was in the thought of Jesus. In other words, the Messianic content of the parables is the primary meaning, and to make them merely stories for moral truths robs them of their vital purpose. The reader will judge the truth of this comment as he reads the interpretations of the parables here set forth. The study of the parables pays a rich dividend in fuller understanding of Jesus Christ, as well as of his message; and since so many parables are rooted in the Old Testament it increases the knowledge and understanding of the writings of Moses and the prophets.

Many attempts at classification of the parables have been made, but no scheme can serve more than a very limited purpose. There are many parables which can be placed in one group or another according to the whim or object of the one who classifies them.

To deal with the parables in the order in which we find them in the gospels, beginning with Matthew, appeared the most practical way. This way has been followed therefore. To facilitate comparison between the gospel records, a Table of Contents is supplied with the references in the gospels where a saying or parable is found. This will enable the reader to find easily all the Scriptures concerning any parable dealt with. Since Jesus spoke in many places and would certainly repeat his words, some sayings are reported in one context in one gospel and in another context in another record. The inclusion therefore in the Table of Contents of more than one Scripture reference does not necessarily mean that the references are to the same incident. This should be remembered, as a different context may give a slightly changed accent to a saying, particularly if the saying has the form of a proverb expressed in general terms.

A glance at this table of Scripture references shows which sayings occur in all the synoptists, which occur in two of them, and which are peculiar to one gospel. There were doubtless reasons why each gospel writer included certain episodes in his record and omitted others. The enquiry into those reasons belongs to the study of the gospels as a whole, but so far as the parables are involved in the investigation, the table will help to supply the information.

It will be noticed that there are no parables in the fourth gospel. The word "parable" occurs in the A.V. (John 10 : 6), but it is more correctly translated "proverb" (see R.V.). John's gospel records aspects of the life of the Master that Matthew, Mark and Luke do not touch upon. The character of the discourses is different, the themes discussed are different. That does not mean that John's gospel has no figurative language; on the contrary figures occur on every page; but they are not in the form of parables, but are drawn from Old Testament types. Almost all the discourses in John's gospel are expositions by the Lord of the foreshadowings in the Law of his own work. A brief chapter has been added on this subject, but for fuller consideration of the fourth gospel the reader is referred to the *Exposition of The Gospel of John.*

A Scripture Index of the Parables, and of other scriptures quoted or referred to, is included at the end of the book.

April, 1947.

CONTENTS

(The parallel references are to the records of the same parable, although these are not always connected with the same incident.)

		Matthew	Mark	Luke
1	Salt	5 : 13	... 9 : 49, 50	... 14 : 34, 35
2	Light	5 : 14		
3	Candle and Bushel	5 : 15	... 4 : 21	... 8 : 16; 11 : 33
4	Adversary	5 : 25	...	... 12 : 58, 59
5	Moth, Rust and Thieves	6 : 19-21	...	... 12 : 33, 34
6	The Eye, Single and Evil	6 : 22, 23	...	... 11 : 34-36
7	Fowls and Lilies	6 : 25-34	...	... 12 : 22-31
8	Good Measure	7 : 2	... 4 : 24	... 6 : 38
9	Mote and Beam	7 : 3-5	...	... 6 : 41, 42
10	Dogs and Swine	7 : 6		
11	Bread and Stone, Fish and Serpent	7 : 9, 10	...	... 11 : 11
12	Two Ways	7 : 13, 14	...	... 13 : 23, 24
13	Wolves	7 : 15; 10 : 16		
14	Trees and Fruit	7 : 16-20	...	... 6 : 43, 44
15	Two Builders	7 : 24-27	...	... 6 : 46-49
16	Physician and Patient	9 : 12	... 2 : 17	... 5 : 31
17	The Bridegroom	9 : 15	... 2 : 19	... 5 : 33, 34
18	The Patched Cloth	9 : 16	... 2 : 21	... 5 : 36
19	Wine Skins and New Wine	9 : 17	... 2 : 22	... 5 : 37-39
20	Harvest and Labourers	9 : 36-38	...	... 10 : 2
21	The Cross	10 : 38; 16 : 24	... 8 : 34	... 9 : 23; 14 : 27
22	Reeds, Storm Troopers, Children at play	11 : 7-19	...	... 7 : 18-33
23	The Yoke of Christ	11 : 29		
24	Sheep in Pit	12 : 11, 12		

	Matthew	Mark	Luke
25 Strong Man Spoiled	12 : 22-30	... 3 : 22-30	... 11 : 14-23
26 Unoccupied House	12 : 43-45	...	... 11 : 24-26
27 Sower	13 : 3-9, 18-23	... 4 : 1-20	... 8 : 1-14
28 Tares	13 : 24-30, 36-43		
29 Mustard Seed	13 : 31, 32	... 4 : 30-32	... 13 : 18, 19
30 Leaven	13 : 23	...	... 13 : 20, 21
31 Hid Treasure	13 : 44		
32 Pearl Merchant	13 : 45, 46		
33 Drag Net	13 : 47-50		
34 Instructed Scribe ...	13 : 52		
35 Blind Leaders	15 : 14; 23 : 16	...	... 6 : 39, 41
36 Children and Puppies	15 : 22-28	... 7 : 24-30	...
37 Rock and Keys	16 : 13-19		
38 Faith as Mustard Seed	17 : 20	...	... 17 : 6
39 Amputated Limbs and Lost Sheep ...	18 : 7-13	... 9 : 41-48	
40 Unforgiving Creditor	18 : 23-35		
41 Camel and Needle's Eye	19 : 16-30	... 10 : 17-22	... 18 : 18-23
42 Labourers in Vineyard..................	20 : 1-16		
43 Fig Tree Withered, and Budding	21 : 18-22 24 : 32-35	... 11 : 12-24 ... 13 : 28, 29	 ... 21 : 29-31
44 Two Sons	21 : 28-32		
45 Wicked Husbandmen	21 : 33-41	... 12 : 1-9	... 20 : 9-10
46 Rejected Stone	21 : 42	... 12 : 10, 11	... 20 : 17
47 Marriage Feast	22 : 1-14		
48 Gnat and Camel......	23 : 23, 24		
49 Cup and Platter......	23 : 25, 26	...	... 11 : 39, 40
50 Whited Sepulchres...	23 : 27, 28	...	... 11 : 44
51 Hen and Chickens...	23 : 37	...	... 13 : 34

52	Lightning	24 : 27	...	... 10 : 18; 17 : 24
53	Vultures	24 : 28	...	... 17 : 37
54	Goodman of the House	24 : 42-44	...	... 12 : 39, 40
55	Faithful and Evil Servants	24 : 45-51	...	... 12 : 41-48
56	Ten Virgins	25 : 1-13		
57	Talents	25 : 14-30		
58	Sheep and Goats	25 : 31-46		
59	Growing Seed		... 4 : 26-29	
60	Two Debtors		...	... 7 : 41-43
61	Tests for Discipleship	8 : 19-22	...	... 9 : 57-62
62	Good Samaritan		...	... 10 : 25-37
63	Friend at Midnight		...	... 11 : 5-13
64	Rich Fool		...	... 12 : 16-21
65	Lord Who Serves		...	... 12 : 35-38
66	Fire and Water		...	... 12 : 49
67	Ass or Ox in Pit		...	... 14 : 5
68	Lowest Place		...	... 14 : 7-11
69	Rules for Hosts		...	... 14 : 12-14
70	Great Supper		...	... 14 : 16-24
71	Tower Builder and Warring King		...	... 14 : 28-32
72	Lost Sheep		...	... 15 : 3-7
73	Lost Coin		...	... 15 : 8-10
74	Lost Son		...	... 15 : 11-32
75	Unjust Steward		...	... 16 : 1-12
76	Rich Man and Lazarus		...	... 16 : 19-31
77	Unprofitable Servants		...	... 17 : 7-10
78	Unjust Judge		...	... 18 : 1-8
79	Pharisee and Publican		...	... 18 : 9-15
80	The Pounds		...	... 19 : 12-27
	Postscript on John's Gospel			

PARABLES OF THE MESSIAH

I

SALT

(Matt. 5 : 13; Mark 9 : 49, 50; Luke 14 : 34, 35)

In these passages we find that three times in his teaching Jesus refers to salt, and always in a figurative sense. While perhaps not strictly parables, they are closely related forms of speech. We take each in turn.

(1) The first is in the Sermon on the Mount, and follows immediately after the Beatitudes. Jesus had declared who are "blessed"; and all the Beatitudes until the last one were expressed objectively: "Blessed are *the poor*"; but in the last, while he began "Blessed are *they*" he at once applied it to the disciples: "Blessed are *ye*, when men shall reproach *you*". This transition to the direct address leads on to saying: "Ye are the salt of the earth: but if the salt have lost its savour, wherewith shall it be salted? It is thenceforth good for nothing but to be cast out, and to be trodden under foot of men" (Matt. 5 : 13). The "blessed", his disciples, are "the salt of the earth". The phrase has become a cliche, forbidden to humorists by the B.B.C., and, spoken as hackneyed words, has taken on a different shade of meaning from when used by Jesus.

Salt preserves and gives flavour to food. The fishermen among Christ's hearers knew how quickly their harvest of the sea corrupted unless taken to the pickling vats of Bethsaida. All his listeners knew that in the warm atmosphere of their land any dead thing quickly became tainted and perished. In what way, then, were the "blessed" like unto salt? The general view, the easy interpretation, is that the disciples of Jesus are the preserving element in society, preventing by their influence the spread of corruption. Some go so far as to say that as Sodom would have been saved for ten righteous men's sake, so the world is not destroyed because of the "Christians" in it. There is an element of truth in these ideas: for "the elect's sake" God does direct the world for the development of His purpose; and the moral principles of Christ's teaching have in measure affected for good some things in "society"; but it remains that the "world" will be destroyed, and that because of the unchecked corruption in it.

It would seem to be rather of the "savour" that Jesus is thinking, for he at once speaks of this being lost, while no mention is made of the preserving power: and men are "salt" as they have the savour of salt—men as they are in themselves and not as they influence their fellows. This is borne out when we remember that Jesus uses two figures in one breath: his disciples are "salt" and they are "the light of the world"; the one saying describes their own quality and the second their relationship to those about. His disciples then, who show meekness, mercy, purity of heart, desire for righteousness, have the wholesomeness and the "savour" that God desires. They can lose this quality, as salt in Palestine does lose its saltness and is then fit for no useful purpose. Thomson, in *The Land and the Book,* tells of an importer trying to cheat, losing money by his salt losing its saltness.

(2) Mark's reference brings in another association of salt, with other ideas involved which Jesus must have had in mind in all his allusions to salt. Passing through Galilee, he foretold his death and resurrection; but the apostles had other preoccupations which prevented them following his thought when he spoke of suffering and death; they were discussing which one of them should be the greater in the kingdom he was to establish. Their minds were so fixed on an immediate restoration of this kingdom that they could not think of Jesus dying. They were so concerned with their own pre-eminence that they had no sympathy for the leader whose mind was fixed on effacement of self, and suffering and sacrifice. Jesus proceeded to teach them that the way to exaltation was by the abasement of self: "If any man desire to be first, the same shall be last of all, and servant

of all". Jesus took a child, and pointed out the need for childlikeness of disposition; he then said that it was better that a disciple should now sacrifice hand or foot or eye, if it be necessary, than by keeping them be cast at last into Gehenna and be completely destroyed. Then he gave the reason for this counsel: "For every one shall be salted with fire, and every sacrifice shall be salted with salt. Salt is good: but if the salt have lost his saltness, wherewith shall ye season it? Have salt in yourselves, and have peace one with another" (9 : 49, 50).

Here again the context is the guide. Jesus had put before them the amputation of desire now, or complete destruction—"where their fire is not quenched"—in the future. To escape the latter everyone must now be "salted with fire"; and the verb "salted" recurs: "every sacrifice shall be salted with salt"; and this second occurrence explains the first. It refers us to the Law of the Offerings. While leaven and honey were forbidden adjuncts of the meal offering, both being agents of fermentation, salt was essential: "Every oblation of thy meat offering shalt thou season with salt: neither shalt thou suffer the salt of the covenant of thy God to be lacking from thy meat offering: with all thine offerings thou shalt offer salt" (Lev. 2 : 13).

The salt with the meal offering was a token of covenant relationship. To partake of a meal together was a "covenant of salt" between men. It was a covenant ratified by a meal. So rigid was this rule that the story is told of a thief who partook of food in a tent, and when caught escaped punishment because the sheik regarded the act of partaking of food, even under those circumstances, as a "covenant of salt". The salt with the offering spoke of the covenant by virtue of which the meal offering was acceptable. Remembering this, and that Lev. 2 : 13 is the source of the phrase used by Jesus, his meaning must be that as every offering must be made in the bonds of covenant (salted with salt) so the cutting off of the desires of sin were essential as a condition of offering (salted with fire). Fire is purifying; to be salted with fire is to be purified as the covenant requires, removing stumbling blocks even at the cost of limbs.

Jesus makes the personal application to the situation before him, when contentious men in self-esteem were seeking precedence over each other. He also uses the phrase on other occasions about salt losing its saltness. They were "salt" as he had before told them: and in this context the greater fulness of his thought is seen. They had savour and wholesomeness as being in God's covenant. They could lose their "saltness" by unworthy thought and rivalry: were, in fact, in danger of doing so then. In sharing the covenant sacrifice which he was making in subduing his will to the Father's will, they would resolve their disputes. When self is placed on the altar contentions regarding precedence do not arise. "Have salt in yourselves, and have peace one with another", he therefore counsels. In other words: "Keep in yourselves covenant principles, as God's people; make the needful sacrifice of self; and your contentions will pass and you will have peace among yourselves".

Paul has an echo of these sayings in Col. 4 : 6: "Let your speech be always with grace, seasoned with salt, that ye may know how ye ought to answer every man". The parallel in Eph. 4 : 29 is instructive, and reads: "Let no corrupt communication proceed out of your mouth, but that which is good to the use of edifying, that it may minister grace unto the hearers".

A corrupt, or putrid word, is unwholesome and unfitted for the mouths of saints. It is not good, does not build up, nor minister grace. Speech seasoned with salt is clean, of good tang, of the quality that belongs to God's covenant—which Paul expresses in characteristic fashion as "with grace" and "ministering grace", using a word which allows the play of graciousness with the deeper meaning of the relationship between God and man made possible by God's favour. Speech "seasoned with salt" is such as may be heard by God acceptably; speech free from the foul and the suggestive, which are so often conspicuous in the talk of men.

(3) The saying in Luke's record forms part of an address to the multitudes crowding around Jesus, in which he warns them of the demands of discipleship. There came a time when men had to decide about him; they could not follow lightheartedly out of curiosity, or to see the sensational cures, or to share in his provisions for their need. Three times he uses the words "cannot be my disciple" (14 : 26, 27, 33). The man who puts first home ties and the affections of the present, and even his own life; the man unprepared to crucify his "self"; the man who cannot finish the task begun, renouncing all that he hath—none of these can be his disciples. "Salt therefore is good", he continues, but "if even the salt have lost its savour, wherewith shall it be seasoned?" To follow him was to take on the tang of salt that made them acceptable. But the "savour" must be retained, or it became unprofitable. So, too, would they if they did not count the cost and in patient continuance endure to the end.

"Wherewith shall *it* be salted?" The emphasis is on the "it". Degenerate salt cannot be "salted"; and how can people who have taken on the quality of salt, losing it, be acceptable? Neither is of use, as Jesus emphasizes. Salt in limited quantities was good for the land; it was mixed with the manure-heap; but "saltless" salt could serve no purpose at all. Men threw it away.

2
LIGHT
(Matt. 5 : 14)

"YE are the salt . . . ye are the light" (Matt. 5 : 14). We have suggested that the first is designed to show what men should be in themselves, while the second sets forth their duty to others. That does not exclude what they must be, for that which gives light is itself light, and darkness does not dispel gloom.

The "great light" is the sun which gives light to the earth. The appointment of the sun to divide the night from the day in the Creator's arrangement of the world in preparation for man is the basis of many figures in both Old and New Testaments. The world natural has analogies in the world spiritual: there is a parallel between the physical and the moral.

First and foremost Christ is the sun of the moral world, and because of this, also the appointed ruler of the world that is to be. "Arise, shine for thy light is come", is the call to Zion in the day when the Redeemer returns (Isa. 59 : 20; 60 : 1), and in the closing words of the chapter the prophet declares: "The sun shall be no more thy light by day; neither for brightness shall the moon give light unto thee: but the Lord shall be unto thee an everlasting light, and thy God thy glory. Thy sun shall no more go down; neither shall thy moon withdraw itself: for the Lord shall be thine everlasting light, and the days of thy mourning shall be ended" (verses 19, 20). The Messiah is "the sun of righteousness" to rise with healing upon a world full of darkness (Mal. 4 : 2).

John traces the parallel between the natural light and the revelation of God's purpose, which gives men light. In the word was life, and "the life was the light of men. And the light shineth in darkness" (1 : 3). That was the prophetic word—a light shining in a dark place, as Peter wrote (2 Pet. 1 : 19), to which men do well to give heed.

At last the purpose was embodied in a Son of God, the word made flesh, and the true light had appeared among men. John records the sayings in which the Son declares himself to be light, the light of the world (8 : 12; 9 : 5; 11 : 9). The Son counselled those who followed him to walk in his light, to believe the light, and so doing they would be "children of light" (12 : 35, 36), or "sons of light"—a Hebrew idiom which expresses their essential characteristic; they are themselves light.

Isaiah (50 : 10), testifying of the instructed and obedient servant of God, smitten and reviled of men, but justified of God, asks a question which was an anticipation of these sayings of Jesus. "Who is among you that feareth the Lord, that obeyeth the voice of his servant, that walketh in darkness, and hath no light?" It is a question that demands for its answer, None. All who follow the Servant walk in light. Therefore God encourages such: "Let him trust in the name of the Lord, and stay upon his God". It is clear that the phrases of Jesus are echoes of this saying of the prophet. The other side is also stated. Men love human philosophies which they regard as light. Doctrines are proclaimed and approved by men which are but fables of human devising. To such "fire-raisers" God says: "Behold, all ye that kindle a fire, that compass yourselves about with sparks: walk in the light of your fire, and in the sparks that ye have kindled. This shall ye have of mine hand; ye shall lie down in sorrow". The sparks quickly die out, and men sink into darkness, lying down at last in sorrow for an eternal sleep. Both these followers and rejecters of the divine light have a similar place in the teaching of Jesus: "I am come a light into the world, that whosoever believeth on me should not abide in darkness; and if any man hear my words and believe not, I judge him not . . . the word that I have spoken shall judge him in the last day" (John 12 : 46-48).

"The gospel of the glory of Christ" is light, shining into the darkness and transforming men and women. In a sentence which joins together the thought of the creative light of Gen. 1 with the Shekinah glory revealed first in the tabernacle, then in the temple, and afterwards in the Son of God, Paul says: "In whom the god of this world hath blinded the minds of them which believe not, lest the light of the glorious gospel of Christ (gospel of the glory of Christ, R.V.), who is the image of God, should shine unto them" (2 Cor. 4 : 4). Using the metaphor boldly, Paul wrote to the Ephesians that "ye were sometimes darkness, but now are ye light in the Lord: walk as children of light". They were not merely in darkness, but were darkness: they have become light, and therefore, taking up the phrase of Jesus, they are "sons of light" (Eph. 5 : 8).

Israel's darkness when Christ appeared was dense: but "the people that walked in darkness saw a great light" (Isa. 9 : 2; Matt. 4 : 16). The state of Christendom at the second advent will be one of "gross darkness" (Isa. 60 : 2), although the world is full of Bibles translated into nearly every tongue. But when all who are enlightened are gathered into the city of God, it is written—and the language reflects the words of Jesus in Matt. 5 : 14-16—"The city hath no need of the sun, neither of the moon to shine upon it; for the glory of God did lighten it, and the lamp thereof is the Lamb" (Rev. 21 : 23).

"Ye are the light of the world"—the words are a testimony to the exalted position of those who know and believe the truth in Jesus, and also to their very grave responsibility. Light shines—it is its nature so to do; so does the light of God's truth. Both forms of light can only be prevented from shining by obstruction. The function of the disciple is to shine—he is failing in duty if light is not radiating from him. This does not apply solely to the spoken word by which the gospel is proclaimed. He who was "the Light" himself preached; but he also walked in light, as he counselled other men to do. Both aspects are included in Paul's words: "Do all things without murmurings and disputings; that ye may be blameless and harmless, the sons of God, without rebuke, in the midst of a crooked and perverse nation, among whom ye shine as lights in the world; holding forth the word of life" (Phil. 2 : 14-16).

3
A CANDLE AND A BUSHEL

(Matt. 5 : 15-16; Mark 4 : 21-25; Luke 8 : 16; 11 : 33)

CLOSELY related to the words of Jesus about Light is the reference to a candle and a bushel: "A city that is set on a hill cannot be hid. Neither do men light a candle, and put it under a bushel, but on a candlestick: and it giveth light unto all that are in the house. Let your light so shine before men, that they may see your good works, and glorify your Father, which is in heaven" (Matt. 5 : 14-16).

The figure must have been used many times by Jesus with such variations as occasion prompted. Mark 4 : 21 gives the saying, with the added words "or under a bed", following the parable of the sower. Luke records the saying twice, once like Mark after the parable of the Sower, and once later in the ministry (8 : 16; 11 : 33).

The emphasis varies on each of the three occasions when the words were spoken, and each, therefore, calls for separate notice.

Men do not do so absurd a thing as to light a candle and then obscure the light; that would be to undo their own action; neither do they risk setting fire to a bushel. Neither does God do absurd things. Men enlightened by God's truth are lights: lights to shine, not to be hidden. As all in a house share the blessing of the light, so by the disciple's shining other men must find it possible to see "good works" and glorify the Father in heaven.

What are bushels? They are vessels for measuring, for buying and for selling. These activities have a right and proper use in life, but they must not be allowed to obscure the light of God's truth. The "cares of this life" can easily be a snare: and, forgetful of the care of the Heavenly Father, His children can act as though He did not exist. Men engrossed only in present things were swept away at the flood; and Jesus says it will be so again when he returns.

A proverb says: "As the door turneth upon his hinges, so doth the slothful man upon his bed" (26 : 14). To hide the light under a bed suggests that ease and sloth are hindrances to its shining. In the setting of the sower parable, Jesus appears to be thinking principally of the duty of the light-bearer as such. Those who hear and understand him, were like lit lamps that any coming into the house may see (Luke 8 : 16). He adds, "For nothing is secret that shall not be made manifest; neither anything hid that shall not be known and come abroad" (verse 17). He had illustrated this saying in his explanation of the parable: the "secret" of it had been "made manifest". Hearing his explanation they became custodians of the knowledge he imparted, and as a consequence had responsibilities as teachers. He stressed that responsibility by adding: "Take heed how ye hear"; "what ye hear" (Mark); and so heeding they would find increase of knowledge. The receptive listeners grow in understanding; the dull and unresponsive lose what they have. Such in this context appears to be the meaning of the words: "for whosoever hath to him shall be given; and whosoever hath not, from him shall be taken even that which he seemeth to have" (verse 18).

On the later occasion (Luke 11 : 33), while the saying is expressed in general terms Jesus is, however, referring to himself. He rebuked his generation for wanting a "sign"; and he recalled that the Queen of Sheba *came* from the utmost part of the earth to hear Solomon; and the Ninevites repented at the preaching of Jonah. He himself was a lamp God had lit—clearly to be seen, "that they which *come* in may see the light". Were they ready to come in, and to listen to him, "to see the light"? He does not pass to the second aspect of repenting. For unless they came and saw they could not repent. He then spoke of the "single eye" and warned them of the darkness in which they were enshrouded. The saying about the "eye" occurs in the context of Matthew (6 : 22) and is considered separately.

Jesus adapts his language to the occasion, and the same words do not bear the identical meaning in every context. We may therefore feel justified in seeing in his sayings certain principles which he adapted in his teaching to the changing circumstances. Thus the people of Israel, planted in the central land of Palestine, were as a city set on a hill which could not be hid. They were a lamp on a candlestick. Had they now moved the lamp and covered it by a bed or bushel, by ease and pleasure or business? The saying applies also to individual disciples.

The rule was there even for Jesus himself, for he so applies it: and in this particular application we may go a stage further. The figure of a lamp is used in the Old Testament of the word of God (Psa. 119 : 105); of God Himself (2 Sam. 22 : 29). The word lights the path of God's servants; and God lightens their darkness. David himself is also "the lamp of Israel" (2 Sam. 21 : 17). But Israel's Messiah too is a lamp, as is shown by the parallelism:

"There will I make *the horn* of David to bud:
I have ordained *a lamp* for mine anointed"
(Psa. 132 : 17).

In a Jewish house a lamp was kept burning all night; a lamp extinguished denoted distress and disaster. For the lamp of the wicked man to be put out was for the disaster of death to befall him. Because of the horn of David that will bud, David's line will be perpetuated: the Messiah is a lamp not to be eclipsed. When Jesus compared himself to a lamp lit by God, did he think of this promise with its guarantee that the darkness would not overwhelm him?

If his disciples in this way connected his language to Old Testament promises, they would see that his coming was not always for the rejection and humiliation they were then witnessing, but to be a light with unhindered shining.

4
THINE ADVERSARY
(Matt. 5 : 25; Luke 12 : 58, 59)

MEN generally dislike to contemplate God's severity. Many who believe in God but do not regard the whole of the Bible as a revelation from Him, so emphasize the other side of God's character—His goodness—that they do not find a proper place for the sterner attributes. Yet, if God is a God of holiness and righteousness, then, when necessary, this severity must find expression.

God is a God of judgment. This has been shown in man's history many times: at the Flood; when human speech was confounded; at the times of national crises in Israel's affairs, when the kingdom was first overturned, and again when Jerusalem was destroyed by Titus. As the vials of wrath are reaching their close another day of judgment, now on a Gentile world, draws near.

God became "the enemy" of His own people, as Isaiah testifies: "They rebelled and vexed his holy spirit: therefore he was turned to be their enemy, and himself fought against them" (63 : 10). Human enemies can be terrible, but when God becomes an enemy there is greater cause for fear. The long and tragic story of Israel's woes is witness.

This statement by Isaiah supplies the key to the saying of Jesus, twice recorded, but in different contexts. The first occurrence is in Matt. 5 : 25: "Agree with thine adversary quickly, whiles thou art in the way with him; lest at any time the adversary deliver thee to the judge, and the judge deliver thee to the officer, and thou be cast into prison. Verily I say unto thee, Thou shalt by no means come out thence till thou hast paid the uttermost farthing". The verses have been thought to be disconnected from the context, and therefore it has been suggested that they are an interpolation. There is, however, a close connection with what precedes. Jesus had pointed out the seriousness of treating one's brother with contempt and disdain (verse 22), rating such conduct with offences that deserved capital punishment. He emphasizes his teaching by adding that if a man has done something to another that might lead him to feel anger and contempt, he had better leave his sacrifice unoffered and go seek to put right his offence. His worship otherwise would not be acceptable. Not only so, but God would become his adversary, and He would demand full penalty for the wrong.

In this setting the "adversary parable" denotes the divine hatred of a man's persistence in wrong towards another—a hatred that will not let the offender escape. Rectify the wrong with your fellow, says Jesus; and so doing, take the opportunity to find agreement with God, for if you fail to agree with God while the chance is here, the consequences will inevitably have to be met.

Roman law, which was operative in Judea, gave a creditor a right to summon his debtors to follow him to the court of the magistrate. While on the way it was possible to effect a settlement without any action by the authorities. Once at the court, the issue was outside the power of the disputants, and the debt became a crime to be dealt with by the State. Once the summons had been issued only a short time remained to make peace, and a man was wise in seizing the opportunity.

Two phrases from the Old Testament illustrate this feature of opportunity. Because God forgives, David says, "Every one that is godly shall pray unto thee, in a time when thou mayest be found" (Psa. 32 : 6). "Seek ye the Lord while he may be found, call ye upon him while he is near; let the wicked forsake his way, and the unrighteous man his thoughts; and let him return unto the Lord, and he will have mercy upon him; and to our God, for he will abundantly pardon" (Isa. 55 : 6).

The second reference to the parable of "the adversary", has the same meaning in principle; it is applied, however, not to individuals as in the Sermon on the Mount, but to the nation of Israel (Luke 12 : 58, 59). In this case it is quite evident that the "adversary" of the parable is God; an application which confirms the interpretation of Matt. 5 : 25, where the meaning is not so obvious but where it is seen to be the correct interpretation when the whole context is taken into account. In the context in Luke, Jesus rebukes the Jews for being weather-wise, but sadly undiscerning in the recognition of the signs of the times. It was a day of visitation without a parallel in human history. God's Son was in their midst, making God's last appeal to the nation. Knowing that they would reject him and that calamities would come upon them in consequence, he said: "I am come to send fire on the earth; and what will I, if it be already kindled?" (verse 49). So it was; and the day of opportunity was nearing its close. He therefore urged agreement with the Adversary at once. God in Christ was calling them to account and if they failed to agree with Him their national freedom would be taken away. God, their judge, would use the Romans as His officers, and the Gentile world would become their gaol. The terms of the parable in this latter case readily find a counterpart in what has befallen the nation.

The parable in both individual and national application is full of solemn warning. It makes more urgent the counsel of Jesus to fear not man, whose powers are limited to the present, but to fear God, who can both guide the present and decide the future.

5
MOTH, RUST AND THIEVES

(Matt. 6 : 19-21; Luke 12 : 33, 34)

JESUS gave counsel concerning men's ambition with regard to wealth, expressed in figures which could easily be expanded into parables. Using the parallelism so often employed by the psalmist and prophets, he says:

"Lay not up for yourselves treasures upon earth,
Where moth and rust doth corrupt,
And where thieves break through and steal:

But lay up up for yourselves treasures in heaven,
Where neither moth nor rust doth corrupt
And where thieves do not break through nor steal:

For where your treasure is, there will your heart be also" (Matt. 6 : 19-21).

The form of society depicted in these verses is simple, where wealth is hoarded in the house. The treasure is in the form of linen, fabrics, or other costly apparel, or in metal. Some may have been buried for security, as mud houses did not offer much resistance to a thief, who gained an entrance by simply digging through the wall. All worldly wealth is subject to influences which can destroy it. In the days of Jesus moths spoilt the fabric, rust the metals, and thieves were a constant danger. The same influences may not operate today—precautions against such simple agents of destruction as moths are more available; and safes and strong rooms offer more protection than mud walls. But, as the wealth in an industrial age takes other forms than in ancient times, in which it appears less tangible, so agents more subtle than of old can destroy with no less certainty. Economic crises, commercial failures, etc., can today bring losses greater and more complete.

In contrast with ephemeral wealth there are treasures which can be stored in heaven, immune from loss by human action. Less apparent these treasures may be; but they are more satisfying to the possessor of them. They are assessed by faith, and "will be found unto praise and honour and glory at the appearing of Jesus Christ" (1 Pet. 2 : 7). A man may be rich in temporal possessions and also rich toward God. Abraham was such, and God called him His friend. But for the most part, men who reckon values in bank balances do not hold treasure in heaven in great esteem. The majority of men are paupers by both standards; and even poor men and women may be consumed by avarice as destructive of peace as in the case of those who, being rich, seek more wealth. But, as Jesus said, rich men generally find it hard to enter God's kingdom; when "to the poor the gospel is preached" there is a greater response.

Possessions test the character, and this test is indicated in the further reason Jesus gives for his counsel. Where the treasure is the heart will be. Human wealth is very relative. The poor today are rich compared with standards in other ages. But whatever its value, the possessor's assessment of it in relation to heavenly wealth is the standard of judgment he applies. If treasure in heaven holds highest place, the heart is drawn thither, and then the saying might even be inverted with truth, that where the heart is, there will the treasure be.

Not many would take the words of Jesus with a prosaic literalness, as though the command forbade any store. He was using a common eastern figure for emphasis. "Lay not up this . . . but lay up that." It has been said: "In Hebrew 'not' often means 'not only—but also' or 'not so much—as'. In other words, 'not' is often used to deny, not absolutely, but conditionally and comparatively".

6

THE EYE: "SINGLE" AND "EVIL"

(Matt. 6 : 22, 23; Luke 11 : 34-36)

"THE lamp of the body is the eye . . ."

By means of the eye we know of the existence of light; it is like a lamp to the body. We "see" by means of the eye, and it therefore easily becomes a figure of mental and spiritual "seeing". In this saying Jesus is not concerned so much with the function of the eye as with the spiritual things of which it had become a figure. At the same time he has something to say about the physical health of the eye because he is thinking of the spiritual wholeness that he desires in men.

If the eye is "single" the body is full of light; if "evil" the body is full of darkness. We have two eyes, but when in proper working order they see but one object. When the eyes are not sound, men may see double; the eye is not single. The malady has its spiritual counterpart as Jesus indicates.

First we must notice that the metaphor was common among the Jews. They were familiar with his meaning; but we may be familiar with his words but not so ready to pick up the meaning. Moses spoke of a man's "eye being evil against thy poor brother" in the year of release, and of his failing therefore to give him anything (Deut. 15 : 9). Solomon warns against eating the bread of "him that hath an evil eye", for as he thinketh in his heart so is he (Prov. 23 : 6, 7). The evil eye is the outward indication of the evil heart, and the heart reveals the real man. Solomon also says that "he that hasteth to be rich hath an evil eye, and considereth not that evil shall come upon him" (28 : 22). It is significant that the figure is thus used in connection with possessions. Wealth, the proverb said, can easily distort the vision: and then there is no clear perception of essential values. "Evil" therefore, as Hatch (*Essays in Biblical Greek*) suggests, has in this context the meaning of "niggardly". The single eye, by contrast, denotes a generous soul. This application of the terms "single" and "evil" in the saying of Jesus is established by the context, for he has been speaking of the treasure upon which men set their hearts. It is also borne out by a number of references where Paul uses the same word. He urges upon the Corinthians the good example of the Macedonians and "of the grace of God bestowed" on them, "how that in a great trial of affliction the abundance of their joy and their deep poverty abounded unto the riches of their liberality" (marg.: simplicity; R.V. marg. Gr. singleness—2 Cor. 8 : 1, 2). With that completeness that Paul feels always marks divine grace, he reminded the same ecclesia that "God is able to make *all* grace abound toward you; that ye *always* having *all* sufficiency in *all* things, may abound to *every* good work . . . being enriched in *everything* to *all* bountifulness" (marg. Or, liberality, Gr. simplicity; R.V. marg. Gr. singleness). He encourages them in their collection for the poor, because thereby the beneficiaries would "glorify God for your professed subjection unto the gospel of Christ and for your liberal (R.V. marg. "singleness") distribution unto them" (9 : 8, 11, 13). In Rom. 12 : 8 the translators have reversed the text and margin of the quotations given: "he that giveth, let him do it with simplicity" (marg. Or, "liberally"). The word occurs in Eph. 6 : 5, 6, and the parallel in Col. 3 : 22, of the single-motived service the bondslave in Christ must give to his master, and Paul repeats his counsel, using the figure of the eye. "Servants, be obedient to them that are your masters according to the flesh, with fear and trembling in singleness of your heart, as unto Christ; not with eye-service, as men-pleasers; but as the servants of Christ, doing the will of God from the heart."

In the pamphlet which was issued to set out the aims of the American R.S.V. translation of the New Testament, entitled: *Introduction to the Revised Standard Version of the*

New Testament, American edition, occurs the following: "If the terms 'single eye' and 'evil eye' are retained in a translation, or are rendered, as in this translation, by 'sound' and 'not sound', it is chiefly because nothing less than a commentary seems available to remind the reader that the eye was regarded as the seat of greed or of the reverse, and that the 'single eye' does not mean unity of aim but generosity, and that 'evil eye' does not in this context mean magic but what, using another part of the anatomy, we might designate as tightfistedness".

It is interesting to notice that Paul uses the word "single" in the passages quoted with the same meaning as Jesus had used it. This suggests a knowledge of the gospel record earlier than is generally regarded as possible for one to have been written. There is the additional parallel that both Jesus and Paul warn men that they cannot serve two masters; men cannot serve God and mammon (Matt. 6 : 24). A man "double eyed" may try to keep an eye on two masters: but it "cannot" be done, Jesus says. It would end, sooner or later, in the displeasure of both masters. The basis of the language is, of course, slavery—where a man is entirely possessed by a master. If two claim his services, he must ignore one.

If a man has power of sight and yet the effect is darkness, it betokens a dark state indeed within the man. "How great is that darkness !" Conversely, as Jesus said when he used the figure of the single eye in the context given by Luke (11 : 33-36), if the eye is single, the whole body is full of light. "If thy whole body therefore be full of light, having no part dark, the whole shall be full of light, as when the bright shining of a candle doth give thee light."

The counsel of Jesus enunciates a principle of wider application than is given to it in the context. Men and women may be prevented from seeing "whole" by other things than lust for wealth. We say a man has a "jaundiced outlook" when the "liverish" mind of the man disables him from seeing any good in others. Prejudice, envy and all the evils that spring from the undisciplined heart, are distorting influences.

Nevertheless, the immediate occasion concerns men's passion for wealth. It is a danger greater even in our industrialized age than in the much simpler times of Jesus. One close observer of men in modern times has written: "When one sees the way in which wealth-getting enters as an ideal into the very bone and marrow of our generation, one wonders whether a revival of the belief that poverty is a worthy religious vocation may not be the spiritual reform which our time stands most in need of . . . We have grown literally afraid to be poor. We despise anyone who elects to be poor in order to simplify and save his inner life. There are thousands of conjunctures in which a wealth-bound man must be a slave, whilst a man for whom poverty has no terrors becomes a freeman. Think of the strength which personal indifference to poverty would give us if we were devoted to unpopular causes. We need no longer hold our tongues or fear to vote the revolutionary or reformatory ticket. Our stocks might fall, our hopes of promotion vanish, our salaries stop, our club doors close in our faces; yet, while we lived, we would imperturbably bear witness to the spirit, and our example would help to set free our generation . . . I recommend this matter to your serious pondering, for it is certain that the prevalent fear of poverty among the educated classes is the worst moral disease from which our civilization suffers".

7
FOWLS AND LILIES

(Matt. 6 : 25-34; Luke 12 : 22-31)

JESUS draws many parables from the countryside, and speaks with an understanding which reveals the sympathetic knowledge of one who observed everything. It has been said: "In the gospels we find . . . faithfulness to living nature . . . a country-bred boy with the same love for bird and beast and the wild open country side.

The Earth
And common face of Nature spake to me
Rememberable things.

"Nature is enough for Jesus . . . She is just splendid and lovable and true as God made her; she slides into his mind whenever he is deeply moved. Think of all the parables he draws from Nature—the similes, metaphors and illustrations; every one of them will bear examination and means more the nearer we look into it and the better we know the living thing behind".

The reference to fowls and lilies in the Sermon on the Mount springs out of his statement that men cannot be bondslaves to two masters, and he calls the one master Mammon, because men are so easily drawn into its servitude. Jesus would have men free from this slavery; free from over-anxiety about the needs of the present. Three times in these verses he says, "Do not be anxious". Our A.V. has "Take no thought", a translation which today can easily mislead. In the seventeenth century "thought" meant "anxious care"; and the R.V. translates "Be not anxious"; in homely speech we would say, "Do not worry".

On the first occasion Jesus says:

"Be not anxious for your life;
What ye shall eat, or what ye shall drink;
Nor yet for your body, what ye shall put on.
Is not the life more than meat
And the body than raiment?"

If we had not life, we should not need food; and if we had not bodies we should not need clothing. We did not give ourselves life or bodies. Ultimately they have their source in God's creative power. If God has made man, is He not then interested in providing for him? That is how Jesus looks at it. So he gives two short parables, to show that, in His care for His creatures, God provides food and clothing.

"Behold the fowls of the air;
For they sow not,
Neither do they reap,
Nor gather into barns:
Yet your heavenly Father feedeth them.
Are ye not much better than they?"

There seems to be good reason for the view that the year during which Jesus gave this address was the "fallow" year for the ground, when men neither sowed nor reaped. The birds were faring well on the corn ungathered. Later in the same year Jesus had compassion on the multitude and fed them—an act of particular benefit when food was getting scarce.

Jesus asks another question also. He uses a word which can mean either "age" or "stature"; the margin of the R.V. gives "age". "Which of you by being anxious can add one cubit to his age?" Men do not try to add a cubit to their height; they do try to add to the length of their lives. But anxiety does not add to length of life—it shortens it, and that is what Jesus means. Too great anxiety about the sustenance of life can shorten the life itself.

He draws a lesson from the flowers of the field:

"Consider the lilies of the field,
How they grow;
They toil not,
Neither do they spin:
And yet I say unto you,
That even Solomon in all his glory
Was not arrayed like one of these."

If Jesus had in mind the scarlet anemone we can see a likeness to the royal robes of Solomon, and the comparison is enhanced. In any case, as a microscope clearly shows, the clothing man makes, however good or gorgeous, does not compare with the wondrous colouring and beauty of the flower of the field.

God clothes the grass of the field, which in a short time is gathered for fuel for the ovens. The grass itself is clothing for the earth, holding the soil which otherwise would be scattered by the wind, thus leaving bare rocks from which nothing could be produced. Over-grazing and forest denudation have produced more than one "dust bowl" making thousands of acres of land unfruitful. The grass itself is clothed, as Jesus said. "The stem is hollow, provided at intervals with knots and invested as if by some mysterious process of electrotype with a thin coating of flint." That coating gives it the strength, with lightness and elegance, to stand upright with a surprising length of stem compared with its diameter.

How simply does Jesus see in these things the hand of the Father in heaven. The world is God's world, full of evidence that He cares for it; and Jesus argues from the smaller to the greater—God cares for His children.

The lesson would be misapplied if it were made an excuse for carelessness or indifference about providing necessary things. It is anxiety, not diligence, that is reproved. "Take no thought" does not mean thoughtlessness. The plant that grows is busy in all its parts—roots, leaves and flowers; more obvious is the industry of the birds in seeking their food, in gathering materials for their nests, and in the untiring labours to feed their young. Yet it is all done with freedom from anxiety.

In effect, Jesus says that anxious efforts to store for the future imply a trust in wealth which is really a worship of mammon, or, in Paul's words, "Covetousness which is idolatry". Men who do not know God act in that way: "after these things do the Gentiles seek"; but men who know God know also that He knows their need. Jesus sums up the lesson: "Seek ye first the kingdom of God, and his righteousness; and all these things shall be added unto you" (Matt. 6 : 33); and gives the wise counsel that each day's cares are enough for that day; the cares of today and tomorrow—a double load—make a burden that taxes the strength, and distracts the mind from essential things.

8
GOOD MEASURE
(Matt. 7 : 2; Mark 4 : 24; Luke 6 : 38)

CONDEMNING a criticizing spirit, Jesus said, "Judge not, that ye be not judged". We may infer the general tendency to this habit from the use of the present tense: "Be not judging". If we are too critical of others we shall be criticized severely ourselves. None are free from faults but all should be careful about passing judgment on others.

In this saying Jesus is not speaking of those decisions that have to be made in many affairs of life. There are matters where it would be wrong to avoid judging, matters where the spirit of toleration is as great an evil as hyper-criticism. There are few fixed standards of right and wrong in the world, and this leads to an easy acceptance of all conduct as being entirely an individual matter. But Jesus himself on occasion was very severe, and he calls for the exercise of discrimination on the part of those who follow him. The instructions to the injured person, if his "brother trespass against" him, to show him his fault, of itself implies a judgment. A collective judgment is called for if the matter has to come before "the church". To "try the spirits", and to "prove all things", to refuse false doctrine and the teachers of it (Gal. 1 : 9; 2 John 10-11)—all these demand the exercise of judgment.

What Jesus condemns is the frame of mind that is always fault-finding. So common is the habit that many proverbs in our own tongue refer to it, such as "people who live in glass houses should not throw stones", or the one about the pot calling the kettle black.

Jesus drives home the lesson by a proverb easily expanded into a parable. "With what measure ye mete, it shall be measured to you again." As Jesus went from place to place he would repeat his addresses. In the "Sermon" recorded by Luke, the idea is expanded.

"Give, and it shall be given unto you;
Good measure, pressed down, shaken together, running over
Shall men give into your bosom."

The words recorded by Matthew are then added.

The scene upon which the saying is based is the market where from time immemorial in the east men have haggled about the prices to be paid. In western lands today and with commodities mass produced and standardized, fixed prices are a frequent rule. Bargaining can bring out evil characteristics, for men have to use their wits to secure value for money, and this quickly leads to sharp practice. Solomon noted how men disparaged the quality of something offered for sale to get it cheaper. "It is naught, it is naught, saith the buyer; but after he is gone his way, then he boasteth."

Jesus noticed the ways of men; he listened to their oaths as they bargained and disputed about prices. They invoked heaven to witness, swore by the altar and other things sacred, just to gain a few pence. He laid down a different rule.

Two men are in the market with produce to sell. The quantity is by measure, not by weight—with possible varying measures when legislation had not made faulty weights and measures an offence against the law. A pile of wheat is for sale. One man fills his measure as lightly as he can. A generous minded soul shakes it down, fills up, and piles on the top: and if the transaction is by barter in each case the response corresponds. To the generous man a return is made with generosity: to the mean man with meanness. The rule is not one only of the market: but the market is a parable of life and also illustrates the rule of God's dealing with men.

In Mark's record the saying is given a particular application. It follows the parable of the sower and is prefaced by the counsel, "Take heed what ye hear: with what measure ye mete, it shall be measured to you again: and unto you that hear shall more be given". We hear instruction from God—how much of it do we receive? and how careful are we in receiving it? If we heed, we receive more. Niggardly application to the Word will not bring a rich harvest of good things from its store. It is also true of dispensers of the Word: by hoarding it there is no increase; but by giving in passing to others the things we have learned, the storehouse of the Word is found to have open doors. The reverse is also true, for Jesus adds: "For he that hath, to him shall be given: and he that hath not, from him shall be taken even that which he hath". This saying is found in other connections: here it indicates that use of the knowledge of God's word brings increase; but neglect of it at last leads to complete forgetfulness, and the knowledge that leads to life is taken away. It was part of the doom pronounced upon Israel, "By hearing ye shall hear, and shall not understand"—they would not give heed; the time came when they could not.

9
MOTE AND BEAM
(Matt. 7 : 3-5; Luke 6 : 41, 42)

At one time men perceived no lightness of touch in any of the sayings of Jesus. Everything he spoke was regarded as heavy and serious, and unrelieved in any way. Then someone saw that on occasion he used a playfulness in his words which would relieve their apparent harshness. As might be expected, once that was perceived it became fashionable to reduce many of the sayings of Jesus to humorous remarks. There is, however, a middle way of viewing Christ's teaching. Jesus was seriously in earnest: and he pressed upon men the urgency of attending to his words. But it is permissible to think of a smile on his lips or a twinkle in his eyes as he drove home a point by some story which has a touch of humour about it.

He condemned the censorious spirit (Matt. 7 : 1-2); then, by the story of the mote and beam, he showed its folly and danger. A censorious spirit is an indication of something being wrong with a man's mind, the gravity of which is enhanced by the fact that he is not aware of his failing. The censorious person does not see his own faults—is indeed quite ignorant of them; otherwise, he would be less ready to criticize others. The real trouble is that he suffers from spiritual pride and self-conceit. He is like a man with a beam in his eye who offers to remove a splinter from the eye of another. This is the language of the carpenter's shop. A small chip of wood gets into the workman's eye, with painful consequences. As the tears flow as nature tries to wash out the intruder, he knows how difficult it is to see at all, let alone perform the delicate operation of removing some object from a fellow's eye. But the critic has a plank—a beam—in his eye; this is impossible of course, but in the story the beam is there *and the man is ignorant it is there*. The story has the humour of the grotesque

—but it is not only an indictment of censoriousness, but a terrible lesson of the moral blindness such a fault induces.

The story shows that a person with a large fault can yet be capable of criticizing another with a smaller fault. Who with experience of life has not met such? The lesson has, of course, a wider application than the particular fault in connection with which Jesus gave it. But to whatever error it is applied there is a two-fold defect. There is an absorption of thought on that which should be avoided, and a neglect of the greater matters that should be encouraged—a concentration on faults, while things that are lovely and of good report are not regarded.

"Thou hypocrite", Jesus calls the beam-eyed one, and calls upon him to remove the beam as a first qualification to deal with the chip. Why "hypocrite"? The word means "play-actor" and in this sense it was used. The man was acting a part: he was being in his action something other than he really was. Such was the fault to which the Pharisees were particularly prone. They made an outward show of religion—long prayers in the street, ostentatious almsgiving, painted faces to indicate fasting—when all the time they were actuated by the desire to be seen of men. It is a danger to which the religious life is peculiarly liable.

The parable is aimed at the man with the beam in his eye: but of course the other had a splinter, and splinters are uncomfortable things in eyes. Faults are, or ought to be, "foreign bodies" in life, and while a man with a small fault, being human, would very easily resent the proffered services of the other to remove it, the man who is aiming at the best will value correction from whatever source it comes. It may be a part of the training of life to accept correction under such circumstances as are depicted in the parable, even though such an attitude may seem to denote an ideal circumspection and self-detachment. A recent writer, however, has rightly said: "Sensitiveness to the judgments of others still remains as essential good, not to be eliminated but sublimated. Nowhere is objectivity with reference to one's self more needed than here. Whatsoever criticism one would listen to with regard to another, let him listen to it with regard to himself. So treated, a man's outspoken enemies are often his best friends, teaching him more unvarnished truth about himself than those who love him would ever tell. Such a man has not ceased being sensitive to the opinions of his fellows, but he is using the quality for well-directed ends—gaining insight into human nature whether in others or himself, achieving mutual understanding and sympathy in his social relationships, neither bulldozed nor embittered by personal criticism, but learning from it and magnanimously refusing to take exaggerated offence at it even when it is unjust".

10

DOGS AND SWINE

(Matt. 7 : 6)

We shall miss the purport of the figures of "dogs and pigs" if we disregard the context, for the saying is really a corrective of the too literal application of the command "Judge not". As we have seen, those words must not be taken in their widest sense, but applied to the critical censorious attitude of mind. Yet judgments must be made, and discrimination shown in many circumstances of life.

The saying about dogs and swine illustrates the introversion (a.b. : b.a.) common in poetry marked by parallelism.

Give not that which is holy unto the dogs,
    Neither cast ye your pearls before swine,
    Lest they trample them under their feet,
And turn again and rend you.

Pigs trample under their feet, and dogs rend with their teeth.

The saying has troubled some to whom it seems unfitting that men should be compared to dogs and pigs. That abhorrence is implied is clear. The dog was the scavenger of the street: the pig was unclean. "Is thy servant a dog?" is an indignant remonstrance (2 Kings 8 : 13); yet Jesus in the same address speaks also of "wolves" and "thistles", and these figures are quite as derogatory. Peter does not hesitate to apply the proverbs of the washed sow that goes back to wallowing in the dirt, and of the dog that returns to its vomit, to the man who has known the truth, and then forsakes it for the world's pleasures. Does Peter in this reference to the same two animals as in Christ's words echo the language that he heard Jesus speak?

It is easy to make the saying an excuse for "hiding one's light", withholding speaking when profession of Christ's name is called for. It should be quite evident that men will treat the word of God as swine treat pearls before we refrain from testifying to the truth of God's saving purpose. It must be clear that they are men who by their actions show that they "judge themselves unworthy" and then there is apostolic example to "turn away" (Acts 13 : 46).

Such men, truly comparable to dogs and swine, can be real enemies of the truth and of those whose aim in life is to follow truth. Aroused to enmity by the faithful life and testimony of Jesus, the evil men of his day opposed him. The servant is not greater than his master, and his experience will correspond to that of his master if his life is like his master's life. "Beware of dogs, beware of evil workers", is apostolic counsel (Phil. 3 : 2); and the final unfitness of "dogs" to enter the city of God is declared in the Lord's last message: "Without are dogs, and sorcerers, and whoremongers, and murderers, and idolaters, and whosoever loveth and maketh a lie" (Rev. 22 : 15).

11

BREAD AND STONE : FISH AND SERPENT

(Matt. 7 : 9, 10; Luke 11 : 11)

JESUS enjoined continual approach to God in prayer, the tense of the verb he used signifying repeated action: keep on asking. The poetic form in which he uttered his counsel would help men and women to remember his words.

"Ask, and it shall be given you;
Seek, and ye shall find;
Knock, and it shall be opened unto you:
For everyone that asketh receiveth;
And he that seeketh findeth;
And to him that knocketh it shall be opened."

The ground of the approach, so insistent and persevering, is the fact that God is the Father of His children. In human life children have a claim on their parents, who, on their part, are desirous to do what they can for their children. But wise parents make a discriminating response—not always giving what is asked, but providing what is good. In both respects there is a parallel between the human and the divine, but the divine is immeasurably greater in both the willingness to provide and in the wise bestowal of what is best. Immeasurably; although Jesus is content to leave it as a suggestion—"how much more"—but a suggestion which has neither doubt nor misgiving. As men are "much better" than the fowls, God is "much more" ready to clothe His children (Matt. 6 : 26, 30). "How much more" ready is God than human fathers to give: "If ye then, being evil, know how to give good gifts unto your children, how much more shall your Father which is in heaven give good things to them that ask him?" (7 : 11).

By two contrasts in Matthew, and three in Luke, Jesus drives home his point. "What man is there of you, whom if his son ask bread, will he give him a stone?" (7 : 9). There was a resemblance between the bread and the stone which enhances the lesson. The child asks for bread and receives something like it in form—but so different in content. The method of baking in the days of Jesus produced a loaf not unlike a stone. The oven, with pebbles forming its floor, was heated with grass and twigs, and then the dough was put in. "In the case of loaves fired in the public oven, these, owing to the glutinous adhesiveness and elasticity of the dough, and the sudden formation within them of vapour on the hot pavement, puff out into air-tight balls." "In travelling through Palestine and partaking of the hospitality of the peasantry, one may notice in the bread the indentations of the pebbles, and small patches of grey ash, with here and there an inlaid attachment of singed grass or charred thorn, the result of the simple baking process."

Such a similarity between a loaf and a stone would suggest that stones be made into bread when Jesus was tempted in the wilderness. Being so like the bread he needed, the stones would make the appeal very potent.

In the second contrast, Jesus said: "If he ask a fish, will he give him a serpent?" It has been suggested that by the word translated serpent "is meant, not a literal serpent but a scaleless fish, therefore prohibited to be eaten (Lev. 11 : 12); serpent-like, found in the sea of Galilee, three feet long, often caught in the nets and of course thrown away like the dogfish of our waters." While the word generally denotes a serpent, Liddell & Scott include "a kind of fish" in their list of meanings of the word. If then the suggestion be correct, and it seems feasible, Jesus in this saying is making a contrast between food allowed by the law of God and that which was "unclean".

Luke adds the third contrast: "If he shall ask an egg, will he offer him a scorpion?" There does not seem sufficient resemblance between an egg and a scorpion to provide a third contrast until we discover that "the scorpion at rest is said to resemble an egg in appearance".

In addition, it is said that "scorpions may be found under every third stone in Palestine"; the creatures were therefore common, and would be familiar to all. The land of Palestine was unfenced, and many a fowl would stray and lay her eggs in some hollow; the resemblance would be readily noticed; and the contrasted qualities of the egg providing wholesome food, and the scorpion with its power for harm, would give point to the illustration.

"If ye then, being evil, know how to give good gifts unto your children, how much more shall your Father which is in heaven give good things to them that ask him?" (7 : 11).

If the idea of "niggardliness" which we found to be involved in the "evil" used in connection with the "eye" (6 : 23) belongs also to its use here, then the meaning could be expanded. If you—whose nature would lead you to keep for yourselves rather than give to others—do so for your children, will not God who is always giving that which is good to His creatures, be always ready to give good things to those who ask Him! But this use of "evil" may restrict its meaning too much. Jesus knew that men possessed natures which were evil, yet even so, parental affection was continually to be seen. God is good; "how much more" will He be ready to give good things to His children. If a human father does not mock his children, neither will the Heavenly Father.

12

THE TWO WAYS

(Matt. 7 : 13, 14; Luke 13 : 23, 24)

One writer has drawn a picture of men going to the Holy City and, travelling the road, they come to the point where they must leave it to climb the hill by which they enter through the gate into the city. The broad way looks inviting—it is spacious and easy. "This is the way", one says. "No", says another who knows more about the place, "that road leads to Gehenna outside the city. We must turn here to climb, or we shall not get in." It may be some such situation was in the mind of Jesus—in any case, it illustrates the saying about the two ways and makes vivid his thought. There is certainly an Old Testament background that would influence his mind.

The thought of destiny based on a choice made once for all and adhered to continually occurs in Moses' words concerning the life in the Messiah (Deut. 30 : 11-13, and Paul's exposition, Rom. 10). "I call heaven and earth to record this day against you, that I have set before you life and death, blessing and cursing: therefore choose life, that both thou and thy seed may live" (Deut. 30 : 19).

More definitely connected with the words of Jesus is the last verse of Psalm 1: "The Lord knoweth the way of the righteous: but the way of the ungodly shall perish". Here are two ways—the one ending in destruction; and while David does not say the way of righteousness ends in life, he says something more than that. He has said inferentially (verse 5) that the godly shall stand in the judgment; and shall be like an evergreen tree (verse 3): but to be known of God includes all other blessings.

Jeremiah has many sayings rooted in the Psalms. In the crisis of Zedekiah's captivity, the prophet declared in words that recall both Moses and David: "Thus saith the Lord, Behold, I set before you the way of life, and the way of death" (Jer. 21 : 8).

"Enter ye in at the strait gate." It is a call to make a choice, to separate from the crowd which drifts along the broad way. In Luke 13 : 24 Jesus says, "*Strive* to enter in at the strait gate". There is a whole exhortation in the word "strive". It enshrines a metaphor taken from the foot race. The verb which describes the runner on the course has given us in English the word *agonize*. But before the race itself there was a period of rigorous training involving self-discipline and attention to everything that made for fitness. The race had to be run strenuously according to the rules, and the one object of reaching the goal had to evoke every effort, that in the harmony of mental purpose and bodily strength the laurel wreath might be obtained. All these thoughts are implicit in the word. The crowd follow the way that calls not for self-discipline, but which appears to offer ease and freedom. The men of faith and purpose are not a large number.

With this counsel concerning the choice of the right way Jesus begins the epilogue of the Sermon. The Beatitudes describe the character of the men who will enter the kingdom. The close of the address tells of the choice they make.

The parable emphasizes—what is indeed declared throughout the Scriptures, but which the speculations of men have obscured—that the present is the day of opportunity. The broad way ends in destruction. It *is* destruction—the end of a man—that is at the end of the broad way. Probation beyond the grave is a fiction to which men are led by the doctrine of the immortality of the soul. With that idea in mind, men have to construe destruction as endless torments, and from the horror of this even a theory of probation beyond the present does not provide a way of escape. For a future probation does not ensure that a man will choose righteousness, and if the soul is immortal, unless there be repeated probation until all are saved, which is universalism, there is no escape from the logical consequence of endless suffering for some. Human speculation produces pitiful results.

The choice of the way now, determines the issues of life or death.

13
WOLVES
(Matt. 7 : 15; 10 : 16)

"BEWARE of false prophets, which come to you in sheep's clothing, but inwardly they are ravening wolves." The use of sheep in figure is frequent and will be noticed later. It is therefore not surprising to find the enemy of the sheep—the wolf—has a place in the teaching of Jesus. The wolf was abundant in Palestine, and very destructive to the flocks. It was large, tawny, usually solitary, or hunting two or three together, their habit being to prowl around the flocks and herds and sometimes to get into the folds. Tristam says: "The wolf is now, as of old, the dread of the shepherds of Palestine. Not so numerous, but much more formidable than the jackal, he lurks about the folds, hunting not in noisy packs, but secreting himself till dark among the rocks. Without rousing the vigilance of the sheep dogs, he leaps into the fold and seizes his victim by stealth." In the animal and its habits, thus described, we are directed by Jesus to find a parallel to the false prophet and his ways. The wolf, however, with whatever cunning and stealth it manages its marauding, remains a wolf: the false teacher affects another form. He pretends to be a sheep—he dresses in sheep's clothing; he is therefore the more dangerous.

In the immediate context in the Sermon, Jesus has been warning his hearers of the narrowness of the way to life, and that few find life. The majority follow the broad way which leads to destruction. Jesus is clear and emphatic on this unpopular view of the destiny of men. Human philosophy nowhere clashes more with divine teaching than on the subject of man's duty and his future. False teachers, putting forward human speculations in place of God's revelation and leading men away from God's truth, are dangerous. They are destroyers of the flock when they beguile to false doctrine or to a way of life contrary to Christ's teaching. Beware of them, said Jesus. It is a call for caution, for scrutiny of professors who would teach, and for discernment and judgment. Such a command as this has to be remembered when interpreting verse 1 of this chapter.

When Jesus sent out the Twelve on a preaching mission he warned them of danger, of opposition, of persecution. "Behold, I send you forth as sheep in the midst of wolves" (Matt. 10 : 16). In this statement Jesus does not describe the opposing parties as sheep dressed as wolves, nor wolves dressed as sheep. In their own true character the apostles were to face the natural enemies of preachers of righteousness. Harmless themselves, they had to be shrewd and resourceful, but never crafty or cunning. "Wise as serpents, but harmless as doves", Jesus said they must be. It is easy to pass by such teaching—sentimental readers tend to ignore it: but a place must be found for all the teaching of Jesus if a man would be a true disciple.

Because the wolf was common, and its menace well known, some references in the prophets might be expected. Ezekiel says that Israel's "princes in the midst thereof are like wolves ravening the prey, to shed blood, and to destroy souls, to get dishonest gain" (22 : 27). Jeremiah and others note its nocturnal habits (5 : 6; Hab. 1 : 8; Zeph. 3 : 3).

The apostle Paul takes up the figure used by Jesus and repeats the warning of Jesus to the elders of Ephesus. "Take heed therefore unto yourselves, and to all the flock, over the which the Holy Spirit hath made you overseers, to feed the Church of God, which he hath purchased with his own blood. For I know this, that after my departing shall grievous wolves enter in among you, not sparing the flock" (Acts 20 : 28, 29).

14
TREES AND FRUIT
(Matt. 7 : 16-20; Luke 6 : 43, 44)

If prophets profess to speak a word from the Lord which is really from their own heart; if while outwardly appearing to be sheep they are really wolves, it behoves the disciple to know how to distinguish the genuine from the false. Jesus supplies a test: "Ye shall know them by their fruits". The change of figure, from wolves to fruit, is abrupt; but the new illustration is well adapted for the lesson Jesus is teaching.

"Do men gather grapes of thorns,
Or figs of thistles?
Even so every good tree bringeth forth good fruit;
But a corrupt tree bringeth forth evil fruit.
A good tree cannot bring forth evil fruit,
Neither can a corrupt tree bring forth good fruit.
Every tree that bringeth not forth good fruit is hewn down
And cast into the fire.
Wherefore by their fruits ye shall know them"
(Matt 7 : 15-20).

Men do not expect grapes from thorns. The idea was not so absurd to Christ's listeners as it sounds to us, for in Palestine "there were thorns with grape-like fruit, and thistles with heads like figs"; yet men were never deceived. The thorn was always a thorn, and it produced its own fruit. The fruit of trees varied as the trees were good or corrupt, conditions depending upon culture and soil. But the results were inevitable either way, and were invariable. So sure were men of this law of nature, that if a tree was corrupt, as is shown by its fruit, without hesitation they hewed it down and burned it. So certainly also were men to be judged by their fruits.

What then is the fruit: in what aspect of life is it to be sought? Is Jesus thinking of doctrine or of moral life as the sphere in which men will reveal themselves? It is probable that both are included; and his test can be applied to both teachers and communities. Jesus has immediately before in his address contrasted the two ways, and men are directed in the broad or narrow way by teachers false or true, even as they are encouraged to pursue the way they travel by the conduct of their companions. There were doctrinal tests in the first century and the apostles uttered grave warnings about teachers who introduced error: but they were not less severe upon those who turned the grace of God into an excuse for immorality.

This comprehensive application may be illustrated from the fact that Paul twice uses the proverb "a little leaven leaveneth the whole", on one occasion of doctrine, and on the other of morals (Gal. 5 : 9; 1 Cor. 5 : 6). The apostle John condemned error in both action and belief: "He that saith, I know him, and keepeth not his commandments, is a liar, and the truth is not in him" (1 John 2 : 4); "Hereby know ye the Spirit of God; every spirit that confesseth that Jesus Christ is come in the flesh is of God: and every spirit that confesseth not that Jesus Christ is come in the flesh is not of God: and this is that spirit of antichrist, whereof ye have heard that it should come; and even now already is it in the world" (1 John 4 : 2, 3). The Lord found fault with ecclesias for condoning false doctrines; and also for declining from their first love, for spiritual death, and for pride and self-satisfaction (Rev. 2 and 3).

That doctrine is not essential to a good life is one of the fallacies of modernism. To have authority, precepts of righteousness must rest on divine sanction. It is possible for a generation which respects God's word to establish conventions which continue even when the respect which the founders had for the Bible has declined. This has in fact happened in the present century: men do not accept as authoritative the Bible upon which their forefathers based their way of life; but the principles of righteousness cannot be maintained without divine commands being recognized. Inevitably decline follows, slowly at first, but at last the fruit of a corrupting tree becomes degenerate. Evolution is regarded by many of its adherents as fundamentally atheistic; and it can, therefore, only inculcate the law of the jungle whence men are supposed to have come.

The absence of fruit proves to be fatal both for men and for communities. The "cursed" ground has to be tilled, even if in sorrow, to bring forth that which is good and serviceable. Man is a husbandman and in his working must conform to nature's rules; thus instructed, he resembles the divine Husbandman. The principle set forth by Paul is applicable in both human and divine spheres: "The earth which drinketh in the rain that cometh oft upon it, and bringeth forth herbs meet for them by whom it is dressed, receiveth blessing from God: but that which beareth thorns and briers is rejected, and is nigh unto cursing; whose end is to be burned" (Heb. 6 : 7, 8).

15
TWO BUILDERS

(Matt. 7 : 24-27; Luke 6 : 46-49)

THE idea that religion is concerned with doing, and that men need not worry about believing, is a part of the shallow thinking so widespread in these last days. The discounting of true faith is a weakness of the credulity of today, for all men have a faith of some sort, and are ready to show it in the most surprising ways.

The demagogues Hitler and Mussolini, who had their short day in Germany and Italy, knew only too well how ready people were to believe, and they exploited this characteristic to the full. It has been said: "A man can no more run away from his faith-faculty than he can run away from his own legs; they are what he does his running away with". The extreme illustration is to be found in the faith shown by so many in no-faith.

"Practise the teaching of Christ, and it is enough" would be a fair representation of most people's idea of the religious life; and if we ask what teaching, we will probably be referred to the Sermon on the Mount. Nothing could better illustrate the smallness of men's grasp of the teaching of Jesus. For, firstly, the teaching of the Sermon is hard: it is difficult to believe, and it is hard to practise. Its meaning is not always easy of understanding despite a superficial simplicity: its practice defies the best efforts of human nature, and reduces men of earnest endeavour to the recognition of human weakness which Paul describes in Romans 7. Secondly, the Sermon is shot through with doctrine concerning a future life, and of man's possible relationship to it. The Beatitudes promise a good to come which will be the fruit of present effort. Jesus plainly declares he will decide men's future. Some call him Lord, Lord, but do not the will of God. In a future day many will call him Lord, Lord, and claim to have done many things in his name, only to hear him say, "Depart". Nowhere is the claim that the future is in his hands more clearly or more boldly made than in the Sermon on the Mount—that he will make decisions which will affect men for ever.

It is a fitting sequence to that claim, and a fitting climax to the Sermon as a whole to compare his hearers to two builders. With a marked rhythmic and balanced parallelism he declares:

Therefore whosoever heareth these sayings of mine and doeth them,
I will liken him unto a wise man which built his house upon a rock:
and the rain descended,
and the floods came,
and the winds blew,
and beat upon that house;
and it fell not;
for it was founded upon a rock.

And everyone that heareth these sayings of mine and doeth them not,
Shall be likened unto a foolish man which built his house upon the sand:
and the rain descended,
and the floods came,
and the winds blew,
and beat upon that house;
and it fell;
and great was the fall of it.

The phrases linked by the word "and" produce a cumulative effect of the growing strength of the storm, as rain, floods and wind all seem to combine to test the building. The rock-founded house resists the storm, the waters rushing around its base leave it unmoved: with all the power of simple statement Jesus says, "It fell not"; and he gives the reason—it was built on a rock.

In the second part the repeated phrases enhance the effect of the terror which the storm brings; the only variation comes at the end, "and it fell"; by repetition its destruction is emphasized—"great was the fall of it". Its walls gave way; the roof fell in; the swirling waters swept away the sand on which it was built; and nothing at all was left of the man's labours. The address ends with the ominous warning that to build other than on Christ's sayings would end in complete ruin.

The utter plainness of it, the staggering demands of it, the amazing claims of the speaker, the awe induced by the picture drawn so graphically—moved the people to astonishment. They marked the dominant note—"he taught them as one having authority".

The language is that of a law-giver and not of an interpreter of the law. "These sayings of mine" have all the force of the "ten words" spoken amidst the thunder and darkness and lightning flash of Sinai. "These sayings" are to govern thought and conscience, and so determine the outward act. Men often mistake sincerity for truth, as if sincerity could take the place of truth. Many of the contemporaries of Jesus were sincere and conscientious enough, but pitiably in the wrong. Their consciences led them to do things which were severely condemned by Jesus. Of such perverted consciences it has been truly said that Jesus was thinking "when he spoke of those who 'tithe mint and anise and cummin', and neglect 'the weightier matters of the law, justice and mercy and faith'. With such men he had his major difficulties. They 'strain out the gnat', he said, 'and swallow the camel'. The Pharisee prayed in the Temple, 'God, I thank thee, that I am not as the rest of men, extortioners, unjust, adulterers, or even as this publican. I fast twice in the week; I give tithes of all that I get.' He was a conscientious person. The elder brother of the Prodigal, who remained at home and did his duty so satisfactorily to himself that he could boast, 'I never transgressed a commandment of thine', was a conscientious person. Simon the Pharisee, who with shocked amazement felt sure that Jesus could not be a prophet because he let a woman of the streets touch him, was very conscientious. The man so interested in righteousness that he tried to get a mote out of his brother's eye, laboured under a heavy sense of duty. Conscience so misused becomes inwardly a disease, and outwardly it has produced some of the darkest evils in human history—bigotry, fanaticism, hypocrisy".

Perverted conscientiousness assumes many forms today. One of the great evils of this century has been the worship of the State. Germany was thoroughly inoculated with the evil doctrine. "Whoever serves Hitler, serves Germany; and whoever serves Germany serves God." The history of the years that followed the utterance of these words show the folly of the saying. "Blood and race" are not rock foundations.

Jesus was himself a builder. It is too restricted a view of his daily work in Nazareth to think only of yokes and ploughs. The village carpenter was a builder also, and Jesus doubtless knew wise people who required their houses to be well founded. Robinson tells of such a house a century ago in the home town of Jesus, and we may not be far wrong in thinking the description would be true 1800 years earlier. He says:

"We were glad towards noon to accept an invitation from Abu Nasir, and join him at his house. Here we found the rooms of stone much cooler than our tent. The house had just been built, and was not yet finished. In order to lay the foundations he had dug down to solid rock, as is usual throughout the country, here to the depth of thirty feet; and then built up arches. The workmanship was solid, but coarse; he assured us it was the best work the masons of Nazareth could turn out" (Robinson, *Biblical Researches*, vol. iii, p. 191).

Men build on sand when they trust in human speculations; they build on rock when they follow Christ's teaching. All men are building, whether they will or not, for life's activities assume some shape; but all efforts can have the quality of permanence only if men build on the foundation Jesus laid in his teaching.

Some results seem fair to look upon; humanistic philosophy may produce a refinement far removed from savagery; but the result has nothing of value to God. But Jesus does not even consider or assess such human schemes; his thought is limited to those who hear his words. The hearer who is also a doer builds a character that has abiding value, and it will survive not only the storms and stresses of the present life, but also the greatest crisis of all—the judgment of Christ himself. "The wicked are overthrown, and are not: but the house of the righteous shall stand" (Prov. 12 : 7). "The house of the wicked shall be overthrown: but the tabernacle of the upright shall flourish" (14 : 11).

The authority with which Jesus spoke was divine—asserted or implied throughout all the discourse. The figure he uses in his closing parable of the Sermon on the Mount is an absolute insistence upon such authority. His teaching is a rock upon which men build safely. This figure of a rock is frequently used in the Old Testament of the Almighty. "The Lord is my Rock"; "Who is a rock, save our God?" "The Lord liveth; and blessed be my Rock; and exalted be the God of the rock of my salvation" (2 Sam. 22 : 2, 32, 47; see also Psa. 28 : 1; 31 : 2; 61 : 2). Isaiah calls God "the rock of ages" (26 : 4 margin), and through him God asks, "Is there a rock beside me?" (44 : 8 margin). The claims of Jesus thus clearly suggest that his words have a divine power and that he is able to use the language which God says is exclusively His. No prophet ever spoke like this; such a form of speech befits only one who has the status of "the Son". It is one of the many sayings which his enemies would readily seize upon that they might charge him with making himself equal to God.

The Sermon is not detached from history. There are events before and after it—events not unconnected with the claims of the Sermon. Jesus had toured Galilee, by word and deed proclaiming the gospel of the Kingdom. "He healed all manner of sickness, and all manner of disease among the people", records Matthew (4 : 23). His works were the evidences that belong to the Kingdom—tokens of what will be when the Kingdom is established. The preacher was virgin-born (chap. 1); declared to be God's Son (2 : 15; 3 : 17); tested in the wilderness without failing (4 : 1-11). These are the background facts which show what manner of man the speaker was. These facts are part of the record and the Sermon must not, cannot, be divorced from them. But the succeeding facts are not less important, for Jesus descends from the Mount to perform a succession of wonderful acts, the details of which, one careful expositor has not hesitated to say, were selected by Matthew for their spiritual significance. A leper is made clean (8 : 37); the palsied servant is given strength

(8 : 6-8); a fevered woman finds calm and rest (8 : 14): so he "took our infirmities and bare our sicknesses" (verse 17). He crosses the lake and a tempest arises; he "muzzles" the storm as a mad dog is muzzled to control it. On the other side of the lake he finds men as tormented with disease as the sea was with the wind. He speaks the word and the demons are cast out.

The man who uttered the Sermon does not promulgate a law, which in its very purity breaks our hearts, and then leaves us. He enters into contact with men, healing and strengthening. If his teaching alone would fill us with dismay, with his presence it becomes an ideal not too far away to move us, not too high that we will not try to reach it. The words of Christ find their expression in the spirit which Jesus Christ even then displayed. Thus encouraged we must *build* on his teaching: "as ye have received Christ Jesus the Lord so walk ye in him; rooted and built up in him, and established in the faith" (Col. 2 : 6, 7). This metaphor of building, which has its source in Christ's teaching, occurs frequently in the counsel of the apostle Paul, although partly obscured by the use in translation of the words "edify" and "edification".

16
PHYSICIAN AND PATIENT
(Matt. 9 : 12; Mark 2 : 17; Luke 5 : 31)

JESUS had an encounter with the scribes in Capernaum. A palsied man was brought to him, borne of four, and Jesus, seeing their faith said to him: "Be of good cheer; thy sins be forgiven thee". The man's condition was probably due to a life of excess; and Jesus knew the man's mind was as sick as his body. Sin and evil are as closely connected as cause and effect, ultimately if not always proximately. The scribes were watching Jesus, and noting his words. Perceiving their evil thought, he asked them which was easier, to say: "Thy sins be forgiven, or to say, Rise up and walk". The first was easier to say, for there could be no disproof: the second produced a visible effect, by which the power of the speaker's words was put to the proof. To establish his power to forgive sins Jesus then commanded the man to get up, take up his mat and go to his house. This healing of sickness is seen to be a real proof that sin was forgiven, when the causal connection of sin and suffering is remembered. In this episode, therefore, Jesus is shown to be a healer of both soul and body.

Jesus next "calls" Matthew, the tax collector, and accepts an invitation to his house. The Pharisees, discomfited in their complaint about Jesus forgiving sins, now attack his disciples. "Why eateth your Master with publicans and sinners?" they ask. Jesus, hearing it, protected the disciples by answering the question. His answer is tinged with irony and contains a rebuke. "They that be whole need not a physician, but they that are sick." That is so, obviously; but the real point is that Jesus takes them at their own estimate of themselves. They did not think they were morally sick; they did not therefore feel the need for the ministrations of Jesus. But they should not grumble at him for going to those who recognized their need. How far their own assessment of themselves was wrong Jesus makes evident by the next saying: "But go ye and learn what that meaneth, I will have mercy, and not sacrifice: for I am not come to call the righteous, but sinners to repentance". This must have been sternly uttered for it contains a strong rebuke. "Go learn"—and they were the teachers of the people; but how truly did they need to learn that mercy is greater than sacrifice. God required sacrifice indeed, but much more did He require that they should exercise mercy.

The quotation (Hos. 6 : 6) was apposite, for in the context in Hosea, God says He will hide Himself "till they acknowledge their offence" and seek Him (5 : 15). The response of Israel in their affliction is foretold: they will say, "Come, and let us return unto the Lord: for he hath torn and he will heal us: he hath smitten and he will bind us up" (6 : 1). God would have "healed" Israel before, but their iniquity stood in the way (7 : 1). Ephraim saw "his sickness" and Judah his "wound", but they went to the Assyrian, "yet could he not heal you" (5 : 13). But though Israel wrought self-destruction, God declared: "In me is thine help" (13 : 9). God would be Israel's physician.

In Jesus God had drawn near, and the use of the figure by Jesus takes up the Old Testament allusions to God's work. "By his stripes we are healed"; "for by his knowledge shall my righteous servant justify many, for he shall bear their iniquities" (Isa. 53 : 11).

17
THE BRIDEGROOM

(Matt. 9 : 15; Mark 2 : 19; Luke 5 : 33, 34)

In the New Testament John the Baptist is the first to use the figure of the Bridegroom. The occasion was when his disciples told him of the success that was attending the teaching of Jesus—"all men come to him". John knew that both his baptism and that of Jesus were of God, and in that large view there was no room for envy. Nor did John show any. On the contrary, his relationship to Jesus excluded it; he was the friend of the bridegroom. "He that hath the bride is the bridegroom: but the friend of the bridegroom, which standeth and heareth him, rejoiceth greatly because of the bridegroom's voice: this my joy therefore is fulfilled" (John 3 : 29). The "friend" was the groomsman, who sought the hand of the bride, and arranged the marriage. When the task was crowned with success and he heard the voice of the bridegroom welcoming the bride, his joy was full. So John—the "friend"—rejoiced to hear that the people were seeking Jesus and were being welcomed by him as the bridegroom welcomes the bride.

Later, John's disciples, possibly at the instigation of the Pharisees (cf. Matt. 9 : 14 and Mark 2 : 18), came to Jesus with the question, Why do the disciples of John and of the Pharisees fast, but not the disciples of Jesus? There was more than one reason, which Jesus gave them in the form of three short parables: The Bridegroom, The Patched Cloth, The Wineskins. The first of these we now consider.

"Can ye make the children of the bridechamber fast, while the bridegroom is with them? But the days will come, when the bridegroom shall be taken away from them, and then shall they fast in those days" (Luke 5 : 33, 34). It has been remarked that whereas John who lived in Judea spoke of the "friend of the bridegroom" (John 3 : 29), Jesus who lived in Galilee spoke of "sons of the bridechamber". The former refers to a practice common in Judea, but not followed in Galilee; the latter was a general term for all invited guests. There is perfect accuracy in the details in the record.

When Jesus referred to himself as the bridegroom he was first of all reminding the disciples of John of the answer of their own teacher. John had the joy of the groomsman; the disciples of Jesus had the freedom and joy of the friends and guests at the wedding. By Rabbinic law the marriage week was a time of unmixed festivity; even the ordinances of the strict fast of the Day of Atonement were modified; everything had to serve the purpose of bringing gladness to bride and bridegroom. In the same way the presence of Jesus then was itself the occasion and reason for joy. "But"—and with that word we see that Jesus recognized that the joy would be short-lived; and he then gives the first public hint of the appointed end of his ministry when he said that the Bridegroom would be taken away. Then, not of command, but arising from the sense of loss, would his disciples fast.

We look at the customs of the land of Palestine of the days of Christ's ministry for the atmosphere of these sayings; but it would be a mistake to restrict our enquiries to manners and customs. They only give the adjuncts, the trimmings of the story. The heart of the story—the very basis of the thought of Jesus—goes back to Old Testament teaching.

Isaiah (ch. 54) compared Jerusalem of the past under the Law to Hagar, and Jerusalem of the future under the Messiah to Sarah. Like Hagar the city was to be "cast off" (verse 6, R.V.); but like Sarah it was also to have children of promise, all spirit-begotten. God says, "Thy maker is thine husband; the Lord of hosts is his name; and thy Redeemer the Holy One of Israel; the God of the whole earth shall he be called" (verse 5). The dullest of Isaiah's listeners must have seen in these words a reference to one in whom God would be manifested, a redeemer of Zion and its people, and a ruler over the whole world. The Messiah is the Maker and Husband, as in a sense the first Adam was the Maker and Husband to Eve.

Jeremiah also uses the figure: "Turn, O backsliding children; for I am married unto you". God was bridegroom to Israel.

Psalm 45 is the marriage ode of the King who is addressed as "O God", whose throne is for ever and ever, and whose queen is in gold of Ophir, in clothing of wrought gold. Psalm 19 tells of the heavens declaring God's glory, in which the sun is as a bridegroom coming out of his chamber. The former is by both apostolic and rabbinic interpretation applied to the Messiah; the latter by Paul in Rom. 10.

The Song of Solomon is a sustained allegory based upon the figure of marriage, which also was given a Messianic significance by the teachers of Israel.

When John applied the figure of bridegroom to Jesus, and Jesus also made use of it in reference to himself, there was implied a claim that Jesus was Israel's Messiah, and that he was a manifestation of God, and one to whom the true Israel was related as "wife".

18
THE PATCHED CLOTH
(Matt. 9 : 16; Mark 2 : 21; Luke 5 : 36)

WHEN the disciples of John and of the Pharisees enquired of Jesus concerning fasting, his answer consisted of three small parables. The first concerns the bridegroom. The second is based on the patching of clothes. In Matt. 9 : 16 and Mark 2 : 21 Jesus is recorded as saying that no one puts a piece of new (raw or "unfulled") cloth on an old garment, for the new piece would pull away and the rent be made worse. Luke's version of the parable speaks of a piece of a new garment being used as a patch, both new and old garments being spoiled. Perhaps in the full reply of Jesus, of which the gospel records can only be a summary, Jesus used both ideas; or more probably, as papyri evidence indicates, the "unfulled cloth" of Matthew or Mark was a colloquial term for a new garment.

An interesting picture of the boyhood of Jesus has been put together from his sayings. In the cottage home with eight or nine mouths to feed, it may have been an anxious Mary that plied her needle to keep her children clothed and tidy. It may be that a suitable patch was not available, and one of the children suggested that another garment too large for immediate use might be cut to supply the patch. It is a child's solution to a pressing need.

The meaning in general terms is clear. The teaching of Jesus was bringing something new as a way of life, and it could not be used to patch up the old forms of Judaism.

The two ways of life were incompatible, and any effort to repair the defects of Judaism by the teaching of Jesus would be disastrous for both.

Is there anything in the figure of a garment that takes us further than the homely idea of childhood's days? There is here, as in most of the teaching of Jesus, an Old Testament background.

Man has been interested in garments since Adam transgressed God's law, and sought by a fig leaf device to cover his shame. But the clothing man invented did not exhibit the divine principles upon which alone sin could be covered. God therefore provided Adam with clothing of skins, illustrating the divine rule that sin could only be covered by blood shedding. This lesson has to be learned by all who would become acceptable to God. Abel discerned it, and *by faith* offered an acceptable sacrifice. The record in Genesis briefly indicates that worship was not left to man's arrangement; God revealed the way men must approach. At the time appointed (at the end of days—margin), by the means commanded (a firstling), offered in the way required (with the fat) (Gen. 4 : 3, 4), —so Abel in faith came to worship God; and he could have said, as David long afterwards wrote: "Blessed is he whose transgression is forgiven, whose sin is covered".

The clothing of the High Priest was an elaborate parable of the preparation of the Lord himself for his office of priest (see *Law of Moses,* chapter XVIII). Isaiah (ch. 61) connects this priestly clothing with the Anointed of the Lord: "The Spirit of the Lord is upon me . . . I will greatly rejoice in the Lord, my soul shall be joyful in my God: for he hath clothed me with the garments of salvation, he hath covered me with the robe of righteousness as *a bridegroom* decketh (that is, robes as a priest, see A.V. margin) himself with ornaments, and as *a bride* adorneth herself with jewels" (verses 1,10). Here the figures of bridegroom and clothing are brought together by Isaiah in a way that could have suggested the same combination in the Lord's answer to the question of John's disciples. But this is not all. The Lord's anointed uses both the figure of bride and bridegroom to illustrate his clothing. The mystical Christ indeed includes both: and therefore in the same context in Isaiah he gives the mourners "beauty for ashes" (verse 3) where "beauty" is the same word as "ornaments" in verse 10.

"Clothing", in a closely related figure in Isa. 6 : 1, stands for the priests of the age to come who are associates of the King: and the figure is used also of Zion's children with which she will be "clothed as with an ornament", "as a bride doeth" (49 : 18)—"beautiful garments" which she will put on when she responds to the Lord's command to "Awake" (52 : 1).

In contrast to this divine clothing Isaiah compares human schemes, plans of worship, and ways of life, to "spiders' webs"—unsuitable material for clothing: "their webs shall not become garments, neither shall they cover themselves with their works" (59 : 5, 6). Israel in the day of their shame when Messiah is revealed will recognize this at last and confess: "All our righteousnesses are as filthy rags" (64 : 6). Jude warns the saints to avoid such a state, "hating even the garment spotted by the flesh" (verse 23).

Paul uses the figure of clothing when he instructs the Colossians that as they had "put off the old man" and "put on the new man" they must eschew the deeds of the one, and cultivate the grace of the other.

This selection of references shows the Bible philosophy of clothes and the impossibility, to use Carlyle's figure of *Sartor Resartus,* for the man to retailor his clothes; the Old Testament references also providing the background of thought to the Lord's parable of the patched garment.

19
WINE SKINS AND NEW WINE
(Matt. 9 : 17; Mark 2 : 22; Luke 5 : 37-39)

THE parable of the wine skins follows the parable of the patched cloth and forms part of the Lord's answer to the Baptist's disciples when they question Jesus concerning fasting. The two parables appear to teach the same lessons. Not really so: for while both parables are part of Christ's explanation why he did not teach his disciples to observe ritual and ceremonies and appointed fasts, there is progress in thought. The lesson of the patched garment is largely negative—the garment could not be mended, and the ceremonial system could not be made to do further service at that time. But the parable of the Wine Skins is not limited to indicating the uselessness of old skins for new wine, but shows that a wise man provides new skins for his new wine so that neither wine nor skins is lost.

A word is necessary about the making of wine in Palestine. The grapes are trodden out in a wine press, the juice being run off to a lower trough. Here for a few days the juice is allowed to go through the first stage of fermentation, which, because of its activity, was called the "tumultuous stage". Wine put into either old or new skins before this process is complete would burst the containers. After three or four days the wine is transferred to the bottles, as described in the following quotation:

"The bottles were partially tanned goat-skins. The apertures where legs and tail had been were sewn up, leaving only that at the neck which is firmly tied when the skin is filled. The wine in the first stage of fermentation, if tied in the skins, would, by reason of the gas generated, burst them. When the tumultuous stage is passed, the new bottle yields sufficiently to permit completion of the process. Bottles once stretched in this way had no further powers of distention, and if used again for the same purpose would, of course, burst."

What, then, is the positive teaching of this small parable? Surely it is not far to seek. Jesus was providing wine—new wine—new teaching, which could not be received by the adherents to the old legalism and formalism. He had therefore to provide "new" men to whom his message could be entrusted. Hence his calling of the twelve and the seventy and the instruction given to them; hence his careful training of the twelve after the crowds were ceasing to follow him from place to place.

"Wine" is used figuratively in the Old Testament. It is used by Isaiah in an unmistakable way for the gospel embodied in the covenants of promise. "Ho, everyone that thirsteth . . . come, buy wine and milk without money and without price . . . Hearken diligently unto me . . . and let your soul delight itself in fatness . . . and I will make an everlasting covenant with you" (55 : 1-3). In a passage which does not present quite so direct a parallel but which requires a related interpretation, the same prophet says, "Thus saith the Lord, as the new wine is found in the cluster, and one saith, Destroy it not; for a blessing is in it: so will I do for my servants' sakes, that I might not destroy them all. And I will bring forth a seed out of Jacob, and out of Judah an inheritor of my mountains: and mine elect shall inherit it, and my servants shall dwell there" (Isa. 65 : 8-9). The cluster was Israel, not to be destroyed for the elect's sake—the elect being the worth-while juice of the grape, while skins and pulp were discarded. Perhaps both these related usages may be found in the promise of the Lord's "feast of fat things, a feast of wines on the lees" which the Lord will make in Zion when the kingdom is established (Isa. 25 : 6). The teaching of the new covenant will be given by that same "elect" which was in the "cluster" and saved by God.

Wine, which in itself can be good and yet can become a great evil, is also used of bad things—false doctrine and evil ways—in several places in the writings of the prophets.

The Lord uses "wine" to represent his own teaching in the enacted parable of the first sign of John's gospel. He changed the water for legal purification into wine for the wedding feast (John 2), an association of ideas also present in the parables of the bridegroom and of the wine skins. In the parable of the Samaritan the injured man had his wounds dressed with oil and wine. Treated as a parable and not merely as an illustration, Jesus was the "Samaritan", despised as such, who gave the gospel of salvation when legalist and ceremonialist passed by on the other side.

There was need for new men to carry the message of the Lord—not less so then than now. "If a man be in Christ he is a new creature" and as such he "contains" the gospel, not for his destruction but for his own and its preservation.

Jesus added a saying to this parable—an epitomized parable: "No man also having drunk old wine straightway desireth new: for he saith, The old is better". Jesus understood human nature with its conservatism, so useful when retaining the good, so hindering when upholding what is false. The saying was his patient and understanding explanation of why some men turned from him, and of why some good men desired to draw his disciples into the ways which they thought essential but which Jesus knew had only limited value.

20

HARVEST AND LABOURERS

(Matt. 9 : 36-38; Luke 10 : 2)

"Jesus went about all the cities and villages, teaching in their synagogues, and preaching the gospel of the kingdom, and healing every sickness and every disease among the people. But when he saw the multitudes, he was moved with compassion on them, because they fainted, and were scattered abroad, as sheep having no shepherd" (Matt. 9 : 35, 36).

Matthew's description of the multitude is based on the language of the prophets concerning Israel: "they were scattered because there is no shepherd" (Ezek. 35 : 5). But God said He would "set up one shepherd over them, and he shall feed them" (verse 23). This "one shepherd", in marked contrast to the hireling shepherds of Ezekiel's days, had compassion on the people. God was Israel's king and the shepherd was appointed by Him. Sent by God to the lost sheep of the house of Israel, Jesus, the Shepherd, sought to gather the sheep by "teaching in their synagogues, and preaching the gospel of the kingdom" (Matt. 9 : 35). In his compassion he said: "The harvest truly is plenteous, but the labourers are few; pray ye therefore the Lord of the harvest, that he will send forth labourers into his harvest" (verses 37, 38).

The quick transition of the figure from sheep to harvest is natural. The "sheep" were also "plants" growing in God's field. The work of shepherding was also in another figure the work of harvesting. Where the rulers spoke contemptuously of those who listened to Jesus as publicans and sinners, Jesus saw in the thronging crowds of Galilee men and women interested in his message, who as wheat ripening needed to be harvested.

The harvest figure was a call for helpers: and since it was God's work the helpers must be co-workers by His arrangement. The work was great—the workers few; so few at that moment that it was really one only, the Lord himself. But he said, "Pray ye, therefore, the Lord of the harvest, that he will send forth labourers into his harvest" (verse 38). Then, acting as God's representative, he sent out the twelve in pairs empowered to preach and heal; and he who had looked with compassion on the people and seen them shepherdless, told the twelve to go to them (10 : 6).

In Luke's gospel the saying about the harvest is given in another but connected context. He records the sending of the twelve in 9 : 1; then in 10 : 1 he says: "After these things the Lord appointed other seventy also"— also, that is, in addition to the twelve; and they were sent out in thirty-five pairs to preach, going before him on his tour. And to the seventy he repeated the words which prefaced his appointment of the twelve.

Much earlier in the ministry he had used the same figure of the harvest to represent his work. When the Samaritan woman hurried to her village home and burst out, "Come, see a man which told me all things that ever I did", the Samaritans streamed out at her bidding to see Jesus. While she was doing this, the perplexed disciples were wondering what Jesus meant by his cryptic allusion to having meat of which they knew not (R.V.), and Jesus was explaining that his meat was to do God's will. One part of that work he had been performing in his talk to the woman: and looking across the plains to the approaching Samaritans he said, "Lift up your eyes, and look on the fields; for they are white already to harvest. And he that reapeth receiveth wages, and gathereth fruit unto life eternal: that both he that soweth and he that reapeth may rejoice together. And herein is that saying true, One soweth, and another reapeth. I sent you to reap that whereon ye bestowed no labour: other men laboured, and ye are entered into their labours" (John 4 : 35-38).

Jesus had been sowing: there was even then a harvesting in that many Samaritans believed on him (v. 39); but there was a fuller harvesting when the outspreading of apostolic labours took Philip to Samaria (Acts 8). The saying of Jesus is so framed that it covers many phases. All God's servants were labourers in this work. "Others had laboured"—the prophets and John; the work of Jesus himself continued it; the Apostles entered into and carried the same work forward.

21
THE CROSS
(Matt. 10 : 38; 16 : 24; Mark 8 : 34; Luke 9 : 23; 14 : 27)

JESUS never underestimated the difficulties involved in following him. He made it clear in plain speech, and also in figure and parable, that he called men to no easy task. Perhaps the figurative forms in which his warning was framed were most emphatic, for no language could be more expressive of the cost of discipleship than the figure of cross-bearing. A man condemned to death by crucifixion had to bear the stake upon which his body would presently hang. Shame, agony, and death were involved in bearing the cross.

From the beginning of his ministry it is evident that Jesus knew that his end would come by crucifixion. He told Nicodemus that as the serpent was lifted up in the wilderness, so he must be "lifted up". The end of his own life being so clearly envisaged, it is not surprising therefore to find Jesus using the "cross" as a figure for all that discipleship would mean—for denial of self, for crucifixion of self.

The first time he employs the figure (Matt. 10 : 38) is in connection with the demand that his disciples must confess him before men. Such a course would entail conflict and sometimes death; but he came not to bring peace but a sword. When men decided to follow him, they would find even their own families in opposition. Following him would test a man's allegiance severely, for it even required that a choice be made between parents and Jesus. The severity of the demand is then expressed in the figure of the cross: "He that taketh not his cross, and followeth after me, is not worthy of me". That his own way involved cross-bearing is clear from this saying, for the disciple is to *follow* him: but that his words literally involved for himself death by crucifixion would not be clear. That it might mean surrendering life was not hidden: "He that findeth his life shall lose it: he that loseth his life for my sake, shall find it". It is a startling paradox, resolved by the context. A man who avoids the cross shall die; the man who accepts the cross shall live. The saying projects the thought into the future when final issues are determined, when men who have chosen the way of self will die, but those who have crucified self will have everlasting life.

The disciples were not unfamiliar with crucifixion, for in their lifetime hundreds of Jews who had taken part in insurrections in Palestine had been hung on crosses on the roadsides. In a general way they would perceive the meaning of cross-bearing though perhaps the figure would seem harsh; there can be no doubt that Jesus used it with a full recognition of what was involved for himself.

The second occasion on which Jesus used the figure was after Peter's confession that Jesus was the Christ, and his well meant but nevertheless satanic remonstrance to his Master. From the time of this confession by Peter, the gospel writers indicate that Jesus emphasized that he would meet his death at Jerusalem (Matt. 16 : 21). On this occasion he uses the simple terms "be killed and be raised again the third day". He then speaks of the duty of disciples, using the figure of "the cross" in a similar way to the previous occasion. For Jesus himself it is evident that being "killed" meant being crucified, and he refers both to that and to his resurrection with the calmness that belongs to assured knowledge. By a picture compressed into a question, the meaning of the double paradox that "losing life is finding life" and that "finding life is losing life", is carried forward. "For what is a man profited, if he shall gain the whole world, and forfeit his life? or what shall a man give in exchange for his life?" (verse 26 : *lose,* A.V.—forfeit his life, R.V.; a different word from verse 25).

The question concerns the day of account when a man, who has so served self that he has acquired possession of the world, stands before Jesus. He has the title-deed of the world; but his life is forfeit, for he was not prepared to lose that life in following Jesus, and he must lose it now. What will he give in exchange for his life when he faces that crisis? Jesus leaves the listener to answer. Without doubt a man would then say, "Whatever I possess is no good to me if my life is taken away; I will give all I possess to have life". Such a decision then will not avail; but Jesus presses the consideration of ultimate issues upon the attention of his hearers that they may be led to make a right decision while life can yet be gained. Jesus establishes the certainty of the picture he has drawn in such a simple way, by adding "For the Son of man shall come in the glory of his Father with his angels; and then he shall reward every man according to his works" (verse 27).

Luke records the use of the figure of the cross on another occasion, when Jesus added two small parables to enforce his meaning, which will be considered later (14 : 26, 27).

In an announcement on the last journey to Jerusalem Jesus spoke again of his own death. Matthew's record uses the word "crucify" which, in this context, could mean nothing else than its own literal dread significance: "The Son of man shall be betrayed unto the chief priests and unto the scribes, and they shall condemn him to death, and shall deliver him to the Gentiles to mock, and scourge, and to crucify him: and the third day he shall rise again" (Matt. 20 : 18, 19).

22

REEDS, CITY-STORMERS, CHILDREN AT PLAY

(Matt. 11 : 7-19; Luke 7 : 18-33)

JOHN the Baptist testified that the one of whom he was the forerunner would have in his hand a fan and would thoroughly cleanse the threshing floor. He also announced him to be the Lamb of God that taketh away the sin of the world. If the prophets searched "what, and what manner of time the spirit of Christ which was in them did signify when it testified beforehand the sufferings and the glory of Christ", may we not think also that John was faced with the same perplexity; not indeed about someone to come, but about one in living association with his own work. The works of Jesus did not altogether fit in with what might have been expected, and he sent to Jesus to ask: "Art thou he that should come, or look we for another?" That it denotes perplexity we may believe: that it showed lack of faith, or instability of character, the eulogy of Jesus does not permit us to believe.

Jesus immediately performed a number of mighty works, and told John's messengers to report to John what they had seen; Jesus added the message of special value to John at the time: "And blessed is he whosoever shall not be offended in me". For the moment John had found in Jesus an "occasion of stumbling"; Jesus called for patience and trust in what he was doing. As the messengers went away, Jesus addressed the crowd concerning John. He would have no misunderstanding about his faithful forerunner. They had heard John's stern words; they knew of his courageous testimony to Herod concerning his illicit union with Herodias. Was he a vacillating weakling after all? "What went ye out into the wilderness to see? A reed shaken with the wind? But what went ye out for to see? A man clothed in soft raiment? Behold, they that wear soft clothing are in king's houses" (Matt. 11 : 7, 8).

The reeds grew luxuriously in the Jordan valley, sometimes reaching a height of 20 feet. Beautiful to look upon they might be: but see them when the wind blows! They respond to every breeze, bending flat and rising again as the wind passes—ever a picture of the weakling, as the oak is of strength. John was not a reed. Neither was he a smooth-tongued courtier, easy going, seeking personal pleasures and gratifying every whim of dress. Such had their place in the king's palace. Where was John? In the king's prison. The softly spoken man-pleaser is not to be found there. John belonged to the court of another king than Herod or Caesar, but was then sharing the "exile" of his Royal Master.

"Bruised reeds" were then to be endured by the Messiah, as he had then to suffer the smoking flax of the rulers of his day who, instead of shining with divine reflection, were darkened in counsel and led the people astray (Matt. 12 : 14-21). There is misunderstanding of the figures of the "broken reed" and the "smoking flax" by some readers. God endures both now; but a day is coming when the true qualities of men will be revealed and unsuitable material discarded.

John was a prophet, more than a prophet: his was the honour of the man who immediately precedes the king: none in all the world was greater than John the Baptist; but, adds Jesus, the least in his Kingdom will be greater than John was then. But John was the last as well as the greatest of the prophets. "The law and the prophets were till John." Now had come the end of the law; and the one of whom the prophets had testified was in their midst. One dispensation was closing, and another dispensation was beginning.

Jesus then speaks of the new order and the manner of men who enter. As given in the A.V. verse 12 reads: "From the days of John the Baptist until now the kingdom of heaven suffereth violence, and the violent take it by force".

A problem of translation exists in connection with the verb, treated in the A.V. as passive, although active in form. Deissman, student of Greek papyri and first century Greek, draws attention to the inscription of the patron of a sanctuary which speaks of a "man forcing himself in". So here Jesus says the kingdom forces itself upon men's attention and forceful (same word) men, take hold of it. The next verse helps the meaning: "All the prophets and the law prophesied until John". The Jews believed prophecy would cease with the coming of Messiah. John, says Jesus, is the last of the prophets—he is the last link in the chain. In that case the days of the kingdom had come, in the sense that the King was in their midst, and the gospel of the Kingdom was pressed upon men's attention. Difficulties would be found which must be overcome, but men imbued with the earnestness of troops who storm a city would gain an entrance. This meaning followed appropriately the words of Jesus concerning the character of John. John was earnest, heroic, strong: so must those be who would enter the Kingdom.

The further words of Jesus that John was in the sense "Elias which was for to come"—evidently not to be understood literally but only by those with ears to hear (verse 15) —also show that he would have them understand that John was the forerunner of the Messiah.

The parable of the market-place children follows naturally. "What", said Jesus, "is this generation like?" and he compared them to children at play in the market, who could not agree. They said:

"We have piped unto you,
And ye have not danced;
We have mourned unto you,
And ye have not lamented."

"Let us play weddings", some of the children said; but the others would not. "Well then, funerals"; still there was disagreement. Neither one game nor the other was pleasing to the fault-finders. Jesus gave the application: John had come calling sternly for repentance and an austere life; Jesus had mixed with the people, attending their marriage feasts, accepting invitations to meals at the houses of Pharisees and publicans. But neither John nor Jesus was acceptable. The men of that generation were like children, who were peevish and complaining. They disliked the message of both John and Jesus and therefore would have neither.

"But", concludes Jesus, "Wisdom is justified of her children". Wisdom, as well as the market place, has her children: but the children of wisdom honour the parent and justify her. Jesus was the wisdom of God (cf. Luke 11 : 49), and men who understood him and his message would not quarrel with him, nor find fault with him.

23
THE YOKE OF CHRIST
(Matt. 11 : 29)

"Take my yoke upon you, and learn of me", said Jesus (Matt. 11 : 29). It is a beautiful, interesting and instructive figure.

First let us get a clear picture of what a yoke is. It was "a bar which connects two of a kind—as the ox-yoke—fastened by bows on the necks of a pair of oxen and by thongs to the horns or the foreheads of the oxen. It consists generally of a piece of timber hollowed or made curving near each end, and fitted with bows for receiving the necks of the oxen, by which means two are connected for drawing. From a ring or hook in the bow a chain extends to the thing to be drawn".

A yoke is, therefore, something which unites two creatures for some particular task. There can be a willing and an unwilling yoking; therefore, the yoke can be a figure of an accepted service or an imposed bondage, of joy or woe, freedom or slavery. In all these senses it was used in the Old Testament (see Jer. 2 : 20; 28; Isa. 9 : 4; 58 : 6; 1 Kings 12 : 4; Lam. 3 : 27, etc.). What then is the meaning attached to its use by Jesus?

As he looked about him he saw men labouring under many yokes: his countrymen were subject to the Romans, which their rulers in pride tried to forget, even claiming that their race was never in bondage to any man (John

8 : 33). They suffered under a yoke of legal observance, "a yoke", as Peter said, "which neither we nor our fathers were able to bear" (Acts 15 : 10). They, in common with all men, but perhaps with an acuter sense of it because of the instruction of God's law, were in bondage to sin, "sold under sin" in Paul's words (Rom. 7 : 14).

The Jews were also familiar with the use of the figure for instruction: "the yoke of the law", "the yoke of the precept", "the yoke of the kingdom of heaven" signified instruction pertaining to these things. Men of Belial were "men without the yoke"—uninstructed men.

The book of Ecclesiasticus, in an appeal to seek learning and instruction, says:

"Put your neck *under the yoke,*
and let your soul *receive instruction*".

Turning now to the words of Jesus, he says: "Come unto me, all ye that labour, and are heavy laden; and I will give you rest. Take my yoke upon you, and learn of me, for I am meek, and lowly of heart, and ye shall find rest unto your souls. For my yoke is easy and my burden (load) is light".

It is a call to discipleship—"Come to me" and "learn of me"—and discipleship is taking his "yoke". It is entering into harness with him as fellow: it is sharing his outlook, approaching life his way, copying his meekness and lowliness of heart. Of such a character are they who learn his way; they are the "babes" of the preceding verses to whom God's will and purpose are "revealed". There is thus a close connection between the invitation to take the yoke and the verses immediately preceding; they form a series which many writers regard as consisting of disconnected sayings—perhaps even not Christ's words—loosely grouped together without having any real association of ideas. Careful study, however, shows that, accepted as the words of Jesus, spoken at one time, a stream of thought flows through all. The teaching of God is hidden from the wise, but revealed to babes. God has delivered all to the Son, to whom the Father is known and through whom the Father is revealed. It is a natural sequel that Jesus invites men to learn of him and enter into the fellowship of service with him.

"My yoke", Jesus said: for he was instructed in the Father's will. He had the open ear, and the "tongue of the learned, that I should speak a word in season to him that is weary", as Isaiah had foretold (50 : 4). The toil of labour, the search for truth, the burden of conscience—all these can be borne when men are yoked to him: for such is the grace and wonder of it, the burdens are cast away and are not to be borne at all. Life in association with the Son of man, yoked with him, is freed from many problems. The frets that come from pride and ambition, from desire for outward show, from self-will, are not to be found with the meek and the lowly of heart. The will of God which Jesus fully obeyed was his yoke which he invited man to share: he was not burdened by the heavy load of false interpretations the scribes imposed upon their followers. In his willing submission to God's will he found the instruction of God to be good and well fitted to his shoulder: and the rest of soul that he experienced he offers to all yoke-fellows.

It was not a new promise. In the days of Jeremiah the message had been heard: "Thus saith the Lord, Stand ye in the ways, and see, and ask for the old paths, where is the good way, and walk therein, and ye shall find rest for your souls" (Jer. 6 : 16). Who is this who now takes God's words on his own lips, and in his own person offers the rest of God? It is a high claim, but not too high when we understand that the speaker is the Son of God, in whom the Father is revealed.

24
SHEEP IN PIT
(Matt. 12 : 11, 12)

THIS short parable of a sheep fallen into a pit on a sabbath and its recovery by the shepherd who shows no sabbatarian scruples about the work, presents no difficulty in its application. If men are ready to rescue an animal, it was also lawful for Jesus to heal a man on the sabbath. But the parable acquires a deeper significance when seen in the framework of the sabbath controversy.

Towards the close of the first year of his ministry Jesus appears to have deliberately provoked interest in his attitude to the sabbath by healing the impotent man: John pointedly focuses attention on this by his words: "on the same day was the sabbath" (John 5 : 9). This third "sign" of John's record "provided Jesus with the opportunity to assert his claims as the Son, with power to perform all healing in everlasting life according to God's will wrought through him" (*Gospel of John,* page 79).

Within a few months the issue was raised by the Pharisees who were watching to find fault. The disciples plucked corn and ate it as they passed through a field—an action forbidden by Jewish tradition based on the method of interpretation of God's law so dear to the lawyers of Israel. The laws concerning the sabbath (Exod. 20 : 8-11; 31 : 12-17) inevitably sooner or later called for interpretation in their application to the details of life. The Tradition of the Elders gradually developed and provided what was recognized as an authorized setting out of what could and could not be done on the Sabbath.

Outside Palestine the pressure of circumstances would tend to make Jews somewhat relax the rigours of these rules. A man might follow his own religious exercises, and his association with his neighbours would not be much affected; but to stop all work every seventh day must have caused endless difficulties in work, in business and social life. In Palestine, with the Jews in the majority, greater importance would be attached to observing the rules concerning the Sabbath. Was not the Sabbath God's sign to them? Did not its preservation form an essential part of their witness to the true and living God? The zealous Jews in their own land were therefore fighting a battle for the faith of their fathers.

We must first look at the answer of Jesus to the critics of his disciples and then trace the significance of his action of healing and of his parable. To the rulers who found fault, he said, "Have ye not read?" and he cited the action of David and *those with him* in eating the shewbread when they were urgently in need of food. The fact that David was the Lord's anointed overruled the law which allotted the shewbread only to the priests. They themselves allowed this, and so doing allowed that one law could override another. But there was something else implicit in the citation by Jesus of David's action; for if that past happening had any bearing upon the action of the disciples —those with Jesus—it could only be found in the fact that Jesus was the Son of David, the Messiah. If David was permitted to do what he did because he was the Lord's anointed, then Jesus is asserting nothing less than that his permission to his disciples to eat is based on the fact that he is the Lord's Christ.

He gives a second illustration of the same principle of one law having overriding power over another law, again introduced by "Have ye not read?" Each seventh day the priests profane the Sabbath by the labour of offering sacrifices—indeed more were offered on that day than on others. In this case the law of the offerings was superior to the Sabbath law and had precedence. But Jesus pressed the lesson still further. The law of the offerings concerned the temple service—the service of God's house. Jesus said, with the emphatic introduction, "But I say unto you", "That in this place is one greater than the temple". There must be some correspondence in the things compared.

He was greater as the dwelling-place of God: he was in Paul's words "the true tabernacle which the Lord pitched, and not men" (Heb. 8 : 2).

After citing Hosea 6 (considered in connection with Matt. 9 : 13) he then adds, "For the Son of man is Lord even of the sabbath". If "the Son of man" is used as a Messianic title, then he claims that as Messiah he is Lord of the Sabbath. Upon what basis can this be? The answer is, and it is consonant with Jewish interpretation of the Sabbath, that that day was a type of Messiah's reign. Their own interpretation of the significance of the Sabbath should have opened their minds to the meaning of the words of Jesus. More authoritative to us than their tradition is the apostle's application of the rest of the Sabbath to the millennial rest (Heb. 4 : 9). If the Sabbath finds its fulfilment in the Kingdom of God, then Jesus as King of God's Kingdom is Lord of both the type and antitype.

In the next incident recorded by Matthew the claim of Messiahship is repeated. A man with a withered arm is in the synagogue, and the Pharisees, Mark adds, are there "watching" him. Mark also gives a fuller statement of the words of Jesus. Seeking whereby they might accuse him the Pharisees ask (Matt. 12 : 10): "Is it lawful to heal on the sabbath days?" His answer (Mark 3 : 4) is a question which enlarges the issue: "Is it lawful to do good on the sabbath day, or to do evil?" That the healing of the man would be "good" could not be questioned. Would they say it would be wrong to do good? But the reference to evil turns the tables. They were there expressly seeking how they might ensnare him. This was evil—yet they found no objection to plot for his death on the Sabbath. Their action was an inversion of the Sabbath intention, and also a hindrance to his work. They sought his death: but his mission was to give life and healing in the fullest of senses. He was angry (Mark) at the hardness of their hearts; and he said unto them:

"What man shall there be among you, that shall have one sheep, and if it fall into a pit on the sabbath day, will he not lay hold on it, and lift it out? How much then is a man better than a sheep? Wherefore it is lawful to do well on the sabbath days" (Matt. 12 : 11, 12).

Is there some inner connection between this little story and the Messianic claim involved in his teaching about the Sabbath? There would seem to be when we remember that he was the great shepherd God had promised in the messages of the prophets; and also that the figure of a pit is not infrequent in the Psalms. "He brought me up out of a horrible pit"; "they have digged a pit for my soul" (40 : 2; 35 : 7). "To go down to the pit" is to "draw nigh unto the grave" (88 : 3, 4); and from this pit of death Israel's Messiah had the power to rescue men. He united the claims to be the Messiah and the Resurrection when he said to Martha that he would raise up the dead "at the last day"—that is, in the day of Messiah. He pointed the same lesson when he raised the sick man from the pit of sickness to health on the Sabbath day.

The whole controversy was brought to a focus when Jesus told them that they practised circumcision on the Sabbath, the importance of the rite, which had its source with the fathers though incorporated in the law, being greater than the Sabbath. Jesus had healed on the Sabbath—making a man "every whit whole"—prefiguring that perfect health that belongs to Messiah's Sabbath (John 7 : 22, 23).

25
THE STRONG MAN SPOILED

(Matt. 12 : 22-30; Mark 3 : 22-30; Luke 11 : 14-23)

A MAN was blind and dumb, and in the language of the first century "possessed of a demon". When Jesus healed him, the people in their amazement exclaimed, "Is not this the Son of David?" that is, "Is not this the Messiah?" The Pharisees, however, sought another explanation. They could not deny the miracle, but at all costs they must deny the inference that thereby his Messiahship was established. They therefore said, "This fellow doth not cast out devils but by Beelzebub, the prince of devils". It was a rash and wicked charge, and Jesus at once replied to it.

"He knew their thoughts", the record tells us. They had not been addressing him, and it would appear that, in fact, they were beyond his hearing. "He called them unto him", says Mark. They learned by experience of continual discomfiture that both his questions and his answers were things to dread. His answer now was simple in its form and obvious in its application. A kingdom divided against itself comes to desolation; civil war disintegrates, it does not consolidate; and this is true also of municipal and family life: where there is internal strife there is weakness and at last dissolution. If Jesus worked by the Satanic power in curing people supposedly under Satan's influence, then Satan was fighting against himself—the absurdity of the reasoning showing how desperate was their difficulty to explain away the miracle.

But their own "sons"—either their own children or their disciples—practised exorcism. Did they explain the power of their "sons" as being of Satanic origin? Obviously not; then the possibility of other agencies in the healing of demoniacs was admitted.

Then comes Christ's counter claim: if he should have done the miracle by divine power, by the Spirit of God, then the Kingdom of God is come unto them. The miracle could not be disputed; the amazement of the people shows how altogether different in method and result was the healing Jesus performed from the cures done by others. It was manifestly done by divine power and by that only: then God was working in their midst. But Jesus calls it the coming unto them of God's kingdom. His words draw a contrast with the kingdom of Satan; they also indicate that if he was doing the mighty works which will be done when God's kingdom comes, then he must be the Messiah through whom by general Jewish consent the prophecies were to be fulfilled.

The kingdom was come nigh them, not only in the presence of the Messiah, but also in those principles and powers upon which the kingdom will be established and maintained, as shown by the works of Jesus. The kingdoms of God and of Satan were in conflict. Thus stated, Satan is a personification of sin and its consequences—disease. Sin was, as it were, enthroned in the world, and since sin was the ultimate cause of all the evils of human life, in those evils its sway was illustrated. The kingdom of God is a kingdom of righteousness, and the effects of righteousness—quietness, assurance, and life—will be the evidence of its establishment. God's kingdom will bring a world-wide extension of the ways of life seen in Jesus; but the issue was then being joined, and Jesus illustrates the conflict by a parable.

"Or else how can one enter into a strong man's house and spoil his goods, except he first bind the strong man? and then he will spoil his house."

Sin was strong, but not invincible. There was a stronger than he, who could bind him as a captive, and liberate his captives. The power of Jesus to do it was shown in his removal there and then of the effects of Satan's power over the demoniac.

Since the work of Jesus is thus seen to be related to the conflict of sin and righteousness in the world, men are not allowed to be neutrals. To espouse the cause of righteousness is a duty; neutrality is a help to the enemy. This Jesus expressed in terms of personal association with himself: "He that is not with me is against me; and he that gathereth not with me scattereth abroad".

The Pharisees accused Jesus of alliance with Satan: his rejoinder was a warning. Jesus clearly was in opposition to Satan since he had destroyed Satan's works. If the Pharisees were not with Jesus, they must be on Satan's side. It was a terrible counterthrust.

In similar figure God had said He was stronger than the Babylonian who had taken captive his people. "Shall the prey be taken from the mighty, or the lawful captive delivered? But thus saith the Lord, Even the captives of the mighty shall be delivered: for I will contend with him that contendeth with thee, and I will save thy children" (Isa. 49 : 24, 25). Israel's enemies have again and again found God to be mightier than themselves: Belshazzar's impious challenge to the truth of the predictions of God's prophets brought the nerve-shattering spectacle of the written doom on the walls of the palace. Many centuries before that day, Pharaoh vainly tried to keep his captives; but when "the selfsame day" of God's promised deliverance dawned, Pharaoh was glad to see the backs of his slaves. "Thou hast ascended on high, thou hast led a host of captives", was the Psalmist's commemoration of it in words which at the same time foretell the Lord's greater deliverance of captives from the bondage of death, as Paul witnesses in his exposition of Psalm 68 in Eph. 4 : 8. This deliverance from death is referred to in Isa. 49 : 9 where the servant of God who was given for a covenant will say "to the prisoners, Go forth; to them that are in darkness, Shew yourselves". He has even now acquired the key of the grave to open that prison house and call out its captives.

Is the figure of the angel from heaven that binds Satan (Rev. 20 : 2) a reminiscence of this short parable of the strong man bound and despoiled?

26
THE UNOCCUPIED HOUSE
(Matt. 12 : 43-45; Luke 11 : 24-26)

It is usual to call this parable The Story of the Unclean Spirit; but such a title puts the emphasis in the wrong place. It draws attention to the occupant, when the state of the house is the first consideration.

This story, like the Rich Man and Lazarus, is based upon current popular beliefs which regarded the world as the abode of unseen spirits—demons—which entered into possession of men and became the cause of their various maladies. A "deaf spirit" might be the cause of deafness, a "dumb spirit" the cause of dumbness, and so on. The "demonized" figure frequently among the cures of Jesus. Possession by demons is a notion that debases and bemuses thought, being destructive of the soundness of mind in which life can be faced with courage, its problems examined, and knowledge of fact secured. Moreover it tends to shift the responsibility for life on to the "demon" when it really belongs to the person.

The idea, however, lends itself effectively to the lesson Jesus wanted to teach: the touch of eeriness attached to it would make it impressive. We have to think of something intangible, evil and repellent, something to be disliked. The "spirit" tenants a man who is the expression of the evil thing. It then leaves him, and roams homeless in the wilderness. In its absence the house is cleaned and made wholesome, but remains unoccupied. The spirit meanwhile is seeking rest, and bethinks itself of its old home. It creeps towards it, peeps within, and finding no occupant, rushes away to gather other boon companions to share the house with it. The one tenant which originally needed an eviction order has now become eight: and as Jesus said, the last state is worse than the first.

What is the meaning of this parable? The primary application Jesus fixes for us, when he added: "Even so shall it be also unto this generation". The story was at once a description and a prophecy: it described that generation at the point when the evil had gone, but was returning. Its last end was still in the future—"shall be"—when Jesus spoke. The meaning is not difficult to find. The nation was sinful, the more blameworthy that they had the Law of God. Through the preaching of John there had been a cleansing process going on; the people had repented and been baptized of John, confessing their sins. But John had directed attention to the greater than himself upon whom they should believe. Instead of doing this, they stopped short; instead of belief, active opposition to God's will as revealed in Jesus was taking hold of them, presently to be shown in their rejection of him. This was followed by their refusal of the appeal through the apostles, after which the nation was given over to its self-will which reached its climax in the frenzied resistance to Rome when the fury and perversity of fanaticism "demonized" the nation and swept to its own destruction.

Jesus had spoken of that generation as "evil and adulterous" (verse 39). They had asked for a sign; but the only sign they were given was one already before them in the Scriptures—the sign of the resurrected prophet whose preaching was heard by Gentile Ninevites. The men of Nineveh condemned that generation, as also did the Queen of Sheba who sought Solomon for his wisdom, for one greater than either Jonah or Solomon was there, sent of God, and revealing God's wisdom, but the generation would not give heed to him. The parable was a warning of doom for their folly of not receiving Jesus as the ruler of the house.

The parable is fundamentally, psychologically, true of human nature: the parable is the story of many a man who has sought with some success to exorcize an evil habit, but instead of developing and enthroning the opposite positive good, has stopped short at the first step. Nature will not allow this. Unless a good habit is given full possession, the old evil asserts itself with sevenfold power, and recovery becomes sevenfold more difficult. "Make free men of your pupils", counsels Wm. James in *Talks to Teachers,* "by habituating them to act, whenever possible, under the notion of good. Get them habitually to tell the truth, not so much through showing them the wickedness of lying as by arousing their enthusiasm for honour and veracity. Wean them from their native cruelty by imparting to them some of your own positive sympathy with an animal's inner springs of joy . . . And in the lessons . . . upon the bad effects of alcohol, lay less stress than the books do on the drunkard's stomach, kidneys, nerves, and social miseries, and more on the blessings of having an organism kept in lifelong possession of its youthful elasticity by a sweet sound blood to which stimulants and narcotics are unknown, and to which the morning sun and air and dew will daily come as sufficiently powerful intoxicants."

Or, in the words of another, "Evil appetites and passions do not yield most readily to direct assault. Passion must be evoked to cast out passion. And if once heart and mind be filled with strong positive interests, the rest will come of itself. For these wholesome incentives will, ever increasingly, occupy the soul, and, if only they be skilfully fostered, will strike up alliances with one another, till the promptings we wish to get rid of will gradually be ousted from their squalid or knavish tenancy. For development and repression are not two things, but one; all genuine development already carries in it repression of much."

But, just as the lesson of the story, being fundamentally true, has its application to the nation of Israel and to individuals, so it would be possible to trace the parallel in broader movements among men. The Reformation did something to cleanse Europe of Romish superstition and for a time enthroned the Bible—but did not go on to a full understanding of it. Decline set in; Higher Criticism found its home in the very land of the Reformation, and the nation accepted the absurdities put forward by Nazi propagandists, and their evil state revealed itself in the horrors of detention camps and all the ghastly practices which the trials of Nuremberg dragged to light. Who can exorcize the evil spirits which hold power in the soul of a nation?

27
THE PARABLE OF THE SOWER

(Matt. 13 : 3-9, 18-23; Mark 4 : 1-20; Luke 8 : 1-14)

ABOUT midway in the second year of his ministry Jesus began to use the parabolic form of teaching more extensively than before. Many of his sayings before this time, as we have already found, were in the form of short parables; but the changing attitude of the people called for an extended use of the parable. The first flush of enthusiasm was passing and the rulers already were plotting to secure his death. In these circumstances his use of stories, based upon everyday things and happenings, served several purposes. The stories are easily remembered and easily recalled when the situation Jesus described is seen again. To those interested they were provocative of thought and would gradually yield their meaning, although many of them would not be fully understood until after his resurrection. But they served another purpose about which some have been critical and others perplexed.

That the parable of the Sower introduced a new style into his teaching was observed by the disciples. They asked him, "Why speakest thou unto them in parables?" He answered, "Because it is given unto you to know the mysteries of the kingdom of heaven, but to them it is not given. For whosoever hath, to him shall be given, and he shall have more abundance: but whosoever hath not, from him shall be taken away even that he hath. Therefore I speak to them in parables: because they seeing see not; and hearing they hear not, neither do they understand. And in them is fulfilled the prophecy of Esaias, which saith, By hearing ye shall hear, and shall not understand; and seeing ye shall see, and shall not perceive: for this people's heart is waxed gross, and their ears are dull of hearing, and their eyes they have closed; lest at any time they should see with their eyes, and hear with their ears, and should understand with their heart and should be converted, and I should heal them. But blessed are your eyes, for they see: and your ears, for they hear. For verily I say unto you, That many prophets and righteous men have desired to see those things which ye see, and have not seen them; and to hear those things which ye hear, and have not heard them" (Matt. 13 : 11-17).

Primarily, the object of teaching is to enlighten; if human teachers fail they can do no more, they have done what was possible and the hearers are the losers. But when a teacher sent from God delivers a message, the hearers sustain an added responsibility to God, for God's word has a divine authority and calls for obedience and not criticism. Not everyone, however, has the capacity either to recognize it as God's word, or to understand and appreciate its message. But the coming of the word has nevertheless made a difference. Those with understanding hearts know more; the unresponsive become more incapable of response; the defiant are accountable, varying in degree, doubtless, and to different judgments in form and time.

The parabolic form of teaching provides a test to those who hear. The humble-hearted store it in their minds and its meaning is understood. The critical, the prejudiced, the bitter, the opposing, by their very attitude do not take to heart the lesson, and the teaching becomes more misunderstood and their attitude to the teacher one of great bitterness and antipathy. It is not for human teachers to aim deliberately at such effects; it is not theirs to judge the hearts of hearers. The Son of God was in a very different position. He knew the effect of the method he chose; he could choose a method to produce a given effect. That he had the right to do so none will question who acknowledge his unique position and divine authority.

Matthew records together eight parables: some writers have thought that the arrangement is Matthew's, but there is no evidence that they were not all spoken on the same occasion. There is a formal division into two groups marked by difference in the audience and in the place where spoken. The second, third and fourth parables are introduced with the words "Another parable put he forth" (verses 24, 31, 33). Jesus after speaking the first few parables, dismissed the multitude "and went into the house". There the disciples enquired the meaning of the parable of the Tares. After his explanation Jesus added three parables, each introduced by the phrase, "Again the kingdom of heaven is like" (verses 44, 45, 47) Jesus then gave the last short parable of "the scribe instructed unto the Kingdom", and "when he had finished these parables, he departed thence".

The first two parables, the Sower and the Tares, are important because to each Jesus gave an explanation. There have been fashions in interpreting the parables. In the first generation after the apostles, much ingenuity was exercised in finding something in the explanation to fit every detail in the parable. This method produced a revolt, and it was maintained that only the central idea mattered and was alone intended, everything else being incidental to the story. In his explanation of the sower, however, Jesus explained that the seed is the word (Mark 4 : 14) and the four kinds of soil represented four different kinds of people. The fowls that devoured the seed were "the wicked one" (Matt. 13 : 19), Satan (Mark 4 : 15), the devil (Luke 8 : 12). The sun which scorched the shallow-rooted plant growing on a layer of rock covered by only a thin covering of soil, was tribulation, affliction and persecution. The thorns were the cares of this world, the deceitfulness of riches, and the lusts of other things. The good ground represented the honest and good of heart who hear the word, keep it, and bring forth fruit with patience. Jesus did not indicate who was represented by the sower: in the first and most important sense he is the sower, but perhaps the absence of identification left open a wider application to include those who continue his work of sowing the seed of the kingdom. The extended explanation which he gave, however, does not discourage the student from looking at details and seeking for meanings conformable to the general lesson of the parable and in harmony with the plain teaching of the word of God.

The parables are all taken from familiar objects, yet there is little that is exclusively Jewish about them. Some of them do gain in vividness with a knowledge of local background and customs; yet the meaning of all can be understood without that knowledge. They have the universality that belongs to the one who spoke them: it is easy to forget that he was a Jew, and the stories, like him, belong to all men, whether Jew or Gentile. Stanley draws attention to this remarkable absence of a reference to any exclusive Jewish practice or thought, while recognizing also the wonderful truth in all local details of the pictures drawn by Jesus. Thus, he writes in *Sinai and Palestine:*

"A slight recess in the hillside, close upon the plain, disclosed at once, in detail, and with a conjunction which I remember nowhere else in Palestine, every feature of the great parable. There was the undulating cornfield descending to the water's edge. There was the trodden pathway running through the midst of it, with no fence or hedge to prevent the seed from falling here and there on either side of it, or upon it—itself hard with the constant tramp of horse and mule and human feet. There was the good rich soil, which distinguishes the whole of that plain and its neighbourhood from the bare hills elsewhere descending into the lake, and which, where there is no interruption, produces one vast mass of corn. There was the rocky ground of the hillside protruding here and there through the corn-fields, as elsewhere through the grassy slopes. There were the large bushes of thorn—the *nabk,* that kind of which tradition says that the crown of thorns was woven—springing up, like the fruit trees of the more inland parts, in the very midst of the waving wheat".

The meaning of the parable, with Christ's own explanation of it, is clear. But some of its lessons are easily overlooked. The quality of the seed is the same upon whatever ground it falls; failure to realize the end in view in the sowing is never the fault of the seed. We might sow seeds of some plant and think that the results would show the germinating power and the quality of the strain of the seed. But the seed of the parable is the word of God, "the incorruptible seed" as Peter calls it (1 Pet. 1 : 23). That in itself cannot fail. As God through Isaiah testified: "As the rain cometh down, and the snow from heaven, and returneth not thither, but watereth the earth, and maketh it bring forth and bud, that it may give seed to the sower and bread to the eater: so shall my word be that goeth forth out of my mouth: it shall not return unto me void, but it shall accomplish that which I please, and it shall prosper in the thing whereto I sent it" (55 : 10-11).

What is revealed by the sower's work is the soil's productiveness. Not all soil provides the conditions suitable for plant-growth, and this is made clear by results when the seed has been scattered upon it. It might be said, therefore, that the seed tests the soil, or, to transfer this to the explanation of the parable, the preaching of the gospel tests and reveals the suitability of men and women for divine purposes. Some are as unresponsive as the hard-trodden path. Some receive the word quickly and enthusiastically, but do not maintain their interest; when trial comes it is found that God's word has not deep rootage—it could not have because of the native shallowness of the person. Others have full possibilities of an abundant yield, but the mind is so much occupied with other interests that the spiritual life is choked. Jesus defines "the thorns" as the care of this world and the deceitfulness of riches; in this as in everything else he spoke unerringly, exhibiting the weakness of human nature which hinders that full service of heart and soul to God's demands. With the same discernment he also indicates the essentials to fruitfulness; the various phrases of the three records are: "hearing the word"; "understanding it"; "receiving it"; "in an honest and good heart, having heard the word, keep it". With Christ's explanation before us, the parable should be thought of as a parable of soils, equally or perhaps more than a parable of the Sower, although the figure of the Sower has a peculiar significance.

There is no suggestion of any mathematical ratio of results. There is no indication of what a person himself may do towards breaking up fallow ground. The parable is rather a declaration of the results which become apparent when the word has been preached. Any parable which is based upon things which have no volition, inevitably cannot indicate the changes which may take place where the will can operate. But the parable clearly shows that the preaching does not gain universal acceptance, and it gives the reasons. The parable reflects what the passing of time was revealing in the experience of Jesus himself. His hearers were becoming "classified" as they showed their reactions to his work and words. The parable was instructive to the disciples also, tempering the enthusiasm which they must have felt at the first wild response given to Jesus, which would lead them to expect results quite contrary to what would prove the case. The instruction still applies to-day as in every age, preventing the deep disappointment that might be felt when the first love of the truth awakens to the fact that all men have not faith.

The very aptness of the story, the seasonal regularity with which the scene would recur to all Christian hearers, must not be allowed to obscure the particular significance which underlay the choice of the sower and his work for the lesson. In the prophecies of Israel's re-gathering, through Hosea, there is a play upon the name Jezreel, which means "God sows". Following the margin of the R.V. we read: "It shall come to pass in that day, I will answer, saith the Lord, I will answer the heavens, and they shall answer the earth; and the earth shall answer the corn, and the wine, and the oil; and they shall answer (Jezreel) whom God soweth. And I will sow her unto me in the land, and I will have mercy upon her that had not obtained mercy; and I will say to them which were not my people, Thou art my people; and they shall say, Thou art my God" (Hos. 2 : 21-23). The same figure is used in Jer. 31 : 27: "I will sow the house of Israel and the house of Judah with the seed of man and with the seed of beast". Isa. 55 : 10 has already been quoted. When Jesus uses the figure of himself, it suggests that the thought is not far away that he is the one in whom God would reveal Himself and who would be Israel's king. As in many of these stories of Jesus, there is an implied Messianic claim in the neglect of which there is failure to perceive the fulness of his teaching.

28
THE TARES
(Matt. 13 : 24-30, 36-43)

OF all the parables, that concerning the tares has been the cause of the most contention. Its interpretation played an important part in the contentions that arose at the time of the Donatists. The rise and work of this body is noticed in *Eureka* II, chapter vii. The Donatists opposed the corruptions which had grown up in Christendom and denied that many who claimed to be Christians were entitled to be so described. They particularly opposed the growing association of Church and State, and consequently by the decrees of Constantine suffered the loss of their buildings used for worship, banishment, and in some cases death. They were opposed by the leaders of the corrupt church, particularly by Augustine, who has the distinction, more than any other of the "fathers", of establishing the doctrines of the immortality of the soul and that the Church was the Kingdom of God as accepted tenets of the Church. The Donatists were exclusive, and one of the arguments used against them was based upon the interpretation of the parable of the Tares, that Jesus taught that the wheat and tares had to grow together until the harvest, and that the discipline which the Donatists called for was not scriptural. The Donatist reply was a denial of the application made by the Augustinians. The latter taught that "the field" was the church where "wheat and tares" should remain together; the Donatists insisted that in the interpretation given by Jesus the field was "the world" and the lesson of the parable had nothing to do with the question whether spurious and heretical Christians should be excluded from the Church.

It is a safe rule in the interpretation of a parable that no meaning shall be attached to it that conflicts with the plain teaching of the Scripture. Judged by this, Augustine was as erroneous in his views on church discipline as on the nature of man. The teaching of Jesus lays down the method to be employed in reclaiming any in error. If recovery was not achieved the offender had to be as "a heathen man" (Matt. 18 : 17). Fuller instruction on this matter is naturally to be found in the epistles and particularly those dealing with ecclesial organization. Paul's counsel concerning the rejection of a "heretic" after the second admonition (Tit. 3 : 10) appears to have the words of Jesus in mind. In other epistles he is quite explicit about the duty of ecclesias "to avoid", "have no company with", "put away", "reject", those that were teachers of errors or who were persistently evil in their ways (2 Thess. 3 : 6; 1 Cor. 5 : 11; 1 Tim. 6 : 3-5; 2 John 8-10). It is quite clear from these commandments given by the apostles who were authorized to teach by their Lord, that it would be a wrong interpretation of the parable to attempt to deduce from it rules of men's duty when there is laxity in a community of professing believers. It cannot mean that false teachers should be allowed to retain their place in ecclesial life.

In later times the Catholics were at pains to reconcile their persecution of heretics with the instruction that wheat and tares must be allowed to grow together until the end of the age. Emphasis was laid on the warning that in gathering up tares the wheat also might be destroyed—and this was taken to mean that the prohibition did not apply where there was no doubt that a man was a heretic; only when the heresy was not fully revealed must toleration be exercised. On this interpretation the reason Jesus gave for not plucking up the tares is made into a conditional prohibition.

Other views are connected with noted names in ecclesiastical history, as men have sought to explain this parable and fix their conduct in the light of it. But we need not follow these views further. Even if his hearers did not grasp his meaning as Jesus spoke, and even if his explanation was not fully understood at the time, yet there must have been some clear intention in the mind of Jesus; this we should seek.

The story is not an improbable one. It is said that Roman law legislated for dealing with such an injurious act as a man over-sowing with weeds some cultivated ground. Trench cites modern illustrations of such over-sowing from India and Ireland.

The Kingdom of heaven, Jesus said, was "like unto a man which sowed good seed". While he slept his enemy sowed "tares". His servants, discovering what had happened when growth began, asked if they should pluck up the tares. The master instructed them that both wheat and tares should remain till the harvest when the reapers should gather up and burn the tares and garner the wheat.

The "tare" is the darnel, about which many who have lived in Palestine have written. In *The Land and The Book* Thomson says: "Let me call your attention to these 'tares' which are growing among the barley. The grain is just in the proper stage of development to illustrate the parable. In those parts where the grain has headed out, they have done the same, and there a child cannot mistake them for wheat or barley; but where both are less developed, the closest scrutiny will often fail to detect them. I cannot do it at all with any confidence. Even the farmers, who in this country generally weed their fields, do not attempt to separate the one from the other. They would not only mistake good grain for them, but very commonly the roots of the two are so intertwined that it is impossible to separate them without plucking up both. Both, therefore, must be left to 'grow together until the time of harvest'."

This general rule to "let both grow together" is not contradicted by the other practice of pulling out an occasional stray stalk (cf. Stanley, *Sinai and Palestine,* p. 426) This was possible, and saved much trouble with the grain, whereas a complete oversowing of darnel would make it impossible to eradicate the weed without great damage to the good crop.

The "darnel", says one who was a native of Galilee, "is a very troublesome weed which occurs in the wheat-fields of Palestine. Women have to be hired to pick it out from the seed which is to be milled, and very careful farmers will even have it picked out from the wheat which is to be used for seed. As a rule the separation of the darnel from the wheat is done after the threshing. By spreading the grain out on a large tray which is set before the women, they are able to pick out the darnel, which is a seed similar in shape and size to wheat but slate-grey in colour".

Even a few grains left with the wheat will spoil all the harvest. The bitterness of the darnel would make all the bread unpleasant to eat as well as making the eater ill.

The story must have seemed hard to interpret to the listeners, and it is not surprising that when the multitude had been sent away the disciples asked Jesus its meaning, the very name by which they spoke of the parable showing what they felt was the essential difficulty. "Declare unto us the parable of the tares of the field." Jesus then enumerated all the points that had significance (Matt. 13 : 37-43) :

"He that soweth the good seed is the Son of man; the field is the world; the good seed are the children of the kingdom; but the tares are the children of the wicked one; the enemy that sowed them is the devil; the harvest is the end of the world; and the reapers are the angels. As therefore the tares are gathered and burned in the fire; so shall it be in the end of the world. The Son of man shall send forth His angels, and they shall gather out of his kingdom all things that offend, and them which do iniquity; and shall cast them into a furnace of fire: there shall be wailing and gnashing of teeth. Then shall the righteous shine forth as the sun in the kingdom of their Father."

At once differences in application between this parable, and the parable of the Sower, appear. Jesus here defines the Sower. Also, in the Sower parable the seed was the word of the Kingdom; here the seed are the individuals, good or bad. These differences have to be kept in mind.

The field is the world, Jesus explained, and for a right understanding of the parable we must not change the world into the church. And since the Son of man is the Sower, the starting point of the parable is his own ministry, to which we may perhaps add the work of those who were specifically appointed to, and endowed with power for, the carrying of his message throughout the world.

28 : THE TARES

After the sowing of the wheat an enemy sows tares in the same field. Other sowers began their work, but what they sowed was a counterfeit of the wheat. It resembled it, but was harmful and useless. The wheat, Jesus said, were children of the Kingdom; the darnel, children of the wicked one. Yet the latter had professions which corresponded to the former. Thus viewed, the parable is a prediction of the growth of a system which would counterfeit the truth taught by Jesus, which would claim to be his church, but which would be of "the wicked one".

In his last letter Paul warns Timothy of perils to come, when men would have a form of godliness but deny its power; when sound doctrine would not be endured, and fables would be followed. He further indicates that this apostasy would assume the form of a counterfeit of the true. "As Jannes and Jambres withstood Moses, so do these men resist the truth: men of corrupt mind, reprobate concerning the faith." How did the Egyptian magicians resist Moses? By imitating his work, by repeating as far as they could the wonders that he had done. So again would truth be resisted, and error established.

No reader of the New Testament epistles and of the Apocalypse can miss the repeated notes of warning which all sound. The warning is not merely of the trials and difficulties that then clouded the sky; the writers look forward to a fuller development of the evils they combated. The atmosphere is charged with the portents of future storm. The history of Christendom could not have been different from what it is and the predictions of the apostles be fulfilled.

In a very short time after the apostle's day "the mysteries" which so captivated men's minds in the pagan world, had so corrupted the teaching of the apostles that a pagan would have felt at home in one of the ecclesiastical buildings, while the apostles would have been strangers. The development of a priesthood, the changing of the significance of baptism, the adoption of the pagan trinity, of the philosophic notion of the soul's immortality, the introduction of pagan rites, such as burning of tapers and other practices unknown in apostolic churches—all marked the change from truth to error, from loyalty to Zion to subservience to Babylon from whence all these errors had ultimately come.

The darnel are the children of the wicked one. The wicked one is a personification of the thinking of the flesh, and the darnel thus represents, not apostate believers in the ecclesia, but the members of the great apostasy of nominal Christianity which by a counterfeit has seduced men from the truth which makes free.

Should such a growth of evil be allowed? Jesus in the parable shows that it would be allowed to the end of the age. It could only be destroyed with its widespread effect, by destroying also the faith established by the labours of the apostles. But there would be a separating time, at the end of the age. The Son of man, the sower, whose labours marked the beginning of the story, will send the angel reapers to gather out of his kingdom all that offends. For the world is his kingdom by divine title, and the time for his possession of it will then have come. It will be a time of judgment for Christendom, when its true nature will be revealed. Then also the children of the kingdom will be revealed in all the splendour of the sunshine. For these children of the kingdom are those of whom Daniel spoke who turn many to righteousness, and this identification Jesus makes when he thus uses the words of the prophet to describe their reward.

The parable has thus nothing to do with rules of ecclesial life. It does not teach a compromise of truth with error. It does not authorize the Papal Church to destroy those regarded by her as heretics. It does indicate the action of the Son of man in the beginning as the planter of truth; it shows that through the ages he has permitted the evil work of men who counterfeited while destroying his work, but that at last in a day of judgment he will eradicate from his kingdom the evil, God-dishonouring notions of men; and associated with his friends, he will then bring light and health to the world.

29
THE MUSTARD SEED

(Matt. 13 : 31, 32; Mark 4 : 30-32; Luke 13 : 18, 19)

To this parable two interpretations have been given which are so opposed that one must be wrong. By treating the series of Matt. 13 as a prophecy of the Gentile times, the Mustard Seed is regarded as a prophecy of a false church which grew to be a political kingdom. This view is reinforced by an extension of the interpretation to the next parable, The Leaven hid in Meal, emphasis being placed upon the fact that leaven in other passages of Scripture is used to represent an evil principle.

The parable of the Mustard Seed is found in three gospels, and a reference to the context in Mark and Luke is of help in fixing the meaning intended by Jesus. Mark gives the parable of the Sower, then instead of the Tares he has the parable of the Candle and the Seed Growing Secretly; he then gives the parable of the Mustard Seed, but does not continue the series as Matthew. Mark, however, adds: "And with many such parables spake he the word unto them, as they were able to hear it. But without a parable spake he not unto them: and when they were alone, he expounded all things to his disciples" (Mark 4 : 33, 34).

There is no doubt that Mark is referring to the same discourse as is recorded in Matt. 13. In the context of the Seed Growing Secretly, it is difficult to apply the parable of the Mustard Seed to the growth of a corrupt political church. This conclusion is confirmed by a study of the parable in Luke's context; in fact, such an interpretation becomes impossible.

The parable as recorded by Matthew reads: "Another parable put he forth unto them, saying, The kingdom of heaven is like to a grain of mustard seed, which indeed is the least of all seeds: but when it is grown, it is the greatest among herbs, and becometh a tree, so that the birds of the air come and lodge in the branches thereof" (13 : 31, 32).

The mustard seed is not literally the least of all seeds, but was the least handled in the ordinary way by the gardener. Relative to the size of the seed the growth is enormous. Most travellers in Palestine have remarked upon it. Thomson refers to some growing in a rich plain which was "as tall as the horse and his rider". The choice of the mustard tree, then, was almost certainly because, in the words of an old writer, it was "the most characteristic emblem, among natural objects, especially of its own class, to mark the disproportion between the first beginning and the final result of any process". The oak and the cedar are larger trees, but the choice of either of those would have failed to bring out the particular lesson Jesus aimed at—how small were the beginnings of things as seen by men. The mustard seed had become proverbial in common speech as a symbol of anything small.

Small beginnings with astonishing results is the teaching of the parable, and applied to the Kingdom that lesson offsets the gloominess that may have been felt from the parables of the Sower and the Tares. As men judge the preaching of the gospel, it would appear to be practically a failure: not really, as the parable of the mustard seed shows, for out of small beginnings great things emerge. With the energy of divinely bestowed life there is growth out of all proportion to the small beginning. No garden herbs so grow. The mustard plant, called a tree in eastern lands, is large enough to accommodate the birds that flock to it to eat of the seed.

But the reference to the birds is not simply a statement of fact: the description given by Jesus is an echo of Old Testament references which in turn lead on to a fuller meaning of the parable. In Nebuchadnezzar's dream of the tree "the leaves were fair, and the fruit thereof much, and in it was meat for all: the beasts of the field had shadow under it, and the fowls of heaven dwelt in the boughs thereof, and all flesh was fed of it" (Dan. 4 : 12). The tree represented first the king himself, and then his kingdom, in the shadow of which many peoples were gathered together (cf. also Ezek. 33). More pertinent still is the epilogue to Ezekiel's parable of the eagles: "Thus saith the Lord God; I will also take of the highest branch of the high cedar, and will set it: I will crop off from the top of his young twigs a tender one, and will plant it upon an high mountain and eminent: in the mountain of the height of Israel will I plant it: and it shall bring forth boughs, and bear fruit, and be a goodly cedar: and under it shall dwell all fowl of every wing; in the shadow of the branches thereof shall they dwell. And all the trees of the field shall know that I the Lord have brought down the high tree, have exalted the low tree, have dried up the green tree, and have made the dry tree to flourish: I the Lord have spoken and have done it". Here the small growing point of the topmost twig of Israel's cedar planted by God in the mountain of Israel is the Messiah—a small scion of Israel's house, who becomes glorious in the land where the last kings of Judah had known shame and dishonour. The resemblance in language suggests that in this parable Jesus was thinking of the Messianic kingdom which would be the great result which would come from small beginnings.

Small indeed are these beginnings; whether we think of the penniless carpenter whose life has already changed history, but whose work will yet issue in more revolutionary changes among men; or of the means employed by him—the preaching of a message which would enlighten men and give them hope, reshaping their lives that they may become fit for rulership in God's kingdom; or the death he died, as a common criminal, a death which many others had known; or the advent as one man, though a divinely sent man, to take over all kingdoms to break them and subdue them as the small stone broke and destroyed the image of Nebuchadnezzar's dream—from whatever point of view, it is "small things" first. The men and women who are called do not include many mighty. The twelve were mostly homely, capable, efficient men of everyday affairs—none of them would have been chosen by the wordly-wise for the work Jesus had in view for them. How astonishing it will be for the Jewish rulers who condemned Jesus and persecuted the apostles to behold Jesus enthroned and the apostles ruling with him!

In the setting in Luke (13 : 1-21) the parable belongs to an occasion other than that referred to in the records of Matthew and Mark. Jesus had been told of the murder, by Pilate, of Galileans in the temple, and it had been suggested that this act was a judgment of God. Jesus replied that it was not because of their greater wickedness that this fate had happened to these Galileans: it was not a judgment of God—but, he added significantly, unless they repented a like calamity would come to them, not as the result of those chances which belong to mortal life, but because God ordained it. This lesson he further pressed home by the parable of the fig-tree to be cut down for fruitlessness. Luke next records the healing on the Sabbath of the infirm woman, in connection with which Jesus refers to men leading animals to water on the sabbath and therefore the fitness that he should release the woman from her bondage. After this he spoke the parable of the mustard seed. While the context in Luke does not permit the parable to be a prophecy of an evil organization wide-spreading under the guise of Christianity, it suggests that while Israel as a fig tree were to be cut down as a nation, which on the face of it seemed the end of the kingdom, yet forces were at work which would restore it. The sabbath healing was a parable of the kingdom (see parable of Sheep in Pit)—an earnest of something to come: a foretaste of what will be in the age to come. Very appropriately Luke next records the discourse which began with the question, Are there few that be saved? in which Jesus declared that there would be an ingathering of Gentiles to sit down with the Fathers of Israel in God's Kingdom.

30
THE LEAVEN
(Matt. 13 : 33; Luke 13 : 20, 21)

THIS short parable, like the parable of the Mustard Seed, has been given two interpretations which are mutually exclusive. Some parables lend themselves to an extended application consistent with the principal lesson; but a parable cannot have two opposing significances. Starting from the idea that because leaven is unquestionably used as a figure for evil elsewhere in the Scripture, it must therefore be so used always, it has been argued that this parable was a prophecy of a false church introducing error into the doctrine of Christ. The woman is identified with the faithless woman of the Apocalypse, and an anti-Roman-Catholic application is made. The three measures of meal are identified with the meal offering which required the same amount of meal, and since this offering denoted fellowship with God, it is suggested that the corruption of error introduced has destroyed that fellowship. A superficial case for this view is made out if the starting point of interpretation is that the parables of Matt. 13 represent successive stages in ecclesiastical history. But, as in the case of the Mustard Seed, the parable of the Leaven is found in a context in Luke 13 which does not support such a view but rather discounts it. The context in Luke has been considered in connection with the parable of the Mustard Seed.

The emphasis of this story rests on the action of the leaven. The three measures of meal was a usual quantity in a baking, and thus appears to have been employed in offerings (Gen. 18 : 6; Judg. 6 : 19; 1 Sam. 1 : 24; and for offerings Num. 15 : 9 and refs.). Since it was a woman's work to grind the corn and make the bread that reference is in harmony with everyday life. The leaven was a piece of dough which had gone sour, kept over from the last baking day—a method of causing bread to rise still in use in parts of this country up to a century ago. All the circumstances in the parable, then, were ordinary ones. But the important point that Jesus makes is that the leaven hidden in the meal influenced the whole. Once there it could not be extracted, and apart from baking, when the heat stopped the process of leavening, nothing could arrest its work.

We must keep in mind that Jesus had already spoken the parables of the Sower and the Tares which revealed how limited were the results to be expected from preaching. So far the instruction left open the extent of the ultimate success of the work. But the parables of the Mustard Seed and the Leaven fill in the information. The Tares ends on the casting out of the weeds at the coming of the Son of man. The Mustard Seed and the Leaven have particular application to the position at that time. Something relatively small producing important effects is the essential point of both parables.

It might be urged that the Kingdom will be introduced by some catastrophic process. The stone breaks the image and grinds it to powder. The nations are broken as a potter's vessel. There is a place for both views. Coercion will destroy existing forms of government when the Lord comes: but only co-operation will build up. The Kingdom will not consist of people held in bondage by the repressive power of omnipotence, but of men and women who, after learning a needed lesson from the display of divine power to establish God's Kingdom, will willingly submit to instruction and guidance. "Come ye, and let us go up to the mountain of the Lord, to the house of the God of Jacob; and he will teach us of his ways, and we will walk in his paths: for out of Zion shall go forth the law, and the word of the Lord from Jerusalem: and he shall judge among the nations, and shall rebuke many people: and they shall beat their swords into plowshares, and their spears into pruninghooks: nation shall not lift up sword against nation, neither shall they learn war any more" (Isa. 2 : 3, 4).

That is a true picture of an enlightened age—divine power recognized, divine wisdom honoured, man willingly seeking to know God and to walk in His ways. The influence of the new rulers incorporated into the world of mankind will influence all.

The parable is true of the present only in the limited sense that leaven works by contact, and Christ's teaching in operation among men has had a remarkable influence, surpassing that of any other teacher. But the world will not be brought to obedience to Christ by preaching; and any interpretation which kindles a hope that the influence of Christ will gradually spread until all mankind is influenced thereby only promotes an idea that is doomed to disillusionment.

31
HID TREASURE
(Matt. 13 : 44)

THIS is the first of the four parables spoken to the disciples "in the house" (verse 36) (see parable of the Sower for comment on the chapter division). At the request of the disciples, Jesus first explained the parable of the Tares, and then spoke three parables without interruption or explanation. He had ended the interpretation of the Tares with the challenge: "Who hath ears to hear, let him hear". The challenge had to do with the issues of life—the tares burned in "the furnace of fire" or the righteous "shining forth as the sun in the kingdom of their Father". The prospects and certainties of a future of glory evoke the thought of the present response to the good news of God's grace. To the reaction which men exhibit to the gospel Jesus therefore turns. "The Kingdom of heaven", said Jesus, "is like unto treasure hid in a field; the which when a man hath found, he hideth, and for joy thereof goeth and selleth all that he hath, and buyeth that field" (verse 44).

It is the story of the man who, suddenly and without any previous search, stumbles across treasure. The discovery was accidental, so far as the finder was concerned. It occasionally happens that treasure trove is discovered in Great Britain; as when a quantity of Roman silver plate and spoons was unearthed in Surrey. These had been buried for safety, it is thought, at a time when Roman strength had declined and other peoples were invading these islands. In Palestine, however, the burial or finding of treasure was quite common. The land had long been a battleground, and the march of armies along the roads north or south with skirmishing parties penetrating into the country districts for food, had been witnessed by many generations of Israelites. Security for portable wealth was sought by hiding it in the earth, and the secret of the hiding place was lost if the owner fled and was unable to return, or lost his life. Recovery then depended upon such a chance discovery as Jesus describes.

There is no need to encumber the interpretation by such questions as the legality or morality of the act of hiding again the treasure while the field was bought: a point of equity may remain even when the legality of the action is established, as appears to be the case. The essential lesson is in the man's response to the discovery—his joy, his surrender of all he possessed in order that he might buy the field.

Jesus many times speaks of joy—his joy, and the joy of the disciples. It is a side of his life that has to be remembered as well as the sufferings which made him a "man of sorrows". The message he delivered was one of glad tidings. When men understand that message and find what is God's purpose, when uncertainty and doubt give place to assured conviction based upon reliable evidence that the good news is from God, they know the joy of the finder of hidden treasure.

Such discoverers appreciate the value of the treasure they have found. The supreme importance of securing it makes the giving up of other valuables easy. It is a paradox of the gospel that the grace of God is free, yet men have to pay a price for it. Isaiah called upon thirsty ones to come to the waters and *buy* wine and milk without money and without price. What he offered was free, yet must be bought. The price in some cases may be heavy as men judge; but men, in love with God and possessed of an ardent desire for the Kingdom which Jesus said must be the first object of men's seeking, know a love surpassing that bestowed on other things. Men in earnest love the Kingdom more than the Rabbis loved the law; more than philosophers love wisdom; more than students love knowledge. Some of the apostles left their nets and other means of livelihood; Paul abandoned his career; but the rich young ruler found the love of his great possessions greater than his desire for eternal life. The love of Jesus constrained many to forsake all to follow him; to love him more than father or mother; to esteem "the treasure" of "the knowledge of the glory of God" greater riches than anything the world can give.

32
THE PEARL MERCHANT
(Matt. 13 : 45, 46)

As the parables of the Mustard Seed and of the Leaven form a pair, so there is an obvious similarity in the parables of the Hid Treasure and of the Pearl Merchant. In both men sell all that they have in order to buy something else; and in both the thing purchased has in their eyes supreme value.

The note struck in this story is quieter than its partner parable. The merchant may be thought of as restrained, grave, and experienced. He has doubtless heard previously of pearls of outstanding quality, but has also found on examination that they did not possess the advertised virtues. A lifetime's experience, as he has travelled from place to place pursuing his business, has given him a trained eye and a quick judgment. He hears of a pearl of superlative quality—perhaps he smiles; he has heard that before. But it does not pay to disregard even such reports; he therefore investigates. His practised eye at once recognizes the worth of the pearl now offered—why has he never heard of it before? The price is high, but not too high for such a pearl. He realizes his stock at a sacrifice; as he does so men wonder at his readiness to sell at the price he will accept; but the wondrous pearl becomes his.

The seeker has got to the end of his quest. So men *seek* for truth; they study many philosophies, learn of many human plans and schemes, yet with longing unsatisfied; then the pearl of God's message is found and while other men fail to understand the full giving to get the one thing, the purchaser experiences the feeling of a need fully met.

The treasure in the field is stumbled upon; there is sudden joy at the discovery. The pearl is found after much searching; there is no reference to joy—exuberance in such a case would not be displayed; but the story breathes the abiding satisfaction which is the end of a long quest.

33
THE DRAG NET

(Matt. 13 : 47-50)

THE Sea of Tiberias was abundant in fish, which naturally formed an important part of the diet of the large population that dwelt along the lake side. Several of the Apostles were fishermen, owners of their own craft, and probably fairly well-to-do, as are many successful small tradesmen to-day. When calling them to follow him Jesus had said he would make them fishers of men (Matt. 4 : 17-22). This saying was a very early use of parabolic language, and in fact contains the germ of the parable in Matt. 13.

The drag-net was "a large net which two or more boats arranged in a circle in the lake, in such a way as to enclose a vast space with a kind of vertical wall. It is kept stretched by means of weights and floats. Then the two extremities are brought together, and the whole with its contents is dragged ashore". This arrangement of the two boats is behind the allusion to "the partners who were in the other ship" (Luke 5 : 7), and this episode in Luke provides a picture of the scene described in the parable.

The interpretation and the story itself are given together—necessarily so, or the correct interpretation would never have been reached. We can think of the preaching of the gospel being like the casting of a net which encloses all kinds of fish. Different types of men and women, and for different reasons, obey the gospel. This has already been indicated in other parables. The essential lesson of the drag-net is that there will be a sorting of the gathered "fish" at the end of the age. The interpretation, however, supplies what would not be apparent in the parable itself, that the angels come forth and sever the wicked from the just. The parallel between the Tares and the Drag-net is obvious, yet there are differences. Belonging to the series spoken in the house, the application of this parable is more circumscribed than that of the Tares. The wide application of the latter we have noticed: the Drag-net concerns those who come within the operations of the gospel.

The fishing goes on throughout the ages; mortal men cast the net and work in the gathering; the angels enter the work visibly at the end. How naturally Jesus speaks of the works of the angels; his several references to them are strong confirmation of the general hints concerning them scattered throughout the Bible. Jesus was as conscious of their existence, and the part they played in his own life, as he was confident about the coming revelation in mighty power when they will again visibly operate in the affairs of men, in the crisis associated with the coming transition of human affairs to the strong hands of the Son of God.

34
THE INSTRUCTED SCRIBE
(Matt. 13 : 52)

It is usual to speak of the seven parables of Matt. 13; yet, although it does not appear to be generally recognized, the one-verse parable about the scribe, which closes the conversation of Jesus and the disciples, is as much a parable as the story of the pearl merchant. Finishing the parable of the Net, Jesus asked his hearers if they had understood what he had told them. They answered, "Yea, Lord"—an answer which in view of the discussion on the meaning of the parables which has since taken place in every generation, appears to have been given rather light-heartedly. The answer, however, does suggest that they felt they had received some clear idea of what Jesus meant to tell them, and this further shows that some of the prophetic and fanciful interpretations since devised could not have been intended as the primary meaning of the seven parables Jesus had spoken.

Jesus answered them: "Therefore every scribe which is instructed unto the kingdom of heaven is like unto a man that is an householder, which bringeth forth out of his treasure things new and old" (verse 52).

"The scribes were a class of learned Jews who devoted themselves to a scientific study of the Law, and made its exposition their professional occupation." The word used by the gospel writers has to do with "letters", but just as that word in English is used not only for everyday correspondence but of a cultured knowledge of literature, so the scribe was an instructed, learned man. Ezra was a scribe of the law, a worthy pattern for all others to follow. That the Scribes of Christ's day, like the Pharisees, had fallen much below the original ideals of their class, is evident; but the function of the Scribes was such that Jesus could refer to them for the basis of his lesson.

A traditional saying of the "Men of the Great Synagogue" laid down three rules for scribes: "Be careful in pronouncing judgment, bring up many pupils, and make a fence about the law". The professional employment of the Scribes, therefore, consisted of the study of the law, teaching it to their pupils, and its administration. Some of the methods and practices which had developed in the pursuit of these aims led to sharp clashes with Jesus, whose teaching contrasted so emphatically with the traditions they had built up.

Jesus spoke of "a scribe instructed unto the kingdom of heaven". That involved a different kind of schooling from that which the Jewish scribes received. The instruction given to the scribes was academic; they were learned in all the lore of the teachers of their nation, and their exposition of Scripture consisted of citing a text and then quoting the opinions of the Rabbis. The scribe of the kingdom is versed in the Word, and his method of teaching consists of reasoning out of the Scriptures and explaining Scripture by Scripture.

Jesus compares such a scribe with a householder. The word is the same as is elsewhere translated "goodman of the house" and "master of the house". In the parable of the Tares the Son of man is the householder, and the use of the word of the instructed disciple in the same context suggests that some parallel was intended between the Lord and the disciple.

The instructed scribe of Christ's own household has a duty towards his fellow-members of the house. That duty is to "bring forth out of his treasure things new and old". The qualified scribe has his "treasure"—the knowledge of God's Word, and to the extent that he has prayerfully studied it, seeking to divide it rightly as a good workman (2 Tim. 2 : 15), so he is a good scribe. Such is the quality of the "treasure" that its full beauties are never fully comprehended, and the most diligent students know how unsearchable are the riches of God's revelation. Hence there is a never failing interest in the "food" the scribe provides, things ever "new" while "old". Without any deviation from first principles of God's word there is a continued freshness in its presentation.

It is probable that the reference to "new and old" had a connection with the disciples' assurance that they had understood the parables the Lord had spoken. They had comprehended in a general way their meaning, but passing time would show them "new" significances not then perceived. Experience would show how the tares were sown, how men reacted to their message, how very different kinds of men responded to their preaching of the gospel.

The short parable is an encouragement to men of every age to follow the Lord as teachers, to be like him students of God's word, like him to present in full loyalty to the Scriptures the unfailing wonder of the grace of God as it is revealed in the many-sided presentation of the oracles of God.

35
BLIND LEADERS

(Matt. 15 : 14; 23; Luke 6 : 39, 41)

A PROVERB is often a compressed parable easily expanded into the usual parable form. We now look at the story of the Blind Leaders. "Jesus answered . . . Let them alone: they be blind leaders of the blind. And if the blind lead the blind, both shall fall into the ditch. Then answered Peter and said unto him, Declare unto us this parable" (Matt. 15 : 14, 15). Jesus could have said something like this: "A certain blind man, who knew not that he could not see, said to another blind man, I will lead you. But as he did not see where the road turned, he fell into the ditch; and dragged in also his follower". But with greater directness of application he affirmed the Pharisees were blind leaders of blind men.

The immediate context concerns the corban law by which the Pharisees evaded duties to their parents and so made void one of the ten commandments. Jesus very severely condemns their casuistry, by which they put the doctrines of men in the place of God's law. The same saying occurs in another context in Luke 6 : 39, as part of the discourse which closely resembles the Sermon on the Mount of Matt. 5-7. This context in Luke's record, and the fact that it was spoken to the disciples, prevents the comfortable detached consideration of the saying which is possible in restricting its reference to the Pharisees. We may appreciate the application to others and endorse the judgment: but it is spoken also as a warning to all disciples. The object lesson of the one must be noted for the guidance of every follower of the Lord. It is a warning of the dangers of being leaders and teachers, which all teachers should take to heart. Luke records:

"And he spake a parable unto them, Can the blind lead the blind? Shall they not both fall into the ditch? The disciple is not above his master: but every one that is perfect shall be as his master. And why beholdest thou the mote that is in thy brother's eye, but perceivest not the beam that is in thine own eye?" (6 : 39, 41).

The connection of thought in Luke is that men should judge themselves before they judge others. Censoriousness is sternly reprobated. If anyone fails to examine self he is blind and, seeking to teach, is a blind leader. His disciples will rise no higher than the teacher, and when fully trained will yet reflect the master's faults. An additional reason for self examination is then given—a man with a grave fault should not correct a man with a smaller one. James echoes the warning of Jesus here: "My brethren, be not many masters (teachers), knowing that ye shall receive the greater condemnation" (3 : 1). The teacher is multiplied in the scholars, and one heretic becomes many: a good teacher of sound doctrine is the means of many rejoicing in truth. But that influence over others which a teacher possesses is the reason why he must bear greater responsibility. The earnest teacher and preacher shirks no toil to make sure that his words faithfully represent the teaching of the Word of God, that he may not know the shame of faulty workmanship (2 Tim 2 : 15). All teachers do well to remember the warning of greater condemnation.

In the chapter of woes (Matt. 23) Jesus five times speaks of the Pharisees as blind. They were astute enough in argument but perverse in their ways; and a blindness of heart and mind had overtaken them. A man could swear by the temple, they said, and the oath did not bind: but if he swear by the gold of the temple, it was binding. Yet, as Jesus pointed out, the gold was sanctified by the temple. So with altar and sacrifice on the altar: the altar sanctified the gift, and an oath by the altar embraced both. Fools and blind! In the light of the trenchant exposure, how deserving the description! They tithed mint scrupulously—garden herbs of small value; but while it was right to tithe and weigh carefully the garnishings of the meal, yet the weightier matters of the law—which could not be weighed in scales—judgment mercy, faith, were neglected. They were like a man pouring out a drink who must carefully strain the water lest a small insect be in it, and yet who swallows a camel—hair, hoofs and all—and does not know it. It is grotesque—grimly, humorously grotesque—and Jesus meant it so to be. They cleansed the crockery they used at a meal; but were unconcerned that the food they ate off that crockery had been obtained by craft and fraud. Careful of externals, which are good in themselves and in their place, but not of vital moment, they yet were indifferent about the essential morality of their acts and thoughts. Blind Pharisees!

How came they to be so blind? We learn something from the healing of the blind man (John 9). Jesus made clay and anointed his eyes therewith; and then sent the blind man to Siloam. Jesus can both make blind and give sight, as he said: "For judgment I am come into this world, that they which see not might see; and that they which see might be made blind". The Pharisees discerned something of the paradox and asked, "Are we blind also?" They claimed to have sight; very well, then they must accept the responsibility of seeing, and their sin remained (verses 29-40). For a fuller discussion of this miracle we must refer to the *Exposition of John's Gospel*.

Jesus, by the act of giving sight, at once claimed to be and proved he was the Messiah. "The blind receive their sight" was one of the evidences given to John in response to his question from prison: "Art thou he that should come? Or look we for another?" It was indeed good evidence to anyone who knew the messages of the prophets. "The Lord openeth the eyes of the blind" (Psa. 146 : 8); "the eyes of the blind shall be opened" (Isa. 35 : 5); God's servant had to "open the blind eyes" (42 : 7). But the prophet declared the nation had "unseeing eyes". They were "deaf" and "blind" (42 : 16, 18). With scorching irony he spoke of them as "the blind people that hath eyes" (43 : 8): and because of their iniquities and sins, their vanity and lying, their violence and blood shedding, the judgment came upon them and they walked in darkness. "We grope for the wall like the blind, and we grope as if we had no eyes" (59 : 1-10). In them was fulfilled the prophecy of Zephaniah: "They shall walk like blind men, because they have sinned against the Lord" (1 : 17). The parable of the Blind Leaders was a terrible indictment, gravely made, and truly spoken. But what a lesson it contains!

36
CHILDREN AND PUPPIES
(Matt. 15 : 22-28; Mark 7 : 24-30)

THE opposition of the rulers and the misguided enthusiasm of the people caused Jesus to seek retirement outside the borders of Israel in Tyre and Sidon. A woman of the district, with a sick daughter, sought him out, and appealed to him to heal her daughter. In Matthew's record the incident is punctuated with a fourfold "And he answered" (verses 23, 24, 26, 28). To her first request he answered nothing. It is evident that she insisted, and the disciples joined, but with another motive, in her appeal that he should grant her the request. The disciples evidently felt it a nuisance that she should follow them, calling after them, and they would be rid of her by Jesus yielding to her importunities.

Jesus answered them: "I am not sent but unto the lost sheep of the house of Israel". It recalled the command that he had given them (10 : 6), and indicates that his prior duty lay with Israel and that he should not use his power for the convenience of getting away from the persistent calls of the woman.

The woman came near and "worshipped" him, contenting herself with the imploring words: "Lord, help me". Jesus then answered her: "It is not meet to take the children's bread, and to cast it to the dogs". The refusal has severity, but not all the harshness of the A.V.; it does repeat, but yet in a form that could not have been pleasing to the woman, the answer Jesus had given to the disciples. The children must be fed ("*first* be filled"—Mark), and it was not fitting their food should be given to dogs. Israelites were children, Gentiles were dogs. Two things relieved the harshness—the word "first", (Mark's account), implying a possible later place for Gentiles; and the word "dog" is a diminutive—"doggies" or "puppies"—and has a touch of the playfulness seen in our slang use of "kiddies" for children. While then "dog" is without question a term of contempt, as in the phrases "dog of an infidel", or "dog of a Jew", the word "puppy" has not the same offensiveness.

The woman accepted the distinction and found in it an opening for a further appeal. The attitude of Jesus was not that of his disciples, and his look would have sympathy. She rejoined: "Truth, Lord: yet the dogs eat of the crumbs which fall from their master's table". The answer sprang from a persistency and wit sharpened by love for her daughter: but it was also based on a recognition that the teacher was of royal descent and perhaps more even than that, for she called him Lord in addition to Son of David. It was one of the cases where a Gentile saw further than the Jews; where a Gentile recognized Jewish privileges, but saw that some fragment of mercy could come to Gentiles. With such a faith revealed, Jesus acknowledged it, "O woman, great is thy faith"; and granted the request—"be it unto thee even as thou wilt".

37
ROCK AND KEYS
(Matt. 16 : 13-19)

In the borders of Caesarea Philippi, in the north of the land, Jesus elicited from his disciples a confession of faith concerning himself. He enquired first what others were saying, and then asked the disciples what they thought. Peter spoke on behalf of the company when he said: "Thou art the Christ, the Son of the living God". It was a remarkable statement for one man to make to another, far more difficult to state then than when the subject has been crystallized in creeds and Statements of Faith after the subject of the confession has been raised from the dead. The answer was gratifying to the Teacher, who replied: "Blessed art thou, Simon Bar-jona: for flesh and blood hath not revealed it unto thee, but my Father which is in heaven. And I say unto thee, That thou art Peter, and upon this rock I will build my church; and the gates of hell shall not prevail against it. And I will give unto thee the keys of the kingdom of heaven: and whatsoever thou shalt bind on earth shall be bound in heaven: and whatsoever thou shalt loose on earth shall be loosed in heaven" (Matt. 16 : 16-19).

These verses have been the subject of controversy for centuries because of the meaning attached to them by the church of Rome, and the tremendous claims based thereon. They form the basis of the pretensions which have led the Roman Catholic Church to demand the submission of men to her teaching and to enforce her claims with all the cruelties that have been inflicted upon so-called heretics. Around the cupola of St. Peter's at Rome the words glitter in golden letters cut in the stone, each twelve feet deep. They encircle the vast building; and are easily read from below. If, however, the meaning which is attached to Christ's words by the Roman Church is the obvious and correct one, it is strange that the writers of the early centuries knew nothing of it. This is common knowledge to all who have read anything of the controversy with Rome; the following extracts give a summary of the facts.

In the book, *The Pope and the Council,* bearing the pen-name of Janus, but written it is said by two of the most capable historians of the Church of Rome, Acton and Döllinger, at the time of the Council which declared the doctrine of Papal Infallibility, occurs the following:

"Of all the Fathers who interpret these passages in the Gospels (Matt. 16 : 18; John 21 : 17) not a single one applies them to the Roman bishops as Peter's successors. How many Fathers have busied themselves with these texts, yet not one of them whose commentaries we possess—Origen, Chrysostom, Hilary, Augustine, Cyril, Theodoret, and those whose interpretations are collected in catenas—has dropped the faintest hint that the primacy of Rome is the consequence of the commission and promise to Peter! Not one of them has explained the rock or foundation on which Christ would build his Church of the office given to Peter to be transmitted to his successors, but they understood by it either Christ Himself, or Peter's confession of faith in Christ; often both together. Or else they thought Peter was the foundation equally with all the other Apostles, the Twelve being together the foundation-stones of the Church (Rev. 21 : 14). The Fathers could the less recognize in the power of the keys, and the power of binding and loosing, any special prerogative or lordship of the Roman bishop, inasmuch as—what is obvious to any one at first sight—they did not regard a power first given to Peter, and afterwards conferred in precisely the same words on all the Apostles, as anything peculiar to him, or hereditary in the line of Roman bishops, and they held the symbol of the keys as meaning just the same as the figurative expression of binding and loosing."

In Littledale's *Plain Reasons against joining the Church of Rome,* we read:

"Archbishop Kenrick of St. Louis, in his speech prepared for, but not delivered in, the Vatican Council, and published at Naples in 1870, declares that Roman Catholics cannot establish the Petrine privilege from Scripture, because of the clause in the Creed of Pius IV, binding them to interpret Scripture only according to the unanimous consent of the Fathers. And he adds that there are five different patristic interpretations of St. Matt. 16 : 18: (1) That St. Peter is the Rock, taught by seventeen Fathers; (2) that the whole Apostolic College is the Rock, represented by Peter as its chief, taught by eight; (3) that St. Peter's faith is the Rock, taught by forty-four; (4) that Christ is the Rock, taught by sixteen; (5) that the Rock is the whole body of the faithful. Several who teach (1) and (2) also teach (3) and (4), and so the Archbishop sums up thus: 'If we are bound to follow the greater number of Fathers in this matter, then we must hold for certain that the word Petra means not Peter professing the faith, but the faith professed by Peter'.—Friedrich, Docum. ad illust. Conc. Vat. I. pp. 185-246."

It is not sufficient to show that the significance attached to the words of Jesus by Rome is not historically well founded; we desire to know as accurately as we can what Jesus himself intended by his words. The extracts given indicate a choice of meanings, and finality in interpretation may not be possible.

There is an evident play upon the meaning of the name Peter—a stone. The name had been given to Simon by Jesus as a token of certain qualities he possessed: and Peter's position in the apostolic band is indicated by the fact that in all enumerations of their names, his comes first. It was characteristic of the man that he should answer for the rest.

"Thou art Peter (*petros*)", said Jesus, "and upon this rock (*petra*) I will build my church." The importance that should be attached to the change in the word, and the exact distinction between the two words, has been much discussed. The general attitude today is to discount any difference. This is in part due to a constant effort to turn back the language of the New Testament into Aramaic, which was generally spoken by Jesus, and in which no distinction is possible. But that leaves unanswered why, granted that Jesus spoke in Aramaic, Matthew should use two words. That the necessities of grammar simply required it, is not admitted by all; and that in classical Greek at any rate the distinction was preserved, is not questioned.

Bullinger in *Figures of Speech,* illustrating the repetition of words derived from the same root, comments thus:

"Here note (1) that *Petros* is not merely Simon's name given by our Lord, but given because of its meaning. '*Petros*' means *a stone, a piece of rock, a moving stone* which can be thrown by the hand. While '*petra*' means *a rock* or *cliff* or *crag,* immovable, firm, and sure. Both words are from the same root, both have the same derivation, but though similar in origin and sound they are thus different in meaning. This difference is preserved in the Latin.

(2) In the case of *petros,* we have another figure: for the word is used in two senses, though used only once. There is a repetition, not of the word but of the thought which is not expressed: 'Thou art *petros*', where it is used as a proper name *Peter,* and there is no figure: but the sense of the word is there as well, though not repeated in words: 'Thou art *a stone*'. Thus there is a metaphor implied.

(3) While *petros* is used for Peter, *petra* is used of Christ: for so Peter himself understood it (see 1 Pet. 2 : 4, 5, 6 and Acts 4 : 11, 12); and so the Holy Spirit asserts in 1 Cor. 10 : 4. 'And that rock was Christ', where we have a pure *metaphor*. So that *petros* represents Peter's instability and uselessness as a foundation, while

petra represents Christ's stability as the foundation which God Himself has laid (1 Cor. 2 : 11; Isa. 28 : 16)".

It is important to remember the Old Testament use of the word Rock. Reference was made to this in considering the parable of the Two Builders (Matt. 7 : 24-28). God was the Rock of Israel, and Jesus was that God in manifestation. This Peter had confessed. The answer of Jesus then can be, "Upon *this* rock, the fact that I am the Son of God, will I build my church"; or "upon myself—*the* rock, will I build my church"—in which case Jesus is builder and foundation; or, the answer may mean: "Upon this confession"—although this differs little, for on this meaning it is not so much the confession as what is confessed that really matters.

What then of the unprevailing "gates of hell"? This is simply a figure of the grave which closes its doors upon all placed therein. Prisoners there have no power to break their bonds; and friends without can do nothing to release the imprisoned. This Hezekiah recognized, saying: "The grave cannot praise thee, death cannot celebrate thee: they that go down into the pit cannot hope for thy truth" (Isa. 38 : 18). The Psalmist speaks of afflicted men whose "soul abhorreth all manner of meat; and they draw near unto *the gates of death*" (Psa. 107 : 18). But men of faith in God's promises are not without hope. The Messianic Psalms speak of a lifting up of the Messiah "from the gates of death; that I may show forth all thy praise in the gates of the daughter of Zion" (9 : 13, 14; for Messianic reference see verse 8). The gates of the citadel of death are not therefore invincible. The church of the Messiah, because it is his church, will be delivered therefrom and be victorious.

If Jesus has "the keys of the grave and of death" (Rev. 1 : 18), he will use them to deliver his people. They have to be subjects of another release, however, before the Lord uses those keys. All need a deliverance from ignorance; all need the way of life to be opened to them. So Jesus speaks of other keys given to Peter—the keys of the Kingdom. "The key of knowledge" had been taken away by the scribes, Jesus said (Luke 11 : 52). But Peter made use of the keys of knowledge for opening the understanding of men, by the preaching of the gospel. This he did when at Pentecost he told the Jews how they might be saved; this he did when he told Cornelius "what he ought to do to be saved". As a teacher, guided by God's Spirit, Peter unfolded authoritatively God's purpose: and as this authority as a teacher was idiomatically referred to as "binding and loosing", so Jesus said that in the use of the keys, Peter would, with heaven's endorsement, speak with authority as he instructed men in the gospel.

38
FAITH AS A GRAIN OF MUSTARD SEED
(Matt. 17 : 20; Luke 17 : 6)

On three occasions Jesus used a parabolic form of speech to illustrate the power of faith to overcome difficulties. As he and the three apostles who were his closest companions came down from the Mount of Transfiguration, they found one group of discomfited men with another group in an antagonistic, aggressive attitude toward them. A man had brought to the disciples his lunatic son, and the disciples had failed to heal him. They had been thinking more of themselves, of their own greatness, than of the great work they were privileged to share with their Master. Crestfallen with failure, harassed by the Scribes, they heard the reproof Jesus uttered about a faithless and perverse generation, and then saw him perform the cure.

"Why could not we cast him out?" they enquired. Jesus answered, "Because of your unbelief: for verily I say unto you, If ye have faith as a grain of mustard seed, ye shall say unto this mountain, Remove hence to yonder place; and it shall remove; and nothing shall be impossible unto you" (Matt. 17 : 20).

The language, of course, has not to be taken literally, as scoffers do when they want to make ridicule. Jesus employs a figure of a great task, too great for human power to accomplish. Characteristically Oriental in form of expression, his hearers would not misunderstand his meaning. Impossible judged by human standards, with faith in God things could be accomplished. The comparison is not with the size of the seed, as though he had said, "If you had faith even the size of mustard seed you could do this"; Jesus is thinking of the life power in even so small a seed. The living energy forces downwards the roots to find sustenance, and upwards the stem with the leaves penetrate to reach the light. The power manifested in a living plant is enormous; examples have been recorded of pavement stones moved and blocks of stones being split thereby. Had the disciples shown a faith like the growing seed they would have overcome their difficulties.

Faith is trust in God, and this implies knowledge of God's will. A faith to achieve what is not in the will of God is both fruitless and futile. But living faith, in harmony with God's will, is, Jesus teaches, charged with power of accomplishment.

Jesus gave the same illustration of faith's power when the disciples had expressed surprise that the fig tree had withered away (Matt. 21 : 21).

On another occasion (Luke 17 : 7) he used the rooting up of a sycamore tree instead of moving a mountain, as a figure of difficulty. He had been speaking of forgiveness to an unlimited number of occasions on repentance; and as the disciples regarded this as difficult to perform, they begged of him, "Lord, increase our faith". This was answered by the reference to faith as a grain of mustard seed. A living seed has power—that power is the expression of its life and is comparable to the power of faith in man. The spirit that forgives is the expression of the living faith of the disciples of Christ.

39
AMPUTATED LIMBS AND LOST SHEEP

(Matt. 18 : 7-13; Mark 9 : 41-48)

THE story of the Lost Sheep occurs also in Luke in a setting that calls for separate consideration there. The context in Matthew gives the parable a slightly different emphasis while having the same major lesson. It therefore seems desirable that something be said on the parable as we come to it in Matthew, and again when we reach Luke's gospel.

The gospel shows the apostles as very human beings with the weaknesses and foibles of men of every age. They truly had very exciting and exhilarating experiences, when, called from the ordinary workaday world, they journeyed with the new teacher throughout their land, saw the crowds who listened to him, caught their enthusiasm or were disturbed by their opposition.

Whatever else may have perplexed them, the teaching of Jesus about the kingdom of God was clear; and there could be no mistake about what that meant. And Jesus was the Messiah, and they were his companions. The people about them thought some of the disciples had importance as associates of the teacher who did so many wonderful things. They could not tell what wonderful thing he might do next. Yes, the disciples felt a sense of importance, and that feeling naturally passed from their relationship to the crowd, to their relationship with each other. There were three whom Jesus always chose on particular occasions; Peter of course had qualities of leadership; he was impetuous and headstrong sometimes, but fearless. We need not be surprised to read that they discussed who was greatest in the Kingdom of Heaven. Jesus took a child, and setting the little one in the midst of them said: "Except ye be converted, and become as little children, ye shall not enter into the kingdom of heaven". He then spoke of the need for humility and the need of appreciating the quality in others instead of riding roughshod over the humbler one. They should not cause any to stumble; to do that to any who believed in Jesus were to risk a fate to which drowning with a millstone around one's neck were to be preferred. "Woe to that man", said Jesus, "by whom the offence cometh." Then he turns the searchlight on the need for self-scrutiny and self-discipline. Not only should one be careful not to cause another to go astray, but there should be watchfulness that each one does not himself stumble. Hand and foot and eye had better be cut off now than the whole man be cut off in judgment at the last. There is metonymy in this form of words about cutting off hand and foot, failure to discern which has caused foolish and extravagant actions by some prosaic literalists, and much anguish of soul to others who would not apply the words literally but who did not perceive their true meaning. Eyes are for seeing, hands for working, feet for walking. Therefore avoid sights, avoid actions, avoid places that cause you to stumble. There may be occasions—and perhaps this particularly is behind the words of Jesus—when things legitimate in themselves are a snare through over-attraction. Eyes, hands and feet are for use, but for use that makes their owner fit for the Kingdom of God. It is good to read good books and to see good paintings; it is good to make things, to enjoy tramping the hills and valleys of God's earth. But if these cause us to stumble by taking the place of essential things, the "amputation" of these legitimate "good things" is the drastic course the wise Teacher enjoins.

Salvation is the essential thing, and all other matters, good and useful and profitable in their place, must subserve this. For this the Son of Man came—to save that which was lost. This he illustrates by the simple familiar story of the shepherd who has a flock of a hundred sheep from which one strays. He leaves the ninety and nine to seek the wanderer, and rejoices more over the one found than the ninety and nine which did not stray.

We miss the point by thinking of the ninety-nine. The shepherd did not, of course, leave them unprotected. A fellow shepherd would keep a watchful eye—it would be folly otherwise with the risk of still more wanderers. The parable does not concern them. The important object is the shepherd's care even for the one. Jesus says the Father is like that: "Even so it is not the will of your Father which is in heaven, that one of these little ones should perish" (verse 14).

It was a challenging view that Jesus put forward then. The Rabbis so readily regarded the people as accursed. On the other hand modern sentiment has often ignored essential things which affect man's relationship to God, and has given to some of these sayings of Jesus an application far removed from his intention. In this context Jesus, by revealing God's care for those "little ones", is driving home the lesson that it is a grave offence to be a stumbling block to one's fellow-believer—"one of these little ones who believe in me". If it is God's will that they should be saved, then men's efforts should be directed in harmony with that will. It should be noticed, however, that Jesus does not ignore the fact that any man can frustrate the will of God for himself. Jesus said the Pharisees and lawyers "frustrated" the counsel of God in not being baptized of John (Luke 7 : 28 margin). So in this parable the contingency of man going astray irrevocably is indicated in the words "if so be that he (the shepherd) find it". God does not impose His will, nor inflict His grace upon any unwilling recipient. The parable is not dealing with human reactions; in the context in Luke, where the parable recurs, another parable was spoken to introduce that aspect. The essential thing here is that God is an example of what men should be in their treatment of others. God is a shepherd with a shepherd's care.

The "seeking" of God involves God's forgiveness, and the discourse moves on to this subject, leading to a parable on forgiveness. The continuation of the theme introduces the next parable.

40
THE UNFORGIVING CREDITOR
(Matt. 18 : 23-35)

If men have to avoid causing others to stumble (see previous parable) (Matt. 18 : 1-13), what is their duty to one who does stumble? If God forgives the erring, as is implied in His seeking, as the shepherd, the straying sheep (Matt. 18 : 12, 13), how should men act to their offending brethren? To this Jesus turns—the carrying forward of his thought being indicated by the word "Moreover" by which he introduces this subject. He then lays down the duty of an injured man towards a brother who has done him wrong. To injure another—and Jesus is thinking of soul, not body—is in his eyes a grievous offence, and the offender is gravely wrong. He has therefore to be won, if possible, to a recognition that his action is wrong, for apart from this recognition, recovery is impossible. Unless sin is recognized for what it is, and is repented of, forgiveness is impossible. An offender is like the straying sheep, though in his anger and self-will he may not recognize that he has left the flock. Jesus puts upon the offended brother the duty of seeking out this man who has strayed. He alone probably knows of the wrong but whether others know or not, he has the greatest responsibility. He must seek out alone the one who has done the hurt, tell him his fault, and so seek to "gain" his brother. This is the whole purpose of this counsel, and it is a perversion of the command to use it as a process of self-justification. The subject discussed by Jesus is the peril of men who are offenders—a peril so great that Jesus calls upon the offended to seek the recovery of the wrong-doer. If he fails, and if others called in to help also fail, a man is shown to be unfit for the society of the brethren, and God regards him as unfit for His flock. He is like a "rogue" animal, mischievous and destructive.

This command that Christ's follower be ready to forgive and also to seek to establish the conditions for forgiveness, led Peter to say, "Lord, how oft shall my brother sin against me, and I forgive him? till seven times?" (verse 21). Jesus answered, "I say not unto thee, Until seven times; but, Until seventy times seven" (verse 22). Peter thought seven times a generous offer. Jesus in effect says, You cannot keep count at all. To talk of counting is to miss what forgiveness means. When forgiveness is extended the past is forgotten by the injured so far as holding a matter against another goes. Ten times seven would not exhaust the obligation—that number could be multiplied by seven, and so stated counting becomes impossible; there is no limit. The figures used by Jesus are fixed by the boastful claim of Lamech that he had the power to avenge offences. There has been a difference of opinion whether the number is seventy and seven (=77) or, seventy-seven fold (=490), but J. H. Moulton says seventy-seven times is unmistakable in Gen. 4 : 24 (LXX), and he adds: "A definite allusion to the Genesis story is highly probable: Jesus pointedly sets against the natural man's craving for seventy-sevenfold revenge the spiritual man's ambition to exercise the privilege of seventy-sevenfold forgiveness".

The parable of the Unmerciful Servant introduced by "Therefore" concerns a king who took account of his servants, and found one owed him £6,000,000. As he had nothing with which to pay, the king, according to law ordered him and all his family to be sold. The servant pleaded for mercy, which was granted and the debt forgiven. The same scene is enacted again between the forgiven debtor and a fellow servant who owed him £10, but with a different sequel. The small debtor was cast into prison by his fellow servant. Upon hearing of this the lord recalled the man, reproved him, cancelled the remission of debt, and had him cast into prison. The lesson Jesus gives: "So likewise shall my heavenly Father do also unto you, if ye from your hearts forgive not every one his brother their trespasses" (verse 35).

There are some fine touches in the story. The large debtor, in keeping with the recklessness of a man so much in debt, says he will pay all. The small debtor promises to pay (so R.V.), for although his debt is not an impossible one he is more deliberate in his offer. We observe also that the first debtor was not only sentenced to be cast into prison, but his family had to share his fate. So it is in life—the effects of sin are not limited to the sinner; others not guilty share the misery of his wrong doing. Then in his application Jesus speaks of "my heavenly Father"—a claim of oneness in spirit with the Father in the exercise of mercy, and a pointed indication that sonship is non-existent where a spirit of forgiveness is not found.

It seems legitimate also to find a place for the cancellation of forgiveness: perhaps we should say that God's anger is aroused when evidence of the right frame of mind for receiving forgiveness is lacking, as seen in an unforgiving spirit. Clearly the man did not appreciate his forgiveness; his conduct towards his fellow servant after the remission of his own debt makes it certain that his plea for clemency was not made because of a sense of guilt, but from a desire to escape consequences. With equal shortsightedness he cast his fellow servant into prison and so made it impossible for him to pay; in seeking vengeance he hurt himself.

From the parable we may also learn how God looks upon an unforgiving spirit. Such a spirit may be nurtured in secret, unknown by our fellows for a time. Where a sinful action of reprisal might be avoided because of the shame that others know of it, no such deterrent operates for a time on sins of thought. But sooner or later nurtured evil thoughts affect action; suppressed anger, malice and envy burst restraints and their existence becomes known by their effects. But before the action reveals the hidden thought to men, the imagination of the heart has been known to God. If we treasure evil thoughts we not only warp our minds, but we also unfit ourselves for God's forgiveness. The words of Paul to the Ephesians may be regarded as a comment on this lesson of the parable. "Let all bitterness, and wrath, and anger, and clamour, and evil speaking, be put away from you, with all malice: and be ye kind to one another, tenderhearted, forgiving one another, even as God for Christ's sake hath forgiven you" (Eph. 4 : 31, 32).

Lastly, we should notice the disparity in the amounts of the debt. The large one is practically an impossible debt between men: but clearly sins can be enormous in God's sight—much greater than offences between men can ever be. Yet God in Christ forgives: and the man who has learned that in his heart, will "from his heart" be ready to forgive an offending brother.

41
A CAMEL AND A NEEDLE'S EYE

(Matt. 19 : 16-30; Mark 10 : 17-22; Luke 18 : 18-23)

A RICH young ruler hurried towards Jesus and knelt at his feet. He may have been thirty years old, or even forty—the word is used of Saul when he must have been thirty, and by Josephus of one about forty. He had, however, the earnestness and zeal of youth, and withal a sincerity that attracted Jesus: "he loved him". "Good Master", the ruler said, "what good thing shall I do, that I may have eternal life?" Jesus answered, "Why callest thou me good? there is none good but one, that is, God: but if thou wilt enter into life, keep the commandments".

Various ideas have been deduced from the answer of Jesus. It was no disclaimer of sinlessness, all agree; but some say that Jesus was asking if the man knew what he affirmed; that since only God is good, Jesus too must be divine. It is better to treat the question of Jesus as an enquiry whether the words were used by the young ruler merely as a courteous form of address, or with a sincere desire to obtain Christ's answer; besides this, the enquiry also turned the man's thoughts to God and to His standard of goodness. Jesus therefore instructed him to keep God's commandments if he would enter into life. This answer was so general in form that it cannot be regarded as complete; nor would it appear that Jesus expected it to be so regarded. The commandments were many, independently of all the various interpretations of the Rabbis, which would also be included in the ruler's thoughts. The next question, Which? was to be expected. In the answer Jesus only directed him to the Second Table of the Law, together with the summary of it, Thou shalt love thy neighbour as thyself. This would be a remarkable limitation if Jesus were giving a complete answer; but he was evidently leading the man to a recognition of his position. The man was not hypocritical when he claimed that he had kept all those; his answer, however, prepared the way for the last word of Jesus: "If thou wilt be perfect, go and sell that thou hast, and give to the poor, and thou shalt have treasure in heaven; and come and follow me" (Matt. 19: 21).

The answer evidently touched a secret weakness—the fascination of riches had a strong hold upon him. To sell all he had was therefore a call to break free from the toils that held him, to break away from the worship of mammon.

Although often treated as the whole of Christ's answer, that renunciation was only half of the demand; it was, however, preliminary to the second half: "Come and follow me". This demand was a call to centre his affection on "treasure in heaven"; it was also a call to enter the line of the cross-bearers, the mark of Christ's followers. Although the young ruler could not meet the demand, his possessions being too great to be renounced, yet Jesus loved him. And as he went away sorrowful we may not be wrong in thinking that Jesus too was sorrowful as he watched him go. It was therefore with a sad note that he pointed out the dangers of riches, as turning to his disciples he said, "Verily I say unto you, that a rich man shall hardly enter into the kingdom of heaven. And again I say unto you, It is easier for a camel to go through the eye of a needle, than for a rich man to enter into the kingdom of God" (verses 23, 24).

Jesus did not say it was impossible—yet he indicated how difficult it was by the hyperbole of the camel going through a needle's eye, which if taken literally would indicate impossibility.

A rather attractive explanation has been put forward in modern times, that the needle's eye was a small postern gate, used after nightfall when the large gates of the city were shut. Only by the load being removed from the camel's back, and with much pushing and pulling, could the animal be got through; so the rich man must get rid of his load of riches if he wished to enter the Kingdom of God.

Against this idea there are two objections. No ancient writer ever gives this explanation; yet if it was customary for camels to get through postern gates such an explanation might have been expected from men familiar with the sight. In addition, the variant form in the Babylonian Talmud, where an elephant takes the place of the camel, points to the saying being proverbial; for whatever may be possible with difficulty for a camel would be quite impossible for an elephant. The saying is hyperbolic—an exaggeration, to describe a thing very difficult to do.

Very difficult, but not impossible. The disciples concluded that it was impossible; they also felt that the saying of Jesus also implied that none could get eternal life. To them a rich man seemed to have so many advantages that if he could not get salvation, no one else could possibly succeed. "Who then can be saved?" they despairingly ask. The answer of Jesus is obscured by the translation of the preposition by the word "with". He said in effect, "If you stand by the side of men, and see it as men see it, it appears impossible; but stand by God's side, see it by His side, and all things, even the salvation of both rich and poor, become possible".

Watching the retreating figure of the young man, Peter asked, since the apostles had left all, what they should have? Jesus promised to them thrones in his kingdom; he also said that all who for his sake had forsaken present advantages, should receive eternal life. He then added words which, while concluding his answer to Peter, are also the text of another parable, the chapter division in the English Bible obscuring the connection. "But many that are first shall be last; and the last shall be first." When he had finished the parable of the Labourers, he repeated this statement: "So the last shall be first, and the first last: for many be called, but few chosen".

Looking at difficulties from God's point of view the humanly possible becomes not only possible but is actually accomplished when part of God's purpose. Sarah laughed at the idea of having a son when she was ninety years old. God, however, promised it and the words of God to Abraham are both a remonstrance against doubt and a call to faith: "Is anything too hard for the Lord?" (Gen. 18 : 14). Jeremiah performed a great act of faith when he bought a field in Anathoth while the Babylonian armies were investing the city of Jerusalem; but he was fortified by his knowledge that God had made heaven and earth by his great power; and he could say: "There is nothing too hard for thee" (Jer. 32 : 17; cf. God's response, verse 27). Mary, the Lord's mother, was encouraged to accept her sublime responsibilities as the mother of God's son by the angel's words: "With God nothing shall be impossible" (Luke 1 : 37). Other things follow from this greatest of all God's acts—that He has given us His own Son for a saviour. Thus the "impossible thing" of law, that sin should be condemned in the flesh, has yet been accomplished, for Christ overcame every impulse that was contrary to His Father's will and so was an acceptable offering for sin (Rom. 8 : 1-3). Paul can therefore say: "I can do all things through Christ which strengtheneth me" (Phil. 4 : 13).

"With God", or "beside God" was always the outlook of Jesus himself. He saw that men chained in bondage to riches and power and office, could yet be released from their slavery and by God's grace become servants to God.

42
THE LABOURERS IN THE VINEYARD
(Matt. 20 : 1-16)

"Many that are first shall be last; and the last shall be first. For the kingdom of heaven is like unto a man that is a householder, which went out early in the morning to hire labourers into his vineyard" (Matt. 19 : 30—20 : 1): and Jesus spake the parable of the Labourers.

That this parable follows, and in fact continues the discussion which began with the question of the rich young ruler, is thus evident (see the preceding parable of the Camel and the Needle's Eye). That it in some way illustrates the facts of that episode and demonstrates the truth of 19 : 30 is also to be expected. That the parable contains difficulties is shown by the fact that only one other parable has had a greater number of interpretations.

The story, briefly, concerns a householder who in the morning hired labourers, agreeing upon their wages of a penny a day, which appears to have been good wages for a day's work. At nine o'clock, at noon, and at three o'clock, other batches were engaged, with the assurance that whatever was right they would be paid. At five o'clock when not long remained before the work would cease, a further batch of men was engaged, these also being told that they would be paid what was right.

At the close of the work the master ordered the last comers to be called first, and they were given a penny: and so with each batch. Seeing this, the first to be employed, contrary to their agreement, expected more than a penny; and when only that sum was paid to them they "murmured", and grumblingly pointed out they had worked longer than the others. The goodman of the house replied—"Friend (mate—or my fellow), I do thee no wrong; didst thou not agree with me for a penny? Take that thine is, and go thy way: I will give unto this last even as unto thee. Is it not lawful for me to do what I will with mine own? Is thine eye evil, because I am good?"

What are the essentials of the story? First and foremost is the spirit of the master. He was clearly not an ordinary employer; did ever any employer act in such a way? Efforts have been made to illustrate the parable from life; the scene is indeed true to life—men in the market place waiting to be hired; an employer engaging men for the day. But no one has matched from Eastern records or experiences the unusual conduct of a man engaging labourers near the close of day and paying them the same as those who have worked all day. It would certainly produce the very result of grumbling that is described. There was something in this unusual conduct that would rivet attention.

The bargain of wages with the first called and not with the others is also unusual, and should be noted. So also the calling of the last for payment before the others was, from an ordinary point of view, not calculated to prevent trouble, but rather to invite it. Only an exceptional employer would do this, and its place in the story is evidently to provide for the grumbling spirit of bargainers to be revealed: it is principally introduced to reveal the master's mind.

Several writers have tried to find in the parable principles of economics that should govern modern life, such as the rights of all for employment and equality of pay based upon, not work done, but readiness to work. But all such efforts miss the significance of the matter.

The concluding words of Jesus—"many be called, but few chosen"—establish that the parable is a portrayal of God's work. God is calling, God is choosing, and the action and spirit of the goodman is designed to show God's spirit and aims. The goodman was uncommercial—he was generous to some without being unjust to others; his action was not that of men generally. Neither are divine actions like those of men. The Psalmist depicted God's way when he said: "With the merciful thou wilt shew thyself merciful; with an upright man thou wilt shew thyself upright: with the pure thou wilt shew thyself pure; and with the froward thou wilt shew thyself froward. For thou wilt save the afflicted people; but wilt bring down high looks" (18 : 25-27).

But the goodman also asserted his absolute rights. He could do as he willed with his own, and the evil eye of a labourer did not prescribe the limits of what he should do. So, too, God is sovereign and will give as He will with His own—paying to bargainers as agreed, generous to those who labour in trust of getting what is right.

We trace the parallel with the circumstances which led to the parable being spoken: first the rich young ruler, and second and in lesser degree, Peter and the rest of the apostles. The rich ruler displayed a legal spirit: "What must *I do* to obtain eternal life?" It was the spirit of Israel, which was based upon pride and self-complacency, and upon a view of the law in relation to life eternal that put the whole emphasis upon works.

In a smaller measure Peter had shown a similar spirit. "We have left all—what shall we have?" "In this", as is said in *Nazareth Re-visited,* "there was a mixture of child-like simplicity with just a trace of complacency verging on vainglory." It was perhaps natural that the influence of the Pharisees and of the general way of thinking among their fellow Jews should give an exaggerated place to "doing" as a condition of favour with God. They could not then see that the only way possible for restoration of man to God's fellowship was through the sacrificial offering of God's Son. Primarily, man can do nothing—he is under sentence of death: his nature is sin-stricken; his will for right is vitiated by sin. He is thrown on God's mercy, and can only accept what God has done. "Not of works, lest any man should boast." Salvation is of grace.

Not that there is no place for works; but good works follow as a consequence of union with Christ, and are not a basis upon which man becomes heir to eternal life. Evil deeds are excluded by that heirship—they are foreign to the state of sonship. The loyalty of sons is thus tested by obedience, and so it becomes also true that a man will be rewarded according to his works (Matt. 16 : 27; 2 Cor. 9 : 6; Rev. 22 : 12). The parable is designed to correct the mercenary spirit, to show that eternal life is not obtainable by keeping the law, whether of Moses or any other. In the words of C. C. Walker: "Looking back, we realize that 'the vineyard of the Lord of Hosts is the House of Israel', and the Jews were the 'husbandmen', for the most part 'wicked husbandmen', 'called' indeed, as the Pharisees, Scribes, and even the good young man, and *thinking to enter into eternal life by observing the righteousness of the law of Moses,* while at the same time many of them posing as 'murmurers against the Good Man of the House', and against 'these last' Galilean fishermen whom the Lord had 'called to his kingdom and glory', and who are proclaimed by Him beforehand to be among the 'chosen'. The whole episode is an eloquent divine enunciation of the truth afterwards more particularly argued out by the Apostles in their epistles, that man is not justified by the works of the law, but by the obedience of faith."

Some have missed the true bearing of the parable by concentration on the "penny" and trying to find a meaning for it. In the parable the payment of the same amount to all was essential to bring out the selfish, calculating character of the one class. The emphasis is wrongly placed when it is centred on the fact that they all had alike. In the answer of the goodman the point is not that he will give to one "even as" to the other, but that the disposal of his own was at his own discretion: "I will give" is the assertion of a sovereign right, exercised for good, but quite lawfully because he was owner. "I will give . . . Is it not lawful for me to do what I will with mine own? Is thine eye evil, because I am good?" All the "penny" can stand for is "the reward"—whatever it may be, in this life or another.

There may be other applications of minor character. Some who have been long in the field of labour view late comers with a patronising air or with some assertion of rights based upon extended service. When disciples hesitated to accept Paul, or opposed him, or treated him as one born out of due time—"this last fellow"—did the parable ever occur to them as depicting the spirit they displayed?

Who then are "first" and who are "last"? or what is "first" and what is "last"? In the context the "first-last" are the rich who turn away, who cannot follow Christ; they are the privileged, the legally minded, the men of the present. The "first-last" is the spirit of self-merit, of complacency with human achievement, of life by law. The "last-first" are the humble, who renounce the present, who follow Christ, who accept the cross for themselves as followers of him who died on the cross, and who therefore do not glory in the flesh, but in the cross of Christ and in the grace of God.

The "first-last" are the Jewish legalists, the men of the present world the "last-first" are the children of faith and of the Kingdom, and heirs of the age to come. These last will be first, for the future is theirs; for Jesus did not say, "So the last are first", but "shall be first". The man who received "payment" and grumbled, and had an evil eye toward the "goodman", was told "to take that thine is and go thy way". He was dismissed from service, and has no place in the future.

"Many are called"—for wherever the invitation of God is heard men are called. The Jews were "called", but not therefore would they be approved: but failure is not a Jewish peculiarity. "Few are chosen" is true, whether the word be translated "choice" or "chosen". The first is regarded as the strict meaning, but the papyri show its use in the latter sense. But the "chosen" will be "choice", because God will choose them on account of their excellence judged by His standards.

43
A FIG-TREE WITHERED, AND A FIG-TREE BUDDING

(Matt. 21 : 18-22; 24 : 32-35)

The cursing of the fig tree was an enacted parable—a parable in deeds, not words—and since it is related to a short parable of the budding fig tree, both might be considered altogether.

In the last week of his life many things were done and said by Jesus which were intended to be a final appeal to Israel. The crisis was at hand, and as events hurried to their inevitable close, Jesus unhurriedly completed his testimony. He rode into the city on an ass, deliberately making the claim that he was the King foretold by Zechariah (9 : 9). He cleansed the Temple, thereby asserting the authority that belonged to the Son of God. It was his Father's house. The assertion was recognized, and the rulers demanded: "By what authority doest thou these things?" (21 : 23). In the evening he went out of the city for lodging, perhaps sleeping in the open air on the slopes of the Mount of Olives.

As he returned to the city in the morning "he hungered". Seeing a fig tree in the way, he came to it only to find leaves. Whereupon he said: "Let no fruit grow on thee henceforth for ever". "And presently the fig tree withered away." When they passed the following day the disciples saw the tree which yesterday seemed so full of life, now dead. They asked, "How did the fig tree immediately wither away?" (R.V.).

The action of Jesus has been the subject of much criticism. To deny the truth of the incident would be a logical thing for those who take a restricted view of the character and person of Jesus. But to accept the account as true and then to criticize is illogical and absurd. If the tree died as the result of the pronouncement of Jesus then we are in the presence of a divine act—an act not to be criticized, but examined that it might be understood. We dismiss therefore at once the charges of petulance and childish impatience which critics have brought against Jesus for this act. The difficulty however which some feel with Mark's expression, "the time of figs was not yet", calls for more sympathy and an explanation. If it was not the time of figs, was it not unreasonable to expect them? The answer is that although not the usual time for gathering figs, the expectation was reasonable. A fruit-like flower precedes the leaves in the fig tree. At the time when Jesus passed, a tree would usually have neither fruit nor leaves. This fig tree, precociously putting out its leaves, gave every promise therefore of figs: but it had none.

There was profession but not practice: it was a fit symbol of the deceitful and hypocritical attitude of one with moral pretensions but of immoral ways. It illustrated a religious pretence; it was a picture of delusion and sham. It was a barren tree—for there was neither an old fig of the last season, nor a new one of that season. There was no token of past fruitfulness nor promise of future.

The fig tree by the wayside was a symbol of the nation of Israel. Jeremiah had compared his contemporaries to figs, good and bad (Jer. 24 : 1-3). The significance, therefore, was not very difficult to understand. But Ezekiel had spoken not only of judgment on Israel in the parable of the eagles and the cedar, but had foretold that the highest branch—the Messiah—would be the means of the nation flourishing again; and, says God, "All the trees shall know that I the Lord have brought down the high tree, and exalted the low tree, *have dried up the green tree,* and have made the dry tree flourish. I the Lord have spoken it and have done it" (Ezek. 17 : 22-24. See also parable of Mustard Seed: cf. also Hosea 9 : 10; Joel 1 : 7).

Who, then, was this that dried up the green fig tree? Not a man certainly; for what man could do it? Must it not be, as he claimed in dispute that same day, that he was the Son of God? Not only so, but his words were a sentence, a divine judgment, on the nation; for not only was the barren fig tree a symbol of Israel in their unfruitfulness, but the sentence upon it was a prophecy of an impending judgment on the nation.

When the disciples asked, "How did the fig tree immediately wither away?" Jesus answered: "Verily I say unto you, if ye have faith, and doubt not, ye shall not only do this which is done to the fig tree, but also if ye shall say unto this mountain, Be thou removed, and be thou cast into the sea; it shall be done. And all things, whatsoever ye shall ask in prayer, believing, ye shall receive".

The answer seems unrelated to the question. It was not really so; but as often with the answers of Jesus he gave a direct application to the hearers. Have faith, he said, and pray, and you will do great things. What was done was an outcome of his faith and prayer. It was also negatively an indication of what was lacking in Israel: they had not faith or sincerity in their worship. Jesus says in effect—be not like those whose end is foreshadowed by that tree. He also said that by faith they could say to "this mountain, Be thou removed". In the central range of hills, Olivet was far from the sea. But what if men of faith do see that mountain cleft by the return of the Messiah? Will not a moved mountain be an irrefutable token that the Messiah has indeed come? (Zech. 14 : 4).

The language of Ezekiel that "God would make the dry tree to flourish" links up with "the parable of the fig tree", which Jesus called upon the disciples to "now learn" after he had told them of the "Son of man coming in the clouds of heaven with power and great glory" (Matt. 24 : 30-31). "Now learn a parable of the fig tree; when his branch is yet tender, and putteth forth leaves, ye know that summer is nigh" (verse 32). He at once explained that this revival of the fig tree would be the sign of his coming: "So likewise ye, when ye shall see all these things, know that it is near, even at the doors" (verse 33).

Luke adds "all the trees" (Luke 21 : 29) which generalizes the reference and tends to make it only an illustration of an approaching change. In this case "parable" becomes a synonym for illustration. But Matthew attributes to the Lord the words, "Now learn a parable of the fig tree", and this suggests that both sayings were uttered, which would be quite possible when we consider that his address would be longer than the few minutes required to read the chapter. The "fig tree" of Israel has certainly undergone a revival during the last century. The budding branches are the sign that the tree will yet flourish and the summer of God's Kingdom is nigh.

In all the trees there are signs that the Kingdom is drawing near. Among the Gentiles, the national isolation of the past is breaking down under pressure of circumstances, and all nations are engaged in activities which will logically eventuate in a world government.

44
THE TWO SONS
(Matt. 21 : 28-32)

THE last fateful week of the life of Jesus was spent in Jerusalem; as he said, it was not fitting that a prophet should perish out of that city. The week began with the challenge that he was Zion's King when he rode into the city after the manner the prophet Zechariah had foretold (9 : 9).

Every day in the last week he engaged in discussion with the authorities and in teaching the people who crowded the courts. Early in the week he had for the second time cleansed the Temple courts of the traffickers, who had spread their tables for changing money, and erected their stalls for the sale of animals for sacrifice, in that portion which should have been kept for any Gentiles who wished to worship Israel's God.

On one of the mornings the chief priests and elders came to Jesus, and asked him by what authority he had done these things, and who gave him the authority. These were questions of first importance, but it was a belated time to ask them. Three years before Nicodemus had come to Jesus as a delegate from the Sanhedrin: what had they done with his report? Before the ministry of Jesus began, the Lord's forerunner—John the Baptist—had been asked for credentials. During the Lord's ministry he himself had repeatedly made claims which rendered such questions superfluous. The rulers were not sincere; they were trying to entangle Jesus.

The answer of Jesus, as always, was masterly; but it has not been understood by many writers. He answered by asking a question concerning John's baptism. This was not to divert the discussion nor to discomfit them. There was a practical connection between his question and theirs.

The baptism of John was an essential part of John's work, and John explained why he demanded obedience to it. "He that sent me to baptize", gives his reason; John's message and baptism were of God. The breaking of the four-centuries silence of God was an important event, and the voice of God through John called men to repentance. Upon the Jewish authorities devolved the duty of examining John's credentials. If the evidence showed that John was sent of God, they should have led the nation in reform; but if John's claims were found to be false he should have been exposed as a false prophet.*

The position of Jesus was not determinable without reference to John's witness, for John had said: "That he (the coming one) should be made manifest to Israel, therefore am I come baptizing with water". The reference of Jesus to the baptism of John was therefore strictly relevant: the rulers should first determine the standing of John and then examine the claims of Jesus. As they refused to decide concerning John, he was quite in order in refusing to answer them.

Here was a remarkable situation—the rulers in God's nation declining to apply the tests God enjoined for determining the genuineness of a claimant to be a prophet of God. What was the explanation?

The people had no hesitation in settling for themselves the status of John. "All hold John as a prophet." The leaders recognized this, and therefore feared to say that John's baptism was of men lest they should alienate the

*For test see Deut. 18 : 21, 22; and for enquiry to John see *Exposition of the Gospel of John*, on 1 : 19-34.

people. The nation was thus divided in its attitude to John. The common people accepted him; the priests and elders rejected him.

While Jesus refused to give a categorical answer concerning his authority, he told the story of a farmer who had two sons:

"But what think ye? A certain man had two sons; and he came to the first, and said, Son, go work to-day in my vineyard. He answered and said, I will not: but afterward he repented and went. And he came to the second, and said likewise. And he answered and said, I go, sir: and went not."

"Whether of the twain did the will of his father? They say unto him, The first. Jesus saith unto them, Verily I say unto you, That the publicans and the harlots go into the kingdom of God before you.

"For John came unto you in the way of righteousness, and ye believed him not: but the publicans and the harlots believed him: and ye, when ye had seen it, repented not afterwards that ye might believe him" (Matt. 21 : 28-32).

The brusque, almost rude refusal of the one son contrasts with the self-righteous, and almost servile attitude of the other. The one repented, however, and went; while the other revealed that his response was only outward and without any intention to perform.

Jesus applied the parable: the publicans and harlots had been like the son who refused to serve the Father, but they had recognized in John's message a call from God to serve Him. The rulers, with all their profession of respect, had proved to be disobedient in refusing the word of God through John.

The parable is another indictment of the rulers. They claimed to be waiting anxiously for the Messianic days, but they refused the forerunner and also the Messiah. Their call for his evidence was a pretence—they were self-satisfied, very "religious" but only outwardly conforming to God's law.

As on many other occasions Jesus elicited from themselves their own condemnation. "Which *did* the Father's will?" It allowed only one answer, and the application was at once made by Jesus.

The story is a continual warning of the danger of the "religious" life: men wrap themselves up in a cloak of smug satisfaction that their religion is "correct", and all is well. On the other hand, the story puts no premium on the outwardly irreligious life. When the one who refused *changed his mind and did the Father's will,* it was well. Religion is obedience.

45
THE WICKED HUSBANDMEN

(Matt. 21 : 33-41; Mark 12 : 1-9; Luke 20 : 9-16)

FOLLOWING a discussion about his authority Jesus had spoken the parable of the Two Sons, in which he had indicted the rulers of professing obedience while failing to do God's commands. There is an abruptness in the opening, "Hear another parable" (Matt.), which he spoke immediately after, which betokens stress of feeling. The circumstances and the thoughts involved in the further parable alike would tend to create this, for it was not only a survey of their national perversity, but a prediction of great calamity to come. The parable needed no interpretation, for it was based upon many familiar Old Testament statements about Israel being God's vine (Isa. 5 : 1-7; Psa. 80 : 8-16; Jer. 2 : 21; Ezek. 15 : 1-16; 19 : 10-14; Hos. 10 : 1). The parable of Isaiah is the basis of Christ's own adaptation of the lesson.

A householder planted a vineyard, hedged it round about, digged a winepress, built a tower, and let it out to husbandmen. God had placed Israel in a favoured land, the very geography of which isolated them from the other nations. But, in addition, God gave them a law which served as a fence, separating them from the Gentiles. God had gathered out the stones (Isa. 5 : 2) in ejecting the Gentile nations; He had made the hilltop fortress of Jerusalem the capital, as a tower. "What more could I do?" God had asked through Isaiah (5 : 4). God had provided every condition for fruitfulness, but instead of judgment he found oppression; and for righteousness, a cry. Therefore God said He would lay His vineyard waste.

But He did more than provide good conditions. He repeatedly appealed to those in charge of the vineyard. In words which summarize their history, "The Lord God of their fathers sent to them by his messengers, rising up betimes, and sending, because he had compassion on his people, and on his dwelling place: but they mocked the messengers of God, and despised his words, and misused his prophets, until the wrath of the Lord arose against his people, till there was no remedy" (2 Chron. 36 : 15, 16).

These successive appeals of God through His prophets, Jesus in the parable puts in the form of servants sent one after the other—all ill-treated, some slain. The facts were so well known that the application could not be missed. Stephen might have been summarizing the lesson of the parable when he said: "Ye stiff-necked and uncircumcised in heart and ears, ye do always resist the Holy Spirit: as your fathers did, so do ye. Which of the prophets have not your fathers persecuted? and they have slain them which shewed before of the coming of the Just One; of whom ye have been now the betrayers and murderers: who have received the law by the disposition of angels, and have not kept it" (Acts 7 : 51-53).

The Just One himself had been betrayed and murdered; it was history when Stephen spoke, but it was not less clear to the mind of Jesus before he suffered. For the owner of the vineyard sent His well beloved son, and as Jesus spoke the parable the husbandmen were fulfilling his words: "This is the heir; come, let us kill him, and let us seize on the inheritance". They perceived that he had spoken this parable against them.

In the parable the owner, in sending his son, said, "They will reverence my son". In actual fact they did not. This outcome was known to Jesus, for it is included in the story, and is its principal point. This apparent contradiction must not be interpreted as indicating that God did not foresee the result of the Son's coming. It is a part of the framework of the parable and is an essential presentation of the case, because the husbandmen's decision in the rejection of the son was not compulsory; it was made voluntarily, and was a true expression of the attitude of the husbandmen. Reverencing the son was something to be expected when men understood and responded to God's approaches. God gives men every opportunity to repent; and in the sending of the Son we have a final answer to the question God asked through Isaiah: "What more could I do?" He spared not His own Son, and through the gift of the Son the infamy of men was fully exhibited.

How could the vinedressers so treat the owner's son? It was not that they wanted the fruit for themselves, but they did not think of the duty of producing fruit. They were so concerned with their office as vinedressers that they thought a request for fruit as something preposterous. In self-centred pride in their appointment they overlooked the duty with which they were entrusted. Instead of realizing that they were a light-bearing nation, God's chosen witnesses, they regarded their national life as an end in itself, for the glory of the nation. The entire absence of any indication of responsibility for fruit in the story is a strong rebuke that the essential duty had been forgotten. They were guilty of a worldly ambition, of desiring to be seen of men and of a craving for adulation—generally God was not only out of their thought, but when His claim was pressed upon them, it was resented.

As the story was told, it made an appeal. As David at once responded to Nathan's parable, and spoke his own sentence, so the iniquity of the vinedressers in the story was at once perceived. Jesus appealed for a verdict. The people answered, "He will miserably destroy those wicked men, and will let out his vineyard unto other husbandmen, which shall render him the fruits in their seasons" (Matt. 21 : 41). We can imagine Jesus repeating with an added emphasis: "He *will* come and destroy the husbandmen, and will give the vineyard unto others" (Mark 12 : 9). As Jesus pronounced the words with the solemnity of a judicial sentence, people were moved to respond, "God forbid"; but it was a judgment divinely approved, and the execution of the sentence came to pass a generation later when, catching the emphasis of a word repeated, the "miserable men were miserably destroyed".

46
THE REJECTED STONE

(Matt. 21 : 42; Mark 12 : 10, 11; Luke 20 : 17)

MEN were engaged in building a house for the accommodation of the government of a state. They had made their plans, and were gathering the material. Many were engaged in the work; but as was usual in the East, the master-builders alone knew the plans and others worked to their directions. In every worth-while building, just above ground level at the principal corner, a special stone was placed. It was selected for its freedom from flaws, and was carefully prepared—its sides being accurately squared. It was, more than any other stone in the building, a "tried stone". All other stones would be built in alignment with it.

A stone was offered the master-builders about which exceptional claims were made. The stone was examined, but certain prejudices in the builders prevented them from discerning its qualities. They rejected it. But another

Master-builder knew of the stone and its perfect suitability for a building he was erecting. He obtained the stone, and it was placed in a structure of unique characteristics. The building was erected in line with the stone, and men marvelled at the beauty and grace of the building.

In a Messianic psalm, accepted as such by both Jesus and his adversaries, the psalm writer described a sufferer to whom God grants an extension of life, to whom God becomes his salvation, and who is revealed to be both king and priest of Israel. This sufferer is rejected by Israel, whose rulers were worldly-wise, but not divinely-wise, and who could not fit the Messiah as he was revealed in their schemes of polity building. But God chose the one whom Israel's rulers rejected, and made him the head stone of the corner of His house and kingdom. Such, in brief, is the prophecy which declares: "The stone which the builders rejected is become the head stone of the corner. This is the Lord's doing; it is marvellous in our eyes" (Psalm 118 : 22, 23).

The psalm probably belongs to the days of Hezekiah, whose life was in many ways a parable of the Messiah. Isaiah, who was contemporary with Hezekiah, twice spoke of the Messiah-stone of Israel. In 28 : 16, 17, "the Lord's doing" is thus described: "Behold, I lay in Zion for a foundation a stone, a tried stone, a precious corner stone, a sure foundation: he that believeth shall not make haste. Judgment also will I lay to the line, and righteousness to the plummet: and the hail shall sweep away the refuge of lies, and the waters shall overflow the hiding place".

The other reference of Isaiah predicts the attitude of Israel to their Messiah, who had to be for a stone of stumbling and a rock of offence to both houses of Israel. How great the stumbling, is indicated by a list of words all joined (and separated) by the word "and". The effect is to pile up a sense of calamity and doom. "And many among them shall stumble, *and* fall, *and* be broken, *and* be snared, *and* be taken" (Isa. 8 : 14-15).

Jesus had told the story of the wicked husbandman; and had elicited an awe-struck assent from his hearers that God would destroy them. He then asks them to consider the words of the psalm: "Did ye never read in the scriptures: The stone which the builders rejected, the same is become the head of the corner: this is the Lord's doing, and it is marvellous in our eyes?" (Matt. 21 : 42). The parable of the rejection of the son was a repetition of this prophecy under another figure. God's Son and Heir was rejected: they could find no place for him in their plans. But the epitomized parable of the rejected stone goes further than the parable of the husbandmen—that stops at the rejection of the heir; the parable of the stone declares that God will use the stone for His building, in which it will have the principal place.

Meanwhile the stone was there before them; its shaping not yet finished but nearing completion. It was still not removed from the quarry where it was being prepared. That quarry was in Israel's public way. Treating the stone as useless, they stumbled over it to their fall and destruction. He was "set for the fall and rising again of many in Israel; and for a sign which shall be spoken against", as Simeon had declared (Luke 2 : 34).

Jesus also said, "The Kingdom of God shall be taken from you, and given to a nation bringing forth the fruits thereof". While this pronounces judgment on Israel, it looks forward to the day of the re-establishment of the Kingdom. Then the stone over which Israel fell will assume another rôle: it will be revealed as the stone cut out of the mountain without hands, to fall upon human kingdoms to grind them to powder. Jesus combined the prophecies of Isa. 8 : 14, 15 and Dan. 2 : 44, when he said: "And whosoever shall fall on this stone shall be broken: but on whomsoever it shall fall, it will grind him to powder" (verse 44).

The statement can be applied to more than one situation. Since the Roman armies which destroyed their national life were "the prince's" armies (Dan. 9 : 26), the nation that stumbled at him were also broken by him. Men who know the truth but stumble at him will find that he will be their judge to their destruction. Lastly the nations at his return will stumble at him. The papacy, itself antichrist, will denounce the true Christ as antichrist. The nations will imagine a vain thing, however, in opposing the Lord's anointed. He is empowered to rule them with a rod of iron and to dash them in pieces as a potter's vessel. This is only another figure for the work described as "grinding to powder".

The "stone" figure had a large place in the thought of the early believers. Both Paul and Peter, after the Lord's example, combine the two prophecies in Isaiah (Rom. 9 : 32, 33; 1 Pet. 2 : 6-8), and Paul elaborates the figure of the temple of which Jesus is the foundation stone (Eph. 2 : 20-22). Peter applies the psalm to Jesus as an indictment of the rulers (Acts 4 : 11). Paul recognized from bitter experience that Christ crucified was a "stumbling block to the Jews" (1 Cor. 1 : 23). How blameworthy in their blindness Israel were, is the more evident if, as seems probable, they used "the stone" as a name of the Messiah.

47
THE MARRIAGE FEAST
(Matt. 22 : 1-14)

MATTHEW links this parable with that of the householder and the short parable of the corner stone. In plain language Jesus had said: "The Kingdom of God shall be taken from you and given to a nation bringing forth the fruits thereof". "They perceived", says Matthew "that he spake of them." "They sought to lay hands on him"—there must have been many whisperings and quiet discussions. Although, then, no verbal question was put to Jesus, the circumstances called for an answer. This Matthew indicates by saying: "And Jesus answered and spake unto them again by parables" (verse 1). This fixes the application of the parable of the marriage feast, and in very thinly veiled form it shows how Jewish indifference to God's approaches would bring its punishment, while the offer of God's grace would be transferred to others.

The basis of this parable was not unfamiliar, for in both the Old Testament and in the teaching of the Rabbis marriage as a figure was used. Rabbinic tradition does not yield much help; but the Old Testament, which formed the very basis of the thought of Jesus, has always relevance.

Isaiah had foretold the theme of the Lord's teaching, as Jesus himself confirmed (61 : 1-2 with Luke 4 : 18). It is remarkable that the prophet should introduce the adorning of both bridegroom and bride to illustrate the "clothing" of the one whose message Isaiah gives. The bridegroom is also a priest. (See the parable of Patched Cloth.) The combination of these metaphors throws light upon the identity of the speaker in the prophecy, and excludes a too rigid application of the passage to Christ as an individual to the exclusion of the Christ-body. Both bride and bridegroom are garbed in salvation and robed in righteousness. "I will greatly rejoice in the Lord, my soul shall be joyful in my God; for he hath clothed me with the garments of salvation, he hath covered me with the robe of righteousness, as a bridegroom decketh himself with ornaments (as a priest—margin), and as a bride adorneth herself with her jewels" (Isa. 16 : 10).

The same speaker is before us in chapter 62; note the "I" of 61 : 10 and 62 : 1, and the repetition of the words "righteousness" and "salvation" in both verses. In verse 4 the land's revival is set forth under the figure of marriage. Hezekiah (2 Kings 21 : 1) became the husband of Hephzi-bah, and that event doubtless provided the occasion and basis of Isaiah's words: "Thou shalt no more be termed Forsaken; neither shall thy land any more be termed Desolate: but thou shalt be called Hephzi-bah, and thy land Beulah: for the Lord delighteth in thee, and thy land shall be married".

Hosea's tragic married life was used by God as a parable of Israel's unfaithfulness to Himself; but a better future is revealed: "I will betroth thee unto me for ever; yea, I will betroth thee unto me in righteousness, and in judgment, and in lovingkindness, and in mercies. I will even betroth thee unto me in faithfulness: and thou shalt know the Lord" (Hos. 2 : 19, 20). The figures used by John and Jesus (Matt. 9 : 15; John 3 : 29) were thus, as we have seen in an earlier parable, but applications and appropriations of the Old Testament allusions.

A king made a marriage (feast) for his son and sent his servants to bid the guests, but they would not come. Others were sent to announce that the dinner was prepared and all was ready. But their own concerns had a prior claim on the invited guests—the king's invitation was spurned, the owning and getting of their own wealth taking precedence. To the insult of refusal was added the offence of ill-treating the servants. The king's invitation was a royal command; refusal was rebellion. The king's anger was a natural consequence, as was also the punishment of the ungracious subjects.

The "king's son" is the Messiah (Psa. 72 : 1), and the Jews were invited to be sharers of his feast. The first invitation was by John and Jesus and was generally rejected: and, such was the long-suffering of the King, the call was repeated in the appeal of the apostles, some of whom were sorely ill-treated. The persistent refusal filled up the cup of Israel's iniquity, and "wrath to the uttermost" (1 Thess. 2 : 16) came upon them. The King's armies were called to destroy their city. As Jesus spoke of "*your* house" a little later, so now Jerusalem is "*their* city". God no longer claimed as His either temple or city; both were appointed for destruction and for long continued desolation. "The armies (of the prince) that shall come shall destroy the city and the sanctuary"— so Daniel had declared (9 : 26). The Roman armies were the prince's armies, or the King's armies, to execute what had been decreed.

The city of the ungracious citizens having been destroyed, the King adjusts his plans. The feast is not to be spoiled by the refusal of churlish self-satisfied men. The servants are now sent forth into highways to gather all they can find: "So those servants went out into the highways, and gathered together all as many as they found, both bad and good: and the wedding was furnished with guests" (verse 10).

The counterpart of this is clear. The Jews spurned the invitation of the apostles, and when they "contradicted and blasphemed" we are told that Paul and Barnabas "waxed bold, and said, It was necessary that the word of God should first have been spoken to you: but seeing ye put it from you, and judge yourselves unworthy of everlasting life, lo, we turn to the Gentiles. For so hath the Lord commanded us, saying, I have set thee to be a light of the Gentiles, that thou shouldest be for salvation unto the ends of the earth" (Acts 13 : 46, 47). The Gentiles received the word with gladness, and the offer of salvation passed away from Israel, and during the present dispensation God visited "the Gentiles to take out of them a people for his name" (Acts 15 : 14).

The parable passes on to the scene when the king comes in to see the gathered guests. He finds a man there without a wedding garment, and accosts him: "Friend, how camest thou in hither not having a wedding garment?" (verse 12). The king orders his servants, his ministers—a different word describing these from the servants who invited the guests—to bind the man and cast him outside into the darkness, where others were bemoaning their exclusion. These "ministers" are the angels.

What is this man's offence? He was clearly conscious of it, and had deliberately attended without the necessary preparation of himself as a guest. In Greek there are two words which are both translated "not"; one describes an objective and the other a subjective fact. In telling the story Jesus states the objective fact that the man had not on a wedding garment (verse 11); when, however, the king says to his guest, "How camest thou in hither *not* having a wedding garment?" (verse 12), the king uses the negative which expresses a fact subjectively known. The man had not, and knew he had not, a wedding garment.

There does not appear to be satisfactory evidence for the explanation sometimes given that all guests were offered suitable garments, and that this man's offence was a churlish disrespect. The man was to blame for not having a wedding garment; he had accepted the invitation, and ought therefore to have done what acceptance involved. We shall be safe in following the use by the Lord himself of the figure of clothing for a marriage. The Lord gave to John a vision of the marriage of the Lamb: "His wife hath made herself ready. And to her was granted that she should be arrayed in fine linen, clean and white: for the fine linen is the righteousness of saints" (Rev. 19 : 7, 8). The garment appropriate for his bride is a robe of righteousness: not her own in the first instance, for no one—the Lord himself excepted—can be declared without sin. But God "counts" men righteous who by faith in His promises are forgiven their sins (Gen. 15 : 6; Rom. 4 : 3-8). Such faith then needs perfecting by works (James 2 : 20-26). The two sides of the matter are before us in the statements that the bride made herself ready, and yet was granted the white linen.

The inclusion in the parable of the rejection of the unprepared (which some have thought to be an addition by Matthew, two parables being joined together) is really necessary to show that the apparently open door to all to come to the feast does not mean that men and women can come on their own terms. There are royal rights to be recognized, essentials of fitness to be regarded. Both the refusal of the one class of men to come, and the deliberate ignoring of the requirements of the divine call by the other, show that though many are called, few are chosen. In these words Jesus reiterates a thought that received considerable emphasis in his teaching at this time in his ministry (cf. Matt. 19 : 30; 20 : 16). The saying was a warning which formed part of the final testimony he was making to the nation.

48
GNAT AND CAMEL
(Matt. 23 : 23, 24)

IN the Sermon on the Mount, near the beginning of his ministry, Jesus pronounced eight blessings. At the end of his ministry he uttered eight woes upon the Scribes and Pharisees. Some of these severe condemnations are expressed in a form which is practically a parable in miniature. In a few lines a picture is drawn with that power which marked all the illustrations of Jesus.

The fifth woe reads: "Woe unto you, scribes and Pharisees, hypocrites! for ye pay tithe of mint and anise and cummin, and have omitted the weightier matters of the law, judgment, mercy and faith: these ought ye to have done, and not to leave the other undone. Ye blind guides, which strain at a gnat, and swallow a camel" (verses 23, 24).

The law required that a tenth of the seed should be contributed to God's service: "Thou shalt truly tithe all the increase of thy seed that the field bringeth forth year by year" (Deut. 14 : 22). "And all the tithe of the land whether of the seed of the land, or of the fruits of the tree, is the Lord's: it is holy unto the Lord" (Lev. 27 : 30).

Mint, dill and cummin were garden herbs, and the punctilious scribes and Pharisees, with what was really show-acting, were careful to insist that these were tithed before any were used. Such scrupulous care over trifles might be compared to a person sitting down to dinner and requiring that the mint used for sauce should be tithed. It was right for the Jew to tithe herbs; but the matter should be placed in right perspective in life. It was really a little thing, to be done without fuss or show: but these Pharisees were particular; not because tithing was an act of obedience to God's law, but because they wished others to see how scrupulous they were in observing the details of the law.

How perverted was their outlook is seen by their omission of judgment, mercy and faith. Three essential virtues are put over against three herbs. The herbs were carefully weighed in order to assess the tithe; but "the weightier matters", which could not be weighed in scales, were neglected by them. Their actions revealed an inverted sense of values; and Jesus calls them "blind guides".

How blind were they? So blind, said Jesus, that they could notice a gnat but could not see a camel. In nine words we have conjured up in our minds a picture of a venerable Pharisee, very serious, very particular about the details of his life that all the traditions be kept. He wants a drink of water, and observes a small insect in it. Ah! that must be got out—it would cause defilement: it was a creature forbidden as food. The water is poured through a piece of linen—the gnat is strained out. He breathes a sigh of content. He has only narrowly escaped consuming the little thing. Pernicketiness allied with religious fanaticism had bred an attitude of superiority that was hateful. More than that: it had perverted his sight—for with all his fastidiousness he swallowed a camel, a hairy dirty, verminous beast, and did not know it. It was absurd—humorously, grotesquely absurd. But so it was intended to be: yet while so ridiculous naturally, it was distressingly true spiritually. The Pharisees strained out gnats and swallowed herds of camels: the tragedy is that while such inconsistencies flourished in a Pharisaic mentality, the same inconsistencies reappear again and again in every age. It needs clear vision, developed under the instruction of Jesus, to avoid this fault.

The A.V. "strained at" is due to a misprint in the first edition that has been reproduced since. "Out" is in earlier translations. "Strain at" is a different figure altogether.

49
CUP AND PLATTER

(Matt. 23 : 25, 26; Luke 11 : 39, 40)

THE sixth of the eight woes in Matt. 23 reads: "Woe unto you, scribes and Pharisees! for ye make clean the outside of the cup and of the platter, but within they are full of extortion and excess" (Matt. 23 : 25, 26).

This piece of hypocrisy was worse than the tithing of pot-herbs. That, at any rate, was required by the law, and became reprehensible only when more important matters were ignored in its favour. But the various washings practised by the Pharisees were only based on tradition. To set these before moral duties was moral perversity. A cup or platter might touch something unclean, and so make ceremonially unclean the food served in it. Fearful of this happening, cups and plates were washed with care. But what of the contents? Jesus wanted to know how they obtained their food; was it by fair dealing or foul; by honest treatment of their work-people or by exaction; by driving a bargain that took advantage of a weaker man, or by just payment? How they came by the food was more important to Jesus than the chance speck of dirt which might defile the vessels that held the food.

Jesus is not thinking about food in itself unclean: but as the R.V. translates it, of vessels "full *from* extortion and excess". If we retain the A.V. it is a metonymy in which the principles—"extortion and excess"—by which a thing is obtained, are put for the thing obtained. If the contents were the fruit of extortion and excess, the Pharisee was more defiled than any ceremonial uncleanness could make him. The very use of such language suggests that dishonest gain entered very much into their life, and that while careful of externals they were morally bad within (Luke 11 : 39).

50
WHITED SEPULCHRES
(Matt. 23 : 27, 28; Luke 11 : 44)

THE figure of sepulchres is found in both Matthew and Luke, but it is used in quite different ways. In the "woe" of Matt. 23 : 27, 28, we read, "Yet are like unto whited sepulchres, which indeed appear beautiful outward, but are within full of dead men's bones, and of all uncleanness. Even so ye also outwardly appear righteous unto men, but within ye are full of hypocrisy and iniquity".

Tombs were whitened so that any passers-by should not accidentally tread on them and so contract defilement. Particularly was this whitening done in Spring when the journey of many pilgrims from the north might have been rendered vain by such a contact which would have prevented the visitor taking part in the Passover service.

The graves so treated looked clean and wholesome in the bright, clear light. But what was inside? "Dead men's bones and uncleanness", Jesus does not hesitate to say. That was a picture of the Pharisees, said Jesus: outwardly fair and clean, but within full of foulness. Did Jesus hint also that men were defiled by contact with them?

In another context and on another occasion Jesus used similar language to the woes of Matt. 23. He was in the house of a Pharisee who observed with dismay that Jesus had not performed the customary ablutions before the meal. Jesus charged the Pharisees with careful observance of outward things but with neglect of the inner essentials. He used the cup and platter, and the pot-herb tithing illustrations as in the "woes" recorded by Matthew, but the figure of the grave carries a severer lesson. "Ye are as graves which appear not, and the men that walk over them are not aware of them" (Luke 11 : 44). Men were not aware how corrupt they were because their true character was hidden; but Jesus reveals how foul they were within, and how corrupting contact with them could be.

51
HEN AND CHICKENS
(Matt. 23 : 37; Luke 13 : 34)

THERE are two records of Christ's lament over Jerusalem, the one in Luke being spoken some months earlier than that recorded by Matthew.

Luke's order gives an interesting context to the saying about a hen and her chickens. The Pharisees approached Jesus with the information that Herod was plotting to kill him and that he had better leave Herod's territory. The motive of the Pharisees is not easy to determine. Some have thought the men who warned him were friendly and wished to help him; but it may be that they seized a known intention of Herod—he "would fain kill Jesus"—to intimidate Jesus and cause him to go into Judea where he would come under the power of the Sanhedrin. The reply of Jesus is aimed at Herod, however, from which we must conclude that Herod's intentions had not been misrepresented, and that they were known to Jesus: and also that these Pharisees had no underlying motive in speaking to Jesus, or he would have exposed them also.

"Go tell that fox, Behold, I cast out devils, and I do cures today and tomorrow, and the third day I shall be perfected. Nevertheless I must walk today, and tomorrow and the day following: for it cannot be that a prophet perish out of Jerusalem" (Luke 13 : 32-33).

"That fox": it puts in a word all that Herod was in character. Craftiness was a mark of the Herod family, and as Farrar has said: "If ever there was a man that richly deserved contempt, it was the paltry, perjured princeling—false to his religion; false to his nation; false to his friends, false to his brethren, false to his wife—to whom Jesus gave the name 'that fox' ".

Luke places next the pathetic words: "O Jerusalem, Jerusalem, which killest the prophets, and stonest them that are sent unto thee; how often would I have gathered thy children together, as a hen doth gather her brood under her wings, and ye would not!" His thoughts, fixed on the evil rulers who had power in the land, would naturally lead him to think of the people ruled—even though they did not recognize him as their appointed king.

Herod in the north, the Sadducees in the south exercising a limited form of government, the Pharisees as the dominant influence over the people, and over all pagan Rome—the strong power that "swift as the eagle flieth" would yet gather to destroy them (Deut. 28 : 49). How defenceless the people were, with rulers that were evil, and misled by their religious guides; and yet how unresponsive to him who would guide them into truth.

They were as chickens, subject to depredation by "foxes" and "eagles", and in a great yearning he wept that they knew not the day of their visitation. How often, on his visits to the Holy City had he tried to teach them—visits which are principally narrated in John, and which are confirmed by this allusion. How often, in a deeper sense, as he speaks the Father's words, had God pleaded with His people, but in vain.

"Your house"—before he had described the temple as his Father's house, but it was now left to them to share their fate—was "left unto you desolate". Yet it will not be desolate for ever, for the prophets tell of the coming of Messiah to the restored temple of God in the midst of a regathered Israel, when the nation which once rejected their king will acclaim him as the "Blessed that cometh in the name of the Lord" (Psalm 118 : 26; see parable of Cornerstone).

God had said that in the day when the enemy ravaged Israel's land, "as mother-birds flying, so will the Lord defend Jerusalem; defending also he will deliver it; and passing over he will preserve it" (Isa. 31 : 5). God did this in the days of Isaiah when He defended Jerusalem; and in a day now drawing near Jerusalem will be again delivered in a time of extremity, and Israel will find protection in the one who comes in the name of the Lord.

The yearning of Jesus over the city yet to be the capital of his kingdom reveals a phase of the travail of the man of sorrows that is sometimes overlooked.

52
LIGHTNING
(Matt. 24 : 27; Luke 10 : 18; 17 : 24)

As an illustration of his second coming, the lightning flash is used by Jesus on two occasions, both near the end of his ministry, the one in Luke 17 : 24 being the earlier by a few weeks.

The reference in Matthew is part of the Olivet prophecy, and reads: "As the lightning cometh out of the east, and shineth even unto the west; so shall also the coming of the Son of man be". Jesus was warning the disciples against false Christs who would attract followers and start insurrections. Any whispering campaign that the Messiah had come and was in the desert had to be ignored by them; for with the unmistakableness of a lightning flash they would know that he had come. The lightning lights up the whole sky; there is no secrecy; it is apparent to all. So when Christ comes there will be no doubt about it.

Luke's reference (17 : 24) had a different introduction. The Pharisees had demanded when the Kingdom of God should come. It was evidently put forward scornfully: If he claimed to be the Messiah, when would he establish his kingdom? He answered that they would not recognize the coming of the Kingdom by watching; neither would men announce it, saying, "Lo here! lo there! for behold the kingdom of God is within (among) you". It was an answer adapted to their mood and attitude. The kingdom was not coming at their behest, nor in the manner that they thought. Moreover, the kingdom, in the person of the king, was in their midst, but they had failed to recognize the signs and had not discerned the truth about the king (Luke 17 : 20, 21).

He turned then to his disciples and said: "The days will come, when ye shall desire to see one of the days of the Son of man, and ye shall not see it. And they shall say unto you, See here; or, see there: go not after them, nor follow them. For as the lightning, that lighteneth out of the one part under heaven, shineth unto the other part under heaven; so shall also the Son of man be in his day" (verse 22-24).

They were experiencing the days of the Son of man, but those days would pass, for (verse 25) Christ had to suffer many things and be rejected. Their longing for his day might be a danger and lay them open to strong temptation to follow false Christs. He therefore adds the information that his coming would be as clearly evident as the lightning which shines across the sky.

"So shall the coming of the Son of man be." Some strange notions of the coming have had a fair publicity through the activities of the Russellites. They claim the *parousia* has reference to the unseen presence of Jesus since his advent in 1914. But such an idea is in sharp conflict both with the figure of the lightning with which Jesus compares his coming and also with the meaning of the word. Abbott-Smith *(Manual Greek Lexicon of N.T.)* points out that it occurs "in late writers as a technical term for the visit of a king". The word occurs in that sense in papyri that have been discovered in Egypt. J. H. Moulton has the following interesting comments on the word:

> "Our Lord in speaking of his coming again uses the word *parousia,* which in the later parts of the New Testament becomes almost a technical term. Now that word as so used, denoting 'advent' or 'presence', had something very much deeper in its meaning. Egyptian papyri of the third and second centuries B.C. give some allusions which utterly puzzled the first editors. I remember one phrase in which even the acuteness of Grenfell and Hunt seemed to be baffled. Two words came together, *stephanou-parousias,* which we have now learned how to read. The Ptolemies, kings of Egypt, after Alexander's

time, were not popular, generally speaking, and I must say I do not think they deserved popularity. Our British sovereign, King George, has lately been up in Lancashire, riding all round the country, going into the cottages and talking with the people, and leaving behind him the most gracious memories. This is one sort of a royal visit. But the royal visits of the Ptolemies were quite different. When they came to distant parts of the country there were appropriate manifestations of enthusiasm but it was all worked up beforehand. The tax-collector came round and extracted from people's pockets money for what was called a 'crown tax'. A free-will offering of a golden crown was made to the king on such occasions, to represent the spontaneous loyalty of the people. That was the type of thing that gives the setting for this word *parousia*. By getting the meaning of 'royal visit', unconsciously the word was prepared beforehand for the time when the King of kings came in great humility, and they called His coming the *Parousia*. And we are relying faithfully upon the promise of another visit, the last and greatest, some day, we know not when."

The other reference in Luke (10 : 18) has for its context the report of the seventy that even evil spirits had been subject to them in their mission. They had entered into the labours of Jesus and, empowered and commissioned by him, had preached the message and healed the sick. The whole effort was an assault on the adversary, sin. Men were turning from darkness to light—from the power of Satan to God. Satan's power over men was illustrated in the effects of sin, in disease and death. The power of Jesus to forgive was demonstrated by his healing of disease (Matt. 9 : 1-8). As the servants of Jesus the seventy had carried the assault into the enemy's land and returned exhilarated with the victory. Jesus responded that he had clearly seen it all—he had witnessed the adversary dethroned and cast out of his kingdom. But he warns them that the personal victory which enrolled their names in heaven, was much more important than the exercise of power in healing sickness.

53
THE VULTURES
(Matt. 24 : 28; Luke 17 : 37)

In the Olivet discourse Jesus foretold the calamities that would attend the close of the Jewish age, and the destruction of Jerusalem. He warned the disciples against false prophets who would claim to be Christ. He pointed out (Matt. 24 : 27) that when Christ did come they would have no doubt that he was there. His return would be as evident as a lightning flash. In verse 28, which is about the "eagles", Jesus resumes and concludes his words about the end of the Jewish age. "For wheresoever the carcase is, there will the eagles be gathered together" (Matt. 24 : 28). The Greek word primarily refers to the eagle but by practically general consent the vulture is indicated in the passages where this proverb occurs. Grimm-Thayer's Greek Lexicon has the following note: "In Matt. 24 : 28; Luke 17 : 37 (as in Job 39 : 40; Prov. 30 : 17) it is better, since eagles are said seldom or never to go in quest of carrion, to understand with many interpreters either the *vultur percnopterus*, which resembles an eagle, or the *vultur barbatus* . . . The meaning of the proverb quoted in both passages is, 'where there are sinners, there judgments from heaven will not be wanting' ".

While the context in Matthew attaches the saying to the impending destruction of Jerusalem, we must remember that the language was proverbial and could be used of any appropriate circumstances. The vulture was a bird of prey, attracted quickly to the dead carcase upon which it preys. Several stories have been told of the vultures' power to discover a dead body and fulfil their work as scavengers. In the Crimean War, the Griffin vultures collected in great numbers around Sebastopol, the Turks saying they came from the ends of the earth, although previously they had been rarely seen in the district. The figure, says David Smith, "is a grim metaphor of the desert, proclaiming an eternal truth of the moral order—that wherever there is evil on the earth, there soon or late judgment will fall", and he quotes a traveller's words as follows:

"It was a bright Syrian day . . . and there was not a speck on the sky from horizon to horizon. But soon a vulture appeared, so high up in the blue vault that it did not seem bigger than a lark. Whether guided by scent or by sight, it came without delay, and with unerring precision steered its course to the dead camel. A veritable bolt from the blue, it dropped on its victim. But the feast was not to be a solitary affair. Soon the air became filled with vultures, screaming and hastening to their prey, and, foul in talon and red in beak, they greedily settled on their victim. And have they not their uses, in helping kindly nature to bury dead things out of sight?"

"The scavenger birds", continues Smith, "are emblems of God's moral judgments which will endure no wicked thing before His eyes. It is the unclean vultures that perform this gruesome yet beneficent office; and when our Lord spoke rather of the 'eagles', He was thinking of Rome's eagle-standards. The word is an interpretation of the parable."

Some strange interpretations have been given to the carcase. One which found favour with some of the so-called "Fathers" of the church, applied the body to Christ and the vultures to the saints that gather to it. Apart from the unsuitability of the symbols for such an idea, the context of the saying both in Matthew and Luke excludes it.

In the address of Jesus recorded by Matthew, the "carcase" was Israel—dying as a body politic when Jesus spoke, and about to breathe its last. Already the birds of prey were in attendance to despoil. False prophets were there; for every crisis provides suitable conditions for their activities. The corrupt state of the nation drew the fanatics that led the people into fratricidal destruction before the final dismemberment was completed by the Romans.

In Luke's gospel (17 : 37) Jesus uses the proverb as part of an answer to a question asked by the Pharisees, concerning when the Kingdom of God would come (17 : 20). Jesus first told the Pharisees that they had already missed the sign of the kingdom, for in the person of the King the kingdom of God was in their midst. He then turned to the disciples and spoke to them. He knew the temptation to listen to false Messiahs that would spring from their desire "for the days of the Son of man"; and in the same way that he compared his coming with the flash of the lightning in the discourse on Olivet (Matt. 24) so here he spoke similar words. He warned the disciples also that the conditions of life in the days of Noah and of Lot would prevail again in the days when the Son of man is revealed. In words that only apply to the destruction of Jerusalem he warns them of the danger of dallying and turning back to retrieve some possession from the doom. He cites the calamity that befel Lot's wife as a warning against turning back and adds the favourite saying about saving life and losing it. Jesus then refers (verses 34-36) to the three situations where one is taken and another left. Two are in bed at night; two grinding at the mill in the morning; two in the field during the day. These situations do not exist at the same time in one land—but they exist in different parts of the globe at one and the same time. The saying of Jesus has, therefore, been thought to indicate the globular form of the earth.

The circumstances described—one taken and the other left—cannot apply to the fall of Jerusalem. Jesus, then, in these verses, has returned in thought to the second advent. This is not surprising: for the fall of Jerusalem was the end of one age, as his second coming will be the end of the Gentile age, and both, without a clear division in time, were in his mind. The day of his coming—his day—being the subject about which he is speaking when the disciples ask the question "Where?" the answer of Jesus that where the body is there the vultures will gather (verse 37) is a general answer in proverbial form. In effect Jesus says that as the vultures gather where a dead body is to be found, so when the earth is ripe for judgment and for the gathering of the saints, he will come.

54
GOODMAN OF THE HOUSE

(Matt. 24 : 42-44; Luke 12 : 39, 40)

NEAR the close of his ministry Jesus urged upon his disciples the need for watchfulness. The warning was required, although probably the disciples at the time did not so regard it. The man who follows Jesus needs always to be alert. Christ's business is pressing and calls for the full use of all the faculties of his disciples. The man who "watches" must see that sleep does not overcome him; sleep would be fatal to the discharge of his duty.

Disciples must be particularly alert concerning the Lord's coming. From the revelation given through the apostles the first generations of believers understood that some time must elapse before the Master returned. How long they could not tell; but to each one the day of Christ's coming was no further away than the day of death, for in the sleep of death time passes unrecorded; to the sleeper the next moment after death is the consciousness that the Lord has come. To every believer of every age, then, the saying is true: "Watch therefore; for ye know not what hour your Lord doth come".

There is always a danger that the long interval between Christ's departure and return would lead to indifference and apathy on the part of his followers. The short parable about the goodman of the house has therefore its use for every generation. Its meaning is obvious, but acquires a vividness when we keep in mind the structure of many houses in Palestine. Built of mud and pebbles, sun-dried, without windows, and with a door so bulky and clumsy that no burglar would seek to effect an entry that way—such was the house Jesus had in mind. The burglars' way was to dig through the wall—a way also chosen sometimes when men wanted to remove their furniture (Ezek. 12 : 5). But the householder would, like Ezekiel, do it in the sight of men, while the burglar chose the hours of darkness and when not expected. "But *know this*", said Jesus, "that if the goodman of the house had known in what watch the thief would come, he would have watched, and would not have suffered his house to be broken up" (verse 43).

They knew it, of course: the meaning is so obvious. But the obvious passes unnoticed unless men are alert. The goodman would have watched to be ready to meet the thief had he known he was coming. The disciples know their master will come: "Therefore be ye also ready: for in such an hour as ye think not the Son of man cometh".

When Paul wrote to the Thessalonians about the Lord's return, he said they knew that he would come "as a thief in the night" (1 Thess. 5 : 1-3). Is the source of this figure the parable in Matthew? The reference to its suddenness is an allusion to Luke's record of the same discourse in which the parable occurs. The only occurrences of the word translated "unawares" in Luke 21 : 34 and "sudden" in 1 Thess. 5 : 3, are in these passages.

From Paul and Jesus we learn that whereas men think of night as the time for sleep, the burgled householder found that it was not always so, and the saints learn that for them the night of Gentile times is the time of watching and not sleeping.

55
THE FAITHFUL AND EVIL SERVANTS

(Matt. 24 : 45-51; Luke 12 : 41-48)

THE short parable of Matt. 24 : 42-44 was followed by two companion pictures of servants good and bad, and the fate of each.

"Who is the faithful and wise servant, whom his lord hath made ruler over his household, to give them meat in due season?" (verse 45). The man is an upper servant in charge of the house, whose duty was to provide the food of the household. It has been thought, therefore, by some that it has reference only to the apostles. Others believing that the clergy are the successors of the apostles, and possessing an authority like theirs, refer the parable to the apostles and clergy. "Pastor" Russell, founder of the movement which has developed into "Jevohah's Witnesses", claimed that "the faithful and wise servant" was none other than himself, and the teaching of "Ransom for All" was "meat in due season".

The parable must have a wide application, however, for in chapter 25 Jesus makes the operative words which describe the servant the basis of two parables. The parable of the Virgins brings out the "wise" phase, and the parable of Talents the aspect of "faithfulness". These two parables are essential parts of the same discourse as that recorded in chapter 24, and but for the chapter break would be readily recognized as an expansion and application of his question: "Who is the faithful and wise servant?" The two parables supply Christ's own answer.

The question form used in the parable invites an examination of the kind of servant that is well-pleasing. That he was an upper servant did not remove him from the servant class. There are teachers, exhorters, and arranging brethren, but all are brethren. "Elders" are to be esteemed for their works' sake; and appreciation shown of those who labour in the word and the doctrine. These are apostolic principles, which are easily overlooked in a democratic age. Brethren with the duties of exhorting and teaching, if faithful and wise, provide meat in due season. The word is suited to the occasion, the essential aim being the building up in faith and knowledge of the Word, exhorting to obedience to the commandments of Christ. The speaker with only one theme which he develops in season and out of season, does not provide a balanced diet. The responsibility of the brother who speaks to his fellow-believers is great; but so also will be his reward if he is faithful.

The unfaithful and foolish servant, "the evil servant", Jesus calls him, deluded by the uncertainty of his Lord's return, "smites his fellow servants" and becomes a glutton and a drunkard. The "smiting of servants" is hateful to the Lord: and the words call for sober thought. They have sometimes been used by those who are not zealous for maintaining the truth, to abuse men who endeavour faithfully to do so. The words are no excuse for toleration of things the Lord disapproves. They are not to be taken literally of physical blows but they are a strong condemnation of men who are overbearing, "who love to have the pre-eminence", and who are not kindly in their treatment of their fellows. How much the Lord abominates such ways, is seen in the severe sentence: "the Lord shall cut him in sunder".

To be cut asunder (divided in two) and be cast out with the hypocrites, describes the fate, and also the classification of "evil servants." A hypocrite is already a divided personality and whatever may be signified by the word translated "cut asunder" which means literally "cut into two parts", there is evidently an indication of a punishment which corresponds to the character of the condemned.

Luke's record of the parables of "the Goodman of the House" and of "the Faithful and Unfaithful Servants", relates them to an earlier period in the ministry than Matthew's gospel. Luke also adds two further comments concerning the punishment of disobedient servants. The servant who tyrannizes over his fellow servants is "cut asunder". His is a positive and grievous fault. There are, however, faults not so serious which call for appropriate punishment. The one who knows his lord's will and fails to do it, is beaten with many stripes; but the one who makes mistakes in ignorance will receive few stripes. The last half of Luke 12 : 48 appears to enunciate the principle of the parables of pounds and talents: a man who receives a gift has to make a return proportionate to the size of the gift: if a man has committed to him a deposit, then more is looked for in return than he received. In the same way defection of duty calls for varying punishments.

56
THE TEN VIRGINS
(Matt. 25 : 1-13)

THE primary significance of this parable is to be found in Christ's words immediately preceding it and in the comment following it. Jesus had asked: "Who then is a faithful and wise steward?" (24 : 45) and in the parable of the Virgins, he shows in what wisdom consists and in the parable following ("the Talents") he emphasizes the quality of faithfulness. The command of Jesus added to the parable of the Virgins is: "Watch, therefore, for ye know neither the day nor the hour wherein the Son of man cometh" (25 : 13). With this guidance we must seek in the parable for those details that inculcate wisdom and watchfulness.

Difference of opinion exists about the details of the marriage customs upon which the parable is based. Some affirm that the virgins assembled at the house of the bride, and from there went out to meet the bridegroom when his coming was announced. Others regard their part to be that of meeting the bridegroom, and going with him to fetch the bride. Another view is that the bridegroom, accompanied by friends, went to the house of the bride, when she and her companions were escorted to his home; on the way a group waiting at some convenient point on the road join the party and go forward with the procession to the festivities. The latter group are, on this view, the virgins of the parable. Fortunately the general meaning of the parable is not dependent upon which of these accounts of the wedding customs is the correct one. The parable is told to bring out the two particular lessons indicated; we introduce incongruity by asking such questions as: If the saints are represented by the virgins, who is the bride? or, How can the saints be both virgins and bride? No parable can set forth every aspect of truth; and unwise efforts to trace correspondences that were not primarily intended can bring farcical results. The whole emphasis of the parable is upon the preparedness of the virgins.

Ten appears to have been a usual number of the company that goes to meet the bridegroom. The division into two equal sections clearly cannot be given a corresponding arithmetical proportion in the number of saints accepted and rejected. The numbers are here only part of the incidentals of the story.

All had lamps, but five were furnished with oil; the others were not. Light is truth in the two aspects revealed in the Scriptures. Paul speaks of the "light of the knowledge of the glory of God": and men are light-bearers as they declare the knowledge of God. Truth is also something *done* as well as something believed. Both light and truth are thus the opposites of evil deeds—as Jesus declared: "Everyone that doeth evil hateth the light, neither cometh to the light, lest his deeds should be reproved. But he that doeth truth cometh to the light, that his deeds may be made manifest, that they are wrought in God" (John 3 : 20, 21).

By knowledge applied to action a man "doeth truth"; thought must express itself in deeds. Men have to shine as lights in the world, holding forth the word of life, and also have to let their lights so shine that men may see their good works and glorify their Father which is in Heaven (Phil. 3 : 15, 16; Matt. 5 : 16).

Oil, which is the basis of light, can thus be regarded as the word of God. Without it there can be no preparation for Christ. The gospel may be understood, but apart from the combustion of the oil in the mind, there is no development that fits for entrance into the marriage feast. Men may accept the gospel and thus make known that they are going to meet the Lord: they set out, but fail to consider the equipment needed. They take the lamp, but do not attend to providing a supply of oil. They make no progress in the knowledge of God, and no growth in spiritual things.

In the parable the bridegroom's absence proved longer than expected. All "fell to nodding" and were overtaken with sleep. This hints at the long interval that would elapse before the Lord's return. So long has it been that relatively all the "virgins" have "fallen on sleep" and lie in the dust. A cry will presently awaken them, and it will then be shown who have prepared and are ready to meet the Lord, and who are poorly equipped and unready for that event.

The dire need of the foolish is expressed in the call, "Give us of your oil". But character cannot be transferred: it is individual and personal. The only answer possible is the one given—that they should go to those who sell and buy for themselves. In this market, application is the purchase price: "Come ye, buy, and eat; yea come, buy wine and milk without money and without price . . . Incline your ear, and come unto me: hear, and your soul shall live", is a prophet's explanation of how the wine and milk of God's covenant can be procured (Isa. 55 : 1, 3). At the present time there is opportunity to buy; it will pass; the apostolic counsel "to buy up the opportunities" has only a present application.

The foolish therefore find themselves not included in the bridal procession; and when they seek admittance the door is closed. Demands for admission bring only the answer: "I know you not".

The form of the petition, "Lord, Lord", and of Christ's answer, "I know you not", links the parable with the similar sayings in the Sermon on the Mount. "Not every one that saith unto me, Lord, Lord, shall enter into the kingdom of heaven; but he that doeth the will of my Father which is in heaven. Many will say to me in that day, Lord, Lord, have we not prophesied in thy name? and in thy name have cast out devils? and in thy name done many wonderful works? And then will I profess unto them, I never knew you: depart from me, ye that work iniquity" (Matt. 7 : 21-23). The protest "I never knew you" occurs both in this quotation from the Sermon on the Mount and in the parable of the Virgins. In the one there is empty profession; in the other empty oil-vessels. In both there has been failure to "do". The verses which follow in Matt. 7 : 24-27 continue the instructions that "hearing" and "doing" are both essential for approval. These parallels confirm that the application outlined is the one intended by Jesus.

"Watch, therefore", is Christ's counsel. Be on the alert, not so much in looking for the coming one, as in recognizing the need for being ready to meet him when the call comes. The preparation is continuous, calling for patience and perseverance. Procrastination is a thief of opportunity as well as of time; and opportunity closes with the coming of sleep. "There will be time" is a vain cry, for not only is there irreparable loss, but such an attitude lulls the mind into a false security. "Ye know not the day nor the hour" of his coming; only today is ours.

The "closed door" of some of these sayings denotes the final exclusion from his presence and kingdom. The horror of this to sensitive souls who believe in the indestructibility of the soul, has led to strange interpretations and much wishful thinking. When the mortality of man is recognized the "closed door" and similar sayings, while teaching solemn lessons, do not raise such problems as the endless suffering of those rejected by Christ. When death—cessation of being—is seen to be the inevitable result of disobedience, the exclusion of those who do not apply themselves to preparation presents no moral difficulty. Jesus himself used the word "fit" as a qualification for God's kingdom; the "unfit" pass away as though they had never been.

The parable gives a picture of what will obtain when the Lord comes: "*Then* shall the kingdom of heaven be likened to ten virgins". To all who are related to divine things such a preview gives an urgency to the command to watch, for the most important lesson is that "they that were ready went in with him to the marriage". (For comments on the figure of the bridegroom, see the parable of the Bridegroom.)

57
THE TALENTS
(Matt. 25 : 14-30)

THERE is an obvious resemblance between the parables of the Talents and the Pounds (Luke 19 : 12-27), with some equally obvious differences. Regarding them as one parable the efforts of some writers to determine which is the original form of the parable, and why one gospel writer varied the story and inserted it in a different place in the order of Christ's ministry, are marked more by ingenuity than faith in the gospel writers. On the face of it, it is practically certain that Jesus, going from place to place, would repeat, and also vary his stories as occasion demanded. The needs of one village were not different from the needs of another—to all the gospel of the kingdom was preached, and while we should not expect a stereotyped form of words, the message would be essentially the same as it was given throughout the land.

When circumstances called for it, the Teacher was able to adapt his message. Why he did so calls for investigation; but patient study is well rewarded. The sceptical, critical approach of many writers disables them from seeing reasons for the variations we find in the gospels; the attitude of a detective determined to find evidence in support of an hypothesis does not lead to open-minded examination.

The parable of the Talents was spoken some weeks after the parable of the Pounds. In the context in Matthew the parable of the Talents was evidently designed to instruct concerning faithfulness in Christ's stewards. "Who is the *faithful* and *wise* steward?" he had asked; and reversing the order in his answers he first illustrated the quality of wisdom in the "ten virgins parable"—and then turns to the other quality, and shows in the parable of the Talents who are the "good and *faithful* servants".

At the time Jesus spoke, none of his hearers would see the full significance of "a man travelling into a far country". A few days later he told the apostles very plainly, but without comprehension on their part, "I go away". The parable, like many other of his sayings, comes within the purpose indicated by his words: "And now I have told you before it came to pass that, when it is come to pass, ye might believe" (John 14 : 29). The course of events—death, resurrection and ascension—were all clear to him, and he patiently continued his teaching as a sower scatters his seed, knowing that the harvest will come in its own time.

To the servants "he delivered *his* goods"—a fact sometimes overlooked. The form in which he gave "his goods" was in money, in talents, worth roughly about £250 each. Not all received the same amount, as in the Pounds, but "to every man according to his several ability" the master distributed his wealth. One had five, another two, and a third one talent. We think of "talents" in modern speech as the natural gifts with which a person is endowed. A man may be a "talented" musician, or artist, or craftsman: and we regard these qualities as essentially his. But what has a man that he has not received? He may use his native gifts and develop them and become proud of his achievements; but when a man becomes a servant of the Lord, he then recognizes that he has "received good at the hand of God" (Job 2 : 10). We may generally regard the opportunities for any kind of service as "talents" entrusted to us. The opportunities may come from the possession of money, of leisure time, or of some particular ability. In a special sense the ascended Lord "gave gifts to men" (Eph. 4 : 8) in the organization of the first century ecclesias, when "diversities of gifts", "ministries", "operations", "given to every man to profit withal", were divided to "every man severally as he will" (1 Cor. 12 : 4-11). Even in these circumstances, there was some sort of illustration of the spirit shown by the one-talent man, in that some grumbled and envied because others possessed "gifts" which they coveted.

Paul explained that in the body, hand and foot, eye and ear, all played their parts for the good of the whole. In the same way there is room for "five" and "one" talent servants in the Lord's household.

Two of the servants applied themselves to the duty of trading with their "talents" with equal relative success. The man with five talents, and the man with two, each doubled the amounts entrusted to them. Both had used their abilities to the utmost. The approbation in each case was the same: "Well done, good and faithful servant; thou hast been faithful over a few things, I will make thee ruler over many things: enter thou into the joy of thy lord" (verses 21 and 23).

The one-talent man hid his talent. He did not steal it or use it for his own advantage; but simply let it remain idle. He gave his reason, shamelessly and boldly: "Lord, I knew thee that thou art an hard man, reaping where thou hast not sown, and gathering where thou hast not strawed: and I was afraid, and went and hid thy talent in the earth: lo, there thou hast that is thine" (verses 24, 25). The choice of the less endowed servant for this graceless rôle raises the question whether there is a greater liability for a man not naturally gifted to feel that he cannot do much, and so to do nothing at all. That the servant was mistaken is evident. The Lord was just—he had only given him responsibility according to his ability, and had a right to expect service to the limit of a man's power. The man expressed fear of his master: "I was afraid . . ." This was unjust on his part; for the master was generous, rewarding good service with a share in his own joy. The servant's faulty views of his master affected the service he gave. Although his estimate of his master was wrong, the man, nevertheless, was judged on the basis upon which he had governed his own life. If he thought of his master as he said, then he should have used his master's wealth in keeping with that view, and have given to the bankers his talent so that the Lord could have had increment. The man was loquacious; faithful men have fewer words; instead of self-examination he unjustly accused his lord and proved himself an unworthy servant. It is possible for people of real but small talent to excuse their failure to use what ability they possess by a rationalizing process of thought. They complain they are neglected, true worth always is; they are not valued aright, others get praise which is not due to them. This spirit of discontent handicaps them, when resolution and application would yield valuable results. The attitude adopted is "Why should *I* do . . . ?"—whether it be a "cutting off of hand" or some duty in connection with the gospel. Anyone so disposed should remember that it was not success that was commended but faithfulness. Men are not equal in ability, but all can use what ability they have to the utmost. "Be not weary in well doing" is apostolic counsel that applies equally to all.

In his messages to the seven churches the same Lord who spoke the parable exhorted his servants: "Be watchful and strengthen the things that remain". "I know thy works . . . and service, and faith." The same qualities are encouraged in these letters as in the parable.

The "reward" bestowed is rulership over many things, and a sharing in the joy of the Lord. The Lord knew the help to endurance that contemplation of future good can be. "For the joy set before him he endured the cross" (Heb. 12 : 2). "Fullness of joy" for evermore—a joy that belongs to the immortal association with the Almighty—is now his (Psa. 16 : 11). It is written of him: "The king shall joy in thy strength, O Lord; and in thy salvation how greatly shall he rejoice!" (Psa. 21 : 1). This joy in possession of divine strength and kingship is now Christ's: that which is his, in the day of his return, will be shared by his brethren (Rev. 2 : 7, 17, 26; 3 : 5, 12, 21). But this should be noticed—the future is the continuation and fruit of present effort. The faithful servant found joy in service and in the wise use of things entrusted to him. Powers which are used develop; the present is the training for the future, and without present development and exercise in Christ's service, qualifications for the future would be absent.

The converse of this is true: neglected powers atrophy and perish, both in the realm of body and mind. It is true also on the spiritual plane. In keeping with this therefore the unused talent was taken away. It was not given to the servant for him merely to look after it, but to use it, and failure to use it was failure of trust. The man therefore was unworthy and unfit for further service. Proved wanting in small things, he could not be given greater.

Is there not finally a cause for his attitude in his view of God? "I was afraid", is his own confession. His character, his life, was determined by the way he thought of God. How could such a man find pleasure in the company of the Almighty? His spirit makes him a stranger. His place is in the darkness outside. "He that overcometh shall inherit all things; and I will be his God, and he shall be my son. But *the fearful* and unbelieving . . . and all liars shall have their part in the lake which burneth with fire and brimstone: which is the second death." "Blessed are they that do his commandments, that they may have right to the tree of life, and may enter in through the gates into the city. For without are dogs, and sorcerers, and whoremongers, and murderers, and idolaters, and whosoever loveth and maketh a lie" (Rev. 21 : 7, 8; 22 : 14, 15).

58
THE SHEEP AND THE GOATS
(Matt. 25 : 31-46)

THE last portion of Matt. 25 is not strictly a parable, although it is so regarded by some. It contains the figures of sheep and goats, and perhaps there are other of Christ's words which have a meaning besides the literal—but with these qualifications it is a description of the judgment when Christ comes. If it is a parable, we must interpret the various parts of it as having to do with some plane of thought other than the one described. In the two parables related earlier in the chapter, the virgins are representative of others who on the spiritual plane correspond to them; the trading of the servants is not in the market place or other commercial business, but represents other forms of service for Christ. One writer, who treats the judgment-picture as a parable, boldly and consistently regards the royal throne and the nations gathered for judgment as "a metaphorical picture of spiritual reality in terms of human life". In that case we should not interpret the visiting of sick and needy in a literal way, but should seek for the spiritual correspondence.

Many think that the words of Jesus now under consideration indicate the sole essentials for acceptance in the day of judgment. But this view sets aside much that Jesus taught as important in relation to that judgment; it also disregards much more in the epistles which, with the authority of inspiration, sets forth certain aspects of responsibility to revealed truth that could not be included in the teaching of Jesus when he preached. The qualities of watchfulness and faithfulness shown in the two parables preceding as conditions of approval by Christ at his return, also prove that such a construction is altogether too narrow. In fact, were we to confine our views to these verses of what the Lord will approve in the day of judgment, we should have to conclude that kindness to needy brethren will be enough to gain Christ's blessing. A person could be guilty of many sins of body and spirit, and yet, by almsgiving, ensure that he would enter into life. A further objection to such a restricted view is that in the last issue salvation would be dependent on merit, even though unrecognized by the meritorious.

We need not discuss the many interpretations that a false theology has imposed upon the parable; nor the difficulties connected with "the everlasting fire" which the doctrine of the immortality of the soul entails. There are also some positive truths concerning both the Lord and those who are his, upon which extended comment could be made, but which do not come within a study of parables.

It might be noted, however, with what sublimity Jesus pictures the future when he knew he was within a few days of shame and death. He could speak with confidence even then of the Son of man coming in glory with angels attending. In the day when he was crowned with thorns, there were legions of angels ready to answer his call; but that was the day of shame, and such help he refused to accept. The throne of his glory yet to be established is the throne of David to which he is heir. Occupation of that throne was not a source of glory to all who succeeded David, neither did all bring glory to it: but it is affirmed of Messiah that "*he* shall be for a glorious throne to *his father's house*" (Isa. 22 : 23)—a statement that indicates Messiah's divine sonship, and the fact that he brings the glory to the throne. In Matt. 25 : 34 Jesus speaks of those "blessed of *my Father*". "All nations" gathered before him does not primarily mean a judgment upon nations, although in a secondary sense of the parable it might be so applied, as Dr. Thomas did. The language of Jesus recalls that of Joel which is a judgment of nations (Joel 3 : 11, 12). The phrase "all nations" in the context of the parable stands in contrast to Jewish exclusiveness. The Jews thought of salvation as limited to Israel: but Jesus, who had on more than one occasion declared that many Gentiles should come from all four corners of the world to sit down with Abraham in the Kingdom of God, thinks of men out of every race as assembled before him in this judgment scene. He said he would draw "all men" unto him—all without distinction of race; having being "drawn" by the knowledge of the gospel, men will be called to the judgment seat of Christ.

Why should the figure of sheep and goats be used for the accepted and rejected? There may be two reasons—based upon the habits and colour of the animals. Sheep are usually white and goats black, the significance of which is clear. Additionally sheep are inoffensive while goats are mischievous. Tristram says: "This constant browsing of goats (on the tender twigs and the foliage of the thymes and dwarf shrubs) is one of the causes which has prevented the restoration of the forests even in the most deserted parts of the Holy Land. Indeed they have extirpated many species of trees which once covered the hills. Though the goats mingle with the sheep, there is no disposition on either side for more intimate acquaintance. When folded together at night, they may be always seen gathered in distinctive groups; and round the wells they appear instinctively to classify themselves apart".

The general differences between sheep and goats have been noted by many writers. Two ancient authors, one Roman and the other Greek, have been cited as follows: "You may often see herds of goats and flocks of sheep mingled at pasture, but easily divided again by the herdsmen". "Sheep whether black or white, betoken good, by reason of their qualities of obedience and fellowship in flocks; but goats bode evil, being solitary and disobedient".

Ezekiel has a parable of sheep which must often have been in the mind of Jesus when he opposed the rulers of his day. The prophet saw in vision Israel as sheep scattered and without shepherd, as Jesus saw them in his experience, when he was moved with compassion for them (Mark 6 : 34). God used the phrase "My sheep" even as Jesus also did. God said he would "judge between cattle and cattle, between the rams and the he goats". The parallel is not exact, for God is indicting the leaders—the rams and he-goats—(cf. Isa. 14 : 9 margin) and not judging between goats and sheep. Yet the objects in view are the same, although the use of the figure is rather different.

In the literary construction of the parable there is a frequent use of parallelism, which adds to its impressiveness.

One consequence of the relationship that exists between Jesus and his brethren is well illustrated in this judgment scene. "*I* was an hungered, and ye gave *me* meat" the judge says. When those to whom he speaks ask in surprise when they saw him hungry, he answers, "Inasmuch as ye have done it unto the least of these my brethren, ye have done it unto me". Christ is the head of the body, and he identifies himself with all the members of the body. When Saul was persecuting the followers of Jesus and the Risen Lord appeared to him, Saul was not asked "Why persecutest thou my followers?" but "Why persecutest thou me?" We are "buried with Christ by baptism into his death". "Our old man is crucified with him." With greater personal emphasis and vividness of figure, Paul says: "I am crucified with Christ". He is our representative when we in baptism make him so by identifying ourselves with him in his death, thereby in symbol acknowledging God's righteousness in imposing death for sin—a righteousness which was upheld by Jesus in his voluntary death. It is at first a surprising but then a comforting thought, that the Lord so closely unites himself with those who are his, both in their suffering and in their needs, that he regards a kindness done to his people as done to himself.

The things commended in the parable are restricted to acts of mercy toward those in *bodily* need or suffering. It would have been inappropriate for the judge to have identified himself with his followers in any more extensive way than this. He both hungered and was thirsty; he was in prison. But he never erred from God's ways; he did no sin; no guile was found in his mouth. Those who are his, without exception, do one or other of these things; and all, without exception, are at some time sick of soul and weary in the way. To feed a sick soul may have greater value than feeding a hungry body; to help the spiritually weary may fill a greater need than restoring physical vigour. The kindnesses which are mentioned in the parable, then, are such only as the Lord could fittingly include and at the same time identify himself with his followers in the actions, and are therefore representative of the much wider range of activity which includes service in spiritual things of equal or even greater importance than physical blessings. In fact, Jesus himself laid greater emphasis upon the spiritual needs of those who sought him than on needs of the body. Loaves and fishes took second place to working the works of God (John 6 : 26-29).

"One of these my brethren"—so he will recognize the accepted. Disciples, children, friends—all these words he used to describe his faithful followers. But "my brethren" takes hold of the King's pronouncement, "I will declare thy name unto my brethren" (Psa. 22 : 22); which, when Paul quotes it, is found to be indicative of Christ's pleasure in them, for, says Paul, "he is not ashamed to call them brethren" (Heb. 2 : 11).

The Lord takes up the idea of "the lake of fire prepared for the devil and his angels" in his own last message through the beloved disciple. "And the beast was taken, and with him the false prophet that wrought miracles before him, with which he deceived them that had received the mark of the beast, and them that worshipped his image. These both were cast alive into a lake of fire burning with brimstone" (Rev. 19 : 20). A comparison of Rev. 12 : 9; 13 : 1, 11; 20 : 2, 10, with the verses quoted will show that under the symbols of beast, dragon, devil, old serpent, satan, the sin-power of the flesh in corporate manifestation in royal and priestly powers, is indicated. This guides us to the meaning of Jesus. His work of subjugation of the world will take time. The resistance will be fierce, for Papal leaders, "the false prophet" of Rev. 19 : 20, will denounce the Lord as antichrist. "Raging nations" will only learn by judgment (Isa. 26 : 21) and "angry nations" will know the "anger of God" (Rev. 11 : 18). If then, with the knowledge they will have of the true facts of the situation, the rejected of Christ are driven forth to take their part in that lake of fire, the circumstances of the punishment will have some correspondence with their own refusal to render obedience to the Lord.

59
THE GROWING SEED
(Mark 4 : 26-29)

THE very titles which have been given to some parables have helped to fix an interpretation which has thus become widely accepted. The name—"the seed growing secretly" —given by many to the parable recorded in Mark 4 : 26-29 has thrown an emphasis upon the secret nature of the growth which, while true, is not the main purpose of the story. "Seed cast into the ground" is a phrase from the parable; but its adoption as a title restricts the aims of the parable.

The parable only occurs in Mark's gospel and is placed between the explanation of the Sower and the parable of the Mustard Seed. Because it is peculiar to Mark, various suggestions have been made such as that it is a variant to the Tares. We need not let the theories and speculations of some modern writers worry us in these things. Textual criticism relates to matters of fact—it is a question of weighing evidence by a comparison of manuscripts which contain various readings. Serious difficulties on questions of text are so few that textual critics speak highly of the accuracy of the text of Scripture. But discussions on "gospels behind the gospels", on earlier versions of the gospel written in Aramaic, on documents used by the gospel writers, are based largely on theories and speculations put forward to explain certain features which exist in the gospels as we have them. The differences of opinion among the critics themselves do not give confidence concerning the accuracy of their explanations.

The parable is short—only four verses: "And he said, So is the kingdom of God as if a man should cast seed into the ground, and should sleep, and rise night and day, and the seed should spring and grow up, he knoweth not how. For the earth bringeth forth fruit of herself; first the blade, then the ear; after that, the full corn in the ear. But when the fruit is brought forth, immediately he putteth in the sickle, because the harvest is come".

The Kingdom of God is "as if" a man "should cast seed into the ground". What that man does is the particular matter that Jesus points to as illustrating some phase of the Kingdom of God. The man sows his seed; he has then done what *he* could. To dig it up to note the progress of germination would not help, but might destroy the disturbed seed. He lives his ordinary life of night and day, sleeping and rising day after day. The germ of life in the seed is active and growth follows—how, the farmer knows not. He may not even think of it; if he does he realizes that the process is beyond his understanding. He knows growth follows sowing of good seed; he knows that in due time harvest will follow; he also knows he can neither hasten nor delay the ripening of the growing corn. His part in preparing has been done; now he can only wait. Because of this the patience of the farmer becomes the example of that patience required of Christ's followers. "Behold, the husbandman waiteth for the precious fruit of the earth, and hath long patience for it, until he receive the early and latter rain" (Jas. 5 : 7). A scientist may give names to the details of the process of germination and growth; he may know some of the changes that take place in the plant organism; but here, as in many modern matters, we may be misled into thinking that the giving of names supplies explanations. We know there is growth: fundamentally, the "how" of the matter is part of the mystery of life.

The earth brings forth blade, ear, and then corn in the ear; finally comes the harvest when work by the farmer is resumed. There is a law of growth; the blade first, the corn last. Nothing can change it, and it is as true of the spiritual as of the natural. Men cannot alter God's order of spiritual life, and if there is a difference at all between natural and spiritual, it is that the higher life is slower in development than the lower. This is true within the natural in the different forms of life; it is true of a comparison between the natural and the spiritual.

The formative processes by which the seed of the word operates in a person's mind are slow. Men may try to hurry growth, and may destroy the life, as does the child when it cannot wait for the growth of the few seeds given to it to plant in a corner of the garden but must dig up the soil to see if any change has taken place. The word of God received in good hearts slowly but surely builds up a new mode of thinking—a renewing of the mind takes place; a transformation follows, a metamorphosis, as Paul describes it (Rom. 12 : 2), using a metaphor from another form of life which illustrates the same law of change and transformation. Hasty teachers do not produce efficient disciples; slow growth is yet sure growth, and reaches harvest at last.

The parable is a call for patience—in oneself, in one's fellow believers; and in the whole present work of God's kingdom. The farmer never doubts; he is content in an assured confidence that the harvest will come. The Lord never doubted; he preached the word, he continued his work. The disappointments of defection of disciples, of departing crowds that never grasped the real significance of his message, of the knowledge that one of the twelve was "a son of perdition", never made his faith waver. The processes God had started would at last reach harvest. The work of seed-sowing in every age is difficult, the thing preached is regarded as foolishness, ears are dull that listen to the sound of the good news; but the work goes on. The "visiting" of God to take out of the Gentiles a people for His name will not be in vain though a person must take the long view to appreciate it. If the farmer counts the seconds there seems no progress; yet when the time draws near for harvest, change in the growing cereals is evident.

With harvest comes a change in the farmer. The contentment of the period of waiting is succeeded by active work. This comes "immediately" the corn is ripe. The slowness of growth gives place to a sudden harvest. So in history; ideas germinate, slowly get a hold in men's minds, then suddenly there is revolution. The slow growth of the centuries in God's work will give place to the harvest cry, "Thrust in the sickle, for the harvest is ripe"; and that whether of the good to be gathered in God's kingdom, or the wicked to be gathered in bundles for the fire of destruction (Rev. 14 : 15, 16).

In the parable of the Sower both soil and sower are important parts of the story: the parable of the Growing Seed is a corrective of wrong inferences. The real activity belongs to the creative energies set into operation by God, and these will not fail. "Wait on the Lord: be of good courage, and he shall strengthen thine heart: wait, I say, on the Lord" (Psalm 27 : 14). "For as the rain cometh down, and the snow, from heaven, and returneth not thither, but watereth the earth, and maketh it bring forth and bud, that it may give seed to the sower, and bread to the eater; so shall my word be that goeth forth out of my mouth: it shall not return unto me void; but it shall accomplish that which I please, and it shall prosper in the thing whereto I sent it" (Isa. 55 : 10, 11).

It shall prosper as God pleases: this was and is true of God's word; it is true also of him who was that word made flesh: for the same prophet says of him, "The pleasure of the Lord shall prosper in his hand" (53 : 10). The yearly miracle of harvest time is a testimony to the certainty of God's "plan of the ages" to be completed in the coming "dispensation of the fulness of times".

60

THE TWO DEBTORS

(Luke 7 : 41-43)

WHILST being entertained at the house of Simon the Pharisee, Jesus told the parable of the Two Debtors. This Pharisee was not unfriendly, but he was uncertain. He wanted to be in touch with Jesus, and asked him to his house, but he omitted the common courtesies extended to guests. He was not prepared to commit himself by frankly espousing the cause of Jesus: at the same time he sought to be counted as a supporter of Jesus, if Jesus should prove to be a prophet.

The social customs then were very different from ours. There was an open door to the house which allowed others to enter with the guests though they did not partake of the feast. "A long table ran all down the centre of the room, and round it on three sides ran three couches . . . upon which the diners lay recumbent on their sides, at full length." A woman slipped in with the guests and was able to approach the feet of Jesus, since it would appear that he had been allotted the lowest place at the table. The woman's character was well known—she was a woman " of the town"; but she had heard Jesus preach and had been moved to a change of life. She had brought with her a bottle of rich perfume. Overcome with emotion she burst into tears which fell on the feet of Jesus, and then in her confusion and in defiance of custom, loosed her hair and wiped the feet of Jesus, afterwards pouring on the perfume.

It would cause a little disturbance at the end of the table where Jesus reclined; Simon noticed it, and recognizing the woman, reflected that Jesus could not be a prophet or he would have known the woman's character, and would have avoided her touch. We can sense in Luke's telling of the incident that the Pharisee was feeling relieved that he had not committed himself too far. Yet his whole reasoning was fallacious. He started with a faulty premise—a premise illustrated in his own attitude to such a woman. In fact Jesus did know the woman's past; he was a prophet. Of the latter fact the Pharisee could have been assured had he faced the evidence of Christ's words and works. The unspoken words of Simon are recorded; they were as clear to Jesus as they are to us on the printed page. With that discernment which was so disconcerting to his enemies he proceeded to answer Simon's unspoken thoughts.

The courtesy of Jesus, when he asked Simon's permission to speak to him, contrasts with the latter's ill-mannered treatment of his guest. Permission being given, Jesus gave the parable of the Two Debtors: "There was a certain creditor which had two debtors: the one owed five hundred pence, and the other fifty. And when they had nothing to pay, he frankly forgave them both. Tell me, therefore, which of them will love him most? Simon answered and said, I suppose that he, to whom he forgave most. And he said unto him, Thou hast rightly judged" (Luke 7 : 41-43).

The answer of Simon, supercilious in tone, suggests that he feared the application of a story told by the prophet. Only too often had Jesus applied some simple anecdote to the weakness and folly of the Pharisees. What unperceived rebuke lay hidden in the story of a money lender who cancelled the unequal debts of two of his debtors?

He was not long in doubt. He had answered rightly, and Jesus administered a rebuke, based upon the conduct of the woman, to the self-satisfied self-righteous Pharisee.

He had not washed the feet of his guest; he had not extended the usual greeting of a kiss; he had offered no oil for anointing the head. He had invited a man to be his guest and had yet shown a reluctance to treat him as such because of that complacent smugness by which the Pharisees thought themselves acceptable to God.

The woman had exceeded the courtesies given to guests. She loved, therefore she gave. She loved because she found in the teaching of Jesus and in the man himself that which enabled her to break with a past of sin and walk again in the ways of righteousness. Her sins, which were many, were forgiven.

But what of Simon's sins? They were "the few", the smaller debt of the parable. Such was Simon's estimate, but whatever they were, they were unforgiven because they were unrecognized by the man himself. In such a state of mind Simon could not appreciate Jesus, nor extend to him a courtesy, nor love him. The "little love" of Simon was no love at all, as conversely his small "debt" was incalculably large.

61

TESTS FOR DISCIPLESHIP

(Luke 9 : 57-62; Matt. 8 : 19-22)

LUKE groups together three sayings of Jesus which concern conditions of discipleship. The first and second of these are found in another context in Matthew (8 : 19-22), but their meaning gains much from the setting in which Luke places them. It would therefore seem that they are either in their proper historical place here, or they have been introduced here by Luke because the episode and the context bear mutually on each other to the added significance of both.

The time was one of great activity, when Jesus enrolled many helpers in his work of preaching. Besides greatly extending the range of the work done, the disciples' participation in the work of preaching was part of their training for future work. First the twelve were sent out (Luke 9 : 1-6), and shortly afterwards the Lord appointed seventy also, sending them in pairs to do some preparatory work in those places he was intending to visit (10 : 1). To both groups he gave power to heal the sick and preach the gospel. Twelve and seventy are suggestive numbers in Old Testament history and type. There were twelve tribes of Israel; and there were seventy nations whose origin is traced in Gen. 10 to the sons of Noah. Both numbers recur in the ritual of the Law: there were twelve cakes of shewbread, and seventy bullocks were offered at the feast of Tabernacles (Num. 29 : 12-34), which is the type of the millenial kingdom and its ingathering of all the nations of the earth. In his choice of the numbers of preachers may we find a hint that the Lord's ministry covers all families of mankind—that the blessing of Abraham is not only for the nation that God promised should spring from him, but also for all the families of the earth, and the blessing comes through Jesus as the seed?

Between these two commissions—to the twelve and to the seventy—we find the record of three men upon whom the Lord laid conditions, and to each one, with a divine discrimination, the appropriate test.

The first was eager; he offered to help saying, "Lord, I will follow thee whithersoever thou goest". A volunteer has great value if the motive is right, and if the man's judgment is sound and discerning. Men may offer help to gain personal advantage; from patronage; from desire to share a popular movement. Jesus had laid down carefully the very great demands discipleship imposed: "If any man will come after me, let him deny himself, and take up his cross daily, and follow me" (Luke 9 : 23). Had the man recognized that "whithersoever" might mean prison and death, and if not these, the self-discipline which Jesus indicated by the figure of cross-bearing? The Master saw clearly what was before himself, and stated it repeatedly (verses 22, 44). The Samaritans, once hospitable, had closed their doors to him (verse 53), and a disciple must be ready for a like humiliation (10 : 10). The Master was to be despised (Isa. 53 : 3); and this, said Jesus, would come to him even in the despite shown to his servants (10 : 16). The man was a scribe (Matt. 8 : 19), one of a class who loved to be called Rabbi, to be saluted in the market place, and to have the best places at feasts (Matt. 23 : 6, 7). Would such endure to eat what men were willing to give (Luke 10 : 8); to spend no time on salutations (verse 4), and to share the contempt with which men would treat the Lord? (verse 16). Jesus denounced his class as "wolves" (Matt. 10 : 16); could he become a "lamb among wolves" (Luke 10 : 3)?

None of these things is mentioned in the answer of Jesus, but all are involved. "I will follow whithersoever—" the man said. "Whither?" answered Jesus; for his way did not lead to comfort, to rest, to security. "Foxes have holes, and the birds of the air have nests; but the Son of man hath not where to lay his head" (verse 58). The action of the Samaritans had illustrated the isolation that was even then his lot; a wayfarer denied the simple things that beast and bird all have.

Jesus did not refuse the man's offer, but he drew by contrast a picture of his own portion among men, and so called for the man's deliberation on the consequences of his choice, that, having counted the cost he would not turn away when difficulties were encountered.

The second man was called by Jesus. He pleaded an excuse which received to our ears a harsh answer: "Suffer me first to go and bury my father". It seems a reasonable request for the man to make, and the attitude of Jesus to men and women in the hour of bereavement does not appear to correspond to the answer. The fault is not in the answer of Jesus but in our failure to understand the idiom of the man's request. It is practically certain his father was not dead, and may not even have been ill. The saying was illustrated about forty years ago in a book on Palestine in which the following incident is narrated: "An American was endeavouring to persuade a stalwart Syrian lad to try his fortunes in Chicago. The lad evidently felt the temptation, but he turned smilingly towards the middle-aged man at his side, and pointing to him answered, 'Suffer me first to bury my father' " (*The Holy Land,* Fulleylove & Kelman).

Three hundred years ago Lightfoot pointed out the meaning of the man's request. He must serve his father so long as the father lived; his father comes "first", then Jesus. He may have been sincere in his answer, for the responsibilities of a firstborn on a father's death were tokens of filial duty (cf. Gen. 46 : 4). But he may have been merely polite in making what was virtually a refusal to follow Christ. Many in Eastern lands have made the duty to parents an excuse for not undertaking some other duty, and have expressed their answer in the same form of words as those recorded by Luke.

Jesus had demanded that men seek first God's Kingdom; he had said that love of parents must be second to love of him. Sternly, therefore, Jesus brushed aside the man's plea. "Let the dead bury their dead." There are many "dead" who do not hear Christ's voice (John 5 : 25), and do not therefore become related to the life in Christ. Let such look after others in like state; the call of Christ is to life and to preaching the word of life, a call away from being engrossed in those activities that are closed by death. "Go preach", for labourers are urgently wanted for the Lord's harvest (Luke 10 : 2-3).

The third man presents another type. While the first had unbalanced enthusiasm and the second lacked enthusiasm, the third was lukewarm.

Like the first, this man offers discipleship, but he couples with the offer a condition, "but let me first go bid them farewell, which are at home at my house" (verse 61). Farewells are natural; but while they are brief in Western lands, a "few days" were suggested for farewell when Rebekah was about to leave home to be Isaac's bride. Salutations also were normally long, and interfered with urgent business; they were therefore forbidden (10 : 4). This man's answer to Jesus recalls Elisha's answer to Elijah, and Christ's answer is based upon the occupation of Elisha and its peculiar dangers.

This man was putting other things "first" before obedience to Christ; and the answer of Jesus is a call to accept unswervingly the rebuffs and hardships which life with him involves. "No man, having put his hand to the plough, and looking back, is fit for the kingdom of God" (Luke 9 : 62). A proverb says, "The sluggard will not plough by reason of the cold; therefore shall he beg in harvest, and have nothing" (Prov. 20 : 4). Solomon also adds another reason for the husbandman's failures: "He that observeth the wind shall not sow; and he that regardeth the clouds shall not reap" (Eccl. 11 : 4). Ploughing had to be done in the rainy season when the hard soil could be turned by the light ploughs which were held with one hand. A cold day or heavy rain were excuses at ploughing time that left empty fields at harvest time. If the hail and rain made the ploughman look back with longing for fireside warmth and comfort, or if he only kept turning to converse with a fellow ploughman just behind him, his furrow would not be straight. The evidence of his unfitness would be left for all to see.

"Not fit", says Jesus sternly; for life itself can be stern. Periods of hardship which chill the spiritual glow, of storm which hurt the face and make seeing difficult—these are tests of courage, of earnestness, of devotion to duty to Christ, of, in Christ's words, "fitness for the kingdom of God".

62
THE GOOD SAMARITAN
(Luke 10 : 25-37)

THE interpretation of this story of the Samaritan who showed compassion on a man in need will depend upon whether we regard it strictly as a parable or as a story by way of illustration and example. If the latter, the meaning is on the face of it. A lawyer tested Jesus by questions. He may not have been putting his questions from any other motive than the desire to have them answered for his own satisfaction. The answer of Jesus, together with his look or his tone, evoked in the lawyer a sense of insufficiency and led him to ask another question because he was desirous of "justifying himself". "Who is my neighbour?" he asked: and in reply Jesus described an action which was an example of neighbourly feeling which he enjoined upon the man as something he must copy. But so to treat the matter takes the story entirely out of the category of parables.

A parable is a story in which something on one plane is used to teach a lesson on another plane. The sheep represent men; the sower, the preacher of the gospel; the seed, the word of God; the soil, different kinds of hearers. In several parables where two men are shown in contrast they represent the classes of men who heard the teaching of Jesus. A nobleman going into a far country represents Jesus going to heaven. If a story is a parable, its meaning is not to be sought in the same circumstances of life as those stated. If the story is a parable a further meaning must be sought.

The lawyer's question was: "Master, what shall I do to inherit eternal life?" The parable is the answer, but the man was gradually led to it. The first reply of Jesus was couched in the terms any teacher of that day would have used to his pupil. "What is written in the law? how readest thou?" The man's answer showed understanding of the law. Inevitably the words of Deut. 6 : 5, the text which they wore in their phylacteries, would be given as describing man's duty to God; but this lawyer with considerable discernment added from Lev. 19 : 18 the law's requirement that a man must love his neighbour as himself. Jesus answered: "Thou hast answered right: this do, and thou shalt live". In its fullest and deepest sense the answer was true: for love to God involves more than keeping tables of laws which the orthodox Jew thought was the basis of favour with God; it involves an appreciation of the disturbed relationships between man and God, and also of God's mercy in providing a way of healing.

The lawyer's attention, however, was fixed on duty to men. Current interpretations restricted the meaning of neighbour to fellow Jew, ruling out the Gentiles as undeserving of inclusion in the term. The Talmud is quoted as teaching: "If a Jew sees a Gentile fallen into the sea, let him by no means lift him out thence. It is written, 'Thou shalt not rise up against the blood of thy neighbour', but this man is not thy neighbour". The lawyer's further question, "Who is my neighbour?" thus reflected a question much discussed among his fellow-lawyers: perhaps he shared the view that only a Jew was entitled to be regarded as neighbour, or he may have had a broader outlook and desired the opinion of Jesus.

Jesus answered by reciting what befell a man journeying from Jerusalem to Jericho. It was not an unusual experience, for the road had earned the name of The Bloody Way. The character of the country and of the way is described by Tristram: "The spot indicated by our Lord as the scene of the parable is unmistakable. About half-way down the descent from Jerusalem to Jericho, close to the deep gorge of Wady Kelt, the sides of which are honeycombed by a labyrinth of caves, in olden times and to the present day the resort of freebooters and outlaws, is a heap of ruins, marking the site of an ancient khan. The Khan el Ahmar, as the ruin is called, possessed a deep well, with a scanty supply of water. Not another building or trace of human habitation is to be found on any part of the road, which descends 3,000 feet from the neighbourhood of Bethany to the entrance into the plain of Jordan. Irregular projecting masses of rock and frequent sharp turns of the road afford everywhere safe cover and retreat for robbers".

The road was unique—no other makes such a descent in so short a distance. The man was truly going *down* to Jericho.

From earliest times men have seen in the parable a representation of man's need and of the sacrificial work of Christ. It is fashionable today to decry such an interpretation and to scoff at the application of some of the details as trifling with the interpretation. But when the facts of Scripture conflict with critical theories some of these scoffers do not hesitate to expunge from the gospel narrative even such matters as Christ's predictions of his own death. If the plain prediction of Christ's death is not possible, any interpretation of a parable which involves such a prophecy must not be allowed. But Jesus saw clearly what would befall him in Jerusalem; he knew that his soul had to be made an offering for sin. His disciples could not at the time receive his teaching, and as a consequence were unprepared for his death, and so suffered the dismay and disappointment of the days during which Jesus lay in the tomb. That the lawyer could not perceive the full significance of the parable is not therefore evidence that Jesus did not have it in mind. In fact many of the Lord's parables must have gained new meanings for the disciples after his resurrection.

Jerusalem was the city of God—the city of blessing. Jericho from ancient times had been a city of curse (Joshua 6 : 26). Man has journeyed from God, has been robbed and despoiled by sin. The representatives of law and sacrifice have passed him by in his need, but a man despised as a Samaritan has brought succour in that need. He has provided healing, taken man in his care and provided a refuge. The oil and wine are used of the gospel message (see, for example Isa. 55 : 1-3). Two pence is the exact price of the redemption money required of everyone included amongst God's people (Exod. 30 : 12, 13). The "Samaritan" has gone away, but will return, when he will provide for any further needs.

How easy it would have been for Jesus to have varied any of these particulars and so have disturbed the parallel. That the parallel is there without straining of detail seems to us strong evidence that it was intended to be such by the speaker. It was "by coincidence" (not "chance" as in A.V.) that the three men passed by as the man lay wounded; and it is "by concurrence" also that the story and its counterpart so fit together.

The parable having been told, Jesus now asks who was neighbour. It would seem the man, being a Jew, was unwilling to name the Samaritan, and therefore answered: "He that showed mercy on him". His first answer had been good: man's duty is to love God and neighbour. "This *do*", Jesus had replied, "and thou shalt live." The parable having shown that a Samaritan could be—must be—included as neighbour, since a Samaritan had done a neighbourly act when two Jews had failed to do it, the man is told to follow the Samaritan's example. "Go and *do* thou likewise", now said Jesus. What is this "doing likewise" but a repetition of the demand Jesus made that if a man would be his disciple he must take up the cross and follow him? In apostolic language the disciple fills up that which is behind of the sufferings of the Anointed; and in another sense a believer is identified with Christ in baptism and "dies unto sin" even as Jesus did (Rom. 6 : 8). But the application particularly suggested by the parable is perhaps that of bringing healing by the preaching of the gospel to men spiritually destitute and naked.

The emphasis moves as Jesus answers the lawyer. "Who is my neighbour?" has changed to "Who has become my neighbour?" The Jewish priest and Levite, recognized as neighbours, failed in the neighbour's part; the Samaritan became neighbour to the wounded man. But the man who performed the neighbour's part to both Jew and Gentile has said, "Follow me". He is *the* exemplar of "compassion"—for of him alone elsewhere in the New Testament is this word used.

63
FRIEND AT MIDNIGHT
(Luke 11 : 5-13)

LUKE alone of the four gospel writers records that on seven occasions Jesus prayed (3 : 24; 5 : 16; 6 : 12; 9 : 18; 9 : 29; 11 : 1; 23 : 46); he also alone records the two parables which teach that men should persist in their prayers to God.

Jesus was praying at a certain place, evidently observed by some of his disciples. They must have been impressed by the earnestness and sincerity of Jesus, for one of them, when he ceased, said unto him, "Lord, teach us to pray, as John also taught his disciples".

The prayers devised by the rulers of Israel were very long and full of repetitions, and were therefore very unsuitable for people who were busy, whether students or men following the daily tasks of life. They therefore arranged shorter prayers called "fountain prayers" which they taught their disciples. While Jesus was very severe in his condemnation of the "much speaking" of the Pharisees, he had himself provided a short form of prayer in the Sermon on the Mount. When, then, he was asked by his disciples to be taught how to pray, he repeated the prayer which has been called the Lord's Prayer. The title is appropriate so long as it indicates that it was the one the Lord provided for the disciples' use. Perhaps the disciple who made the request was thinking more of the way of prayer than of any particular form of words to be used in prayer. If so, the way of prayer cannot be imparted as words may be taught; the practice of prayer has its secrets which a man can only know for himself by graduating in the school of Christ. But method and form of petition are initial steps, and it was therefore appropriate that the prayer, "Our Father", should be again enjoined.

After this Jesus spoke the parable of the three friends. A man, travelling, as many did, in the evening to avoid the heat of the day, arrived at midnight at a friend's house seeking a night's lodging. Hospitality required that the lodging be provided, but at that time of night it did not extend to supplying a meal. A proverb said: "He who arrives after sundown goes supperless to bed"—for a host should be given time to prepare a meal which did him credit as host. The host in this case, however, felt it a duty to supply a simple meal, but was in the embarrassing position of having no food to put before his visitor. He therefore went off to another friend, roused him from sleep and asked for the loan of three loaves—small cakes, of which three would provide a meal. Such a request was hardly reasonable at that hour, and the grumpy answer is understandable. The borrower had used the word Friend, but the disgruntled and disturbed friend made no such rejoinder. Instead, he exclaimed, "Don't bother me". He then, to use a modern term, "rationalized" and put forward excuses which are not without a humorous side. The door was shut, the children were in bed. Of course they were—for it was midnight; where else did the knocker at the door think they were? Poor man, how to be pitied! The excuses were foolish as reasons for not giving help, and show how unwilling the man was to respond to the request. "I cannot rise and give thee", really means in his case "I won't".

But the man outside the door was not to be put off. Unwillingness to trouble was matched by a determination not to be refused by such paltry excuses. The man who would not respond to the call of friendship was made more than willing by the shamelessness (as the word importunity here means) of the petitioner who knocked and knocked until the man whose comfort prevented him acceding to the request at first, now for comfort's sake gets up and gives the loaves. The children in bed and asleep, which was the reason for refusal, becomes one of the best reasons for providing the man with the loaves he wants, for how can children sleep when a man makes such a noise? So at last, whether the demand is for three or many more, the aroused friend is ready to give.

It is a story based on the circumstances of ordinary homely folk, in a home such as is described in a recent book on Palestine: "In one large recess we see a pile of neatly-folded bedding and bolsters, to be taken out at night and spread on mats upon the floor. Thus the living room of the day becomes the sleeping room of the night. In the richer homes there may be a special guest chamber and more privacy for certain members of the family. In a poorer home one room may have to serve, not only for the family, but for the animals as well. There is usually a dais, or raised platform, reserved for the household. A small light is kept burning during the night. The idea seems to be that everything a man possesses should be safely housed and barricaded during the hours of darkness, and one can easily understand the head of the house being most unwilling to unbar his door once the household has settled down for the night."

In words he had before used in the Sermon Jesus draws out the lesson he would teach (Matt. 7 : 7): "Keep on asking, keep on seeking, keep on knocking, and so it shall be given you, ye shall find, and it shall be opened to you".

Does that mean that God is like the "friend" who can only be stirred by the brazen persistence of a man determined to get what he wants? Not at all. God is never like that. It may seem that at times He does not hear, or that

He is long in answering. All who "ask" feel that to be so at one time or another, and Jesus knew that men would so feel. He knew when he told the story that someone could answer, "Yes, that is all right with men: you can wear down their unwillingness by being a nuisance, but you cannot do that with God. No noise we may make can disturb Him". Jesus anticipates the objection by an assertion. Both verses 8 and 9 contain statements beginning with "I say unto you". In verse 8 the phrase opens a comment on the parable which points out the result which follows in the nature of the case from the man's persistence; but, in verse 9 by an emphasis on the "I" not reproduced in our translation, he puts in contrast to the statement of fact in verse 8 an assertion made on his own authority that if men ask they will receive. He supports this by recalling that human parents are responsive to the calls of their children, and do not mock them with harmful substitutes for what they have asked (see on Matt. 7 : 7-12). He then draws the lesson which is the key to the reason for telling the story: "How much more shall your heavenly Father give the Holy Spirit to them that ask?" The "how much" is not measurable except to say that it is the measure of the difference between a human and the divine Father.

In Matt. 7 : 7 Jesus used the same language about "asking". He spoke then of God giving "good things". Here he uses the words "the Holy Spirit", or more correctly "holy spirit". The absence of the definite article gives a wider meaning to the words than when it is present; and the "good things" in the statement in Matthew guides us to that meaning. The contrast with the good things which "the fathers of our flesh" give to us, suggests that the heavenly "Father" will give us those spiritual things which have abiding value, whereas the fatherly gifts of men have only temporary worth.

64
THE RICH FOOL
(Luke 12 : 16-21)

THIS parable arose out of an interruption during a discourse of Jesus. The request which was made appears to be so unrelated to what Jesus was saying that it would seem that the man who made it was not interested in the words Jesus was speaking but was preoccupied with his own real or fancied grievance. The interrupter is described as "one of the company", and he said: "Master, speak to my brother that he divide the inheritance with me". He did not ask Jesus to adjudicate; he was so confident that he was being defrauded that in the hearing of all the company he asked for the decision against his brother. The answer of Jesus was a refusal to do as requested, and the parable which followed lays bare the man's error.

"Man", Jesus said, "who made me a judge or a divider over you?" The words are so like those spoken to Moses (Exod. 2 : 14) when he would have intervened in the quarrels of the two Hebrews that it is difficult to resist the thought that Jesus had them in mind. It was not his work to settle such disputes—there were proper courts for that purpose; but had he essayed to do so, would both brothers have accepted his decision? The question "Who made me a divider?" raises the issue of his authority. It was not his function then to adjudicate; but, in keeping with this fact, neither would the brother against whom his decision was solicited have acknowledged any binding force in the answer of Jesus in such a matter.

The man was at fault; but the principal error upon which Jesus puts his finger was not the act of making a claim against his brother: Jesus says the impulse behind his request was wrong. That he was covetous is seen by the warning of Jesus addressed to all who were about him: "Take heed, and beware of covetousness: for a man's life consisteth not in the abundance of the things which he possesseth" (verse 15). The man thought that the division of the inheritance was essential to his life, but Jesus says that a man's life does not consist in wealth; a man is what he is, not what he has. True wealth is bound up with our relationship to God; or, in the words of Jesus in concluding the parable, in being "rich towards God". To know God is life, to know the saving truth is to be possessed of a "treasure". True riches are those things which are pleasing to God. In rare cases a man may have earthly riches and so regard them that they do not interfere with his hold on the "true riches". Abraham is an outstanding case. On the other hand it does not follow that poverty is a virtue, for a poor man can be eaten up with covetousness as much as a rich man, and also miss the real wealth. Yet it remains true that "the poor" tend to appreciate the gospel more than the rich who, because of their possessions, are too busy with the present life to be concerned with a future. This fact is illustrated in the parable.

"The ground of a certain rich man brought forth plentifully: and he thought within himself, saying, What shall I do, because I have no room where to bestow my fruits? And he said, This will I do: I will pull down my barns, and build greater; and there will I bestow all my fruits and my goods. And I will say to my soul, Soul, thou hast much goods laid up for many years; take thine ease, eat, drink and be merry" (verses 16-19).

There is no suggestion that the rich farmer had acquired his riches unjustly. He was successful and prosperous; but he was also self-centred. He was like Nabal "the fool" of the Old Testament in this respect, as the pronouns both "fools" used show plainly. "Shall *I* take *my* bread", said Nabal, "and *my* water, and *my* flesh that *I* have killed for *my* shearers, and give it unto men, whom *I* know not whence they be?" (1 Sam. 25 : 11). So this farmer, complacently egoistic, "talks to himself", and says "What shall *I* do", and he decides he will "pull down" and "build" and "bestow", so that he can say to his soul, "Take thine ease". "My barns", "my fruits", "my goods"—the centre and circumference of his thought was "I" and "my". The goal before him was eating, drinking and being merry—all bodily creature comforts.

He had no thought for others: the abundance could have made many glad—the orphan and widow, the poor and needy were always there. But he also had no thought that the fruitful seasons which had made him rich were due to the rain from heaven and the multiplying power of each seed having life, and that these were matters beyond his power—that, while he might have been industrious and capable in managing his farm, behind his prosperity was the power of God. He heeded not the warning "If riches increase, set not thine heart upon them". He fulfilled the proverb, "The prosperity of fools shall destroy them" (Prov. 1 : 32).

God made an assessment of the man. "Thou fool"—clear, and emphatic, and true; for the folly was apparent in that he had not power over his own life, when that was required of him. He was planning for "many years" ahead, but God said "this night". What then of his plans, his barns, his fruits, his goods? They ceased to be his—the tenure of his life is the limit of the time a man can call them his; wealth cannot buy off death. No man can redeem his brother nor give to God a ransom that he should not taste of death. Wise men die, also the fool; the poor man, and also the rich. It has been well said that "The rich man, used to finding in his wealth the key to all doors, stands before the door of the Kingdom of God as helplessly absurd as a camel contemplating the passage of a needle's eye".

The issue might be crystallized in this way: when a man is stripped of all that men count wealth, in the day when he is as stripped of everything as in the day of his birth, is he then rich or poor? The man in the parable had much to say; but "God said" also; and the judgment of

God reveals the real poverty or wealth of a man when the end of his days is reached. "Thou fool", God said: and Jesus says, "So is he that layeth up treasure for himself, and is not rich toward God" (verse 21). Jesus then repeats the counsel about anxiety for temporal needs, and about observing God's care for His creatures which he had spoken in the Sermon on the Mount. The words are appropriate in this connection. Why should not Jesus have repeated himself as occasion called for it? There is no reason to conclude that if the lesson was spoken in the connection given by Luke, therefore it could not also form part of the Sermon on the Mount recorded by Matthew; nor conversely that because it is part of the Sermon on the Mount it should not have been spoken again when a fitting occasion presented itself.

65
THE LORD WHO SERVES
(Luke 12 : 35-38)

AFTER telling the parable of the rich Fool, and repeating the counsel that he had given in the Sermon on the Mount about the folly of anxiety and the necessity for putting the Kingdom as the first desire, Jesus spoke about "watching servants" in similar language to that which he used at the close of his ministry, as recorded in Matt. 24 : 42-51. The "good man of the house" occurs in verse 39, as in Matt. 24 : 42. We have already considered these verses. But Luke also gives the little parable of the Lord who serves. The opening sentences recall the parable of the virgins, but differ in that here the servants wait their Lord's return from a wedding. "Ye yourselves like unto men that wait for their lord, when he will return from the wedding; that when he cometh and knocketh, they may open unto him immediately" (verse 36).

The master had attended a wedding as a guest, and since the festivities lasted several days, the time of his return would not be known. He arrived late at night, when one might expect to find the house in darkness and the servants asleep. But such was the loyalty and respect of the servants that he found the house with lights burning and the servants ready to serve him a meal. They were ready to open the door "immediately". Jesus said, "*Blessed* are those servants, whom the lord when he cometh shall find watching". Beatitudes concern rare qualities, and the inclusion of this watching attitude among them shows that it does not belong to the everyday things. Servants that are always ready give joy and pleasure to their master; and the watching, alert, servants of the Lord Jesus are a joy to him. This is shown in a striking way by an action of service by the master in the parable: "Verily I say unto you, that he shall gird himself, and make them to sit down to meat, and will come forth and serve them" (verse 37).

At the end of his ministry, Jesus girded himself with a towel and washed the disciples' feet as an example of humility. "Gird yourselves with humility", Peter commands, in words based on that unforgettable experience (John 13 : 5-17; 1 Pet. 5 : 5). The lesson of the parable is different: the Master's action in the parable is performed to bestow honour on faithful servants.

A similar inversion of roles is found in Rev. 3 : 20, 21, where the language is reminiscent of the words of Jesus recorded in the gospels. "Behold, I stand at the door and knock: if any man hear my voice, and open the door, I will come in to him, and will sup with him, and he with me." Jesus is the one who knocks. To proud and self sufficient Laodiceans he administered rebuke, but because he loved them, he said "Be zealous, therefore, and repent". With the rebuke he names a gracious appeal. He is standing at the door and knocking; if they will hear his voice and open to him, receiving him as guest, he will sup with them. He will do more: the guest will then become host, for he adds, "and he with me". In a sense this happens each first day when disciples prepare the table of memorials of bread and wine. Their table becomes "the Lord's table", for where two or three are met together in his name, he is there.

The Apocalypse also tells us that in the day of the marriage of the Lamb, it will be granted to the bride to "be arrayed in fine linen, clean and white"; and upon those who form the bride rests the benediction: "Blessed are they which are called unto the marriage supper of the Lamb" (Rev. 19 : 8, 9).

What is this service of the Lord that he bestows upon his servants? What is this "grant" of wedding robes? What is the feast to which he will invite them? When Isaiah speaks of the "feast of fat things", he is describing the blessings of the new covenant, and he associates the feast with the swallowing up of death in victory (Isa. 25 : 6-8). Since the Lord Jesus laid down his life that death-stricken men might have life, what is the festival at which he serves but the completing of that work in the bestowal of life and immortality upon his faithful servants? This bestowing of life will be on his part an act of condescension and of grace; life will not be given because of any servant's merit, for in another parable Jesus taught the disciples to think of themselves as unprofitable (Luke 17 : 7-10). As the greatest of his services is the conferring of everlasting life, the parable is fittingly prefaced by "Blessed". There can be no higher honour for mortals. The ecstatic language of the Song is needed to describe the mutual responses of the Bridegroom and the Bride when they sit down in the kingdom of God: "I am come into my garden, my sister, my spouse: I have gathered my myrrh with my spice; I have eaten my honeycomb with my honey; I have drunk my wine with my milk; eat, O friends; drink, yea, drink abundantly, O beloved" (Song 5 : 1).

66
FIRE AND WATER
(Luke 12 : 49)

THE Lord describes the effects of his first coming in startling ways. "I am come to send fire on the earth; and what will I if it be already kindled?" It had been written (Isa. 49 : 6) that the Lord's servant would be a light of the Gentiles. Isaiah also contrasts the light of this servant of God with human fire-raisers. "Who is among you that feareth the Lord, that obeyeth the voice of his servant, that walketh in darkness, and hath no light? let him trust in the name of the Lord, and stay upon his God. Behold, all ye that kindle a fire, that compass yourselves about with sparks: walk in the light of your fire, and in the sparks that ye have kindled. This shall ye have of mine hand; ye shall lie down in sorrow" (Isa. 50 : 10,11).

In this statement the prophet speaks of light for guidance in life's way. Those who hear the voice of God's servant do not walk in darkness; they obey the injunction to trust in God. But the fires men kindle give off smoke and sparks which, as Isaiah implies by his ironic challenge that men should walk in the light of them, do not guide men. The end of such "lighters" is sorrow and death.

There are many thoughts connected with the Lord's words about the "fire on earth" that are related to Isaiah's statement. By the preaching of the gospel Jesus was starting a fire which should set the world aflame. Men who believe would walk in the light; and so doing would find in the Gospel message itself a purifier, besides being brought providentially into circumstances of chastening that cleanses as fire. Others in unbelief would oppose the truth and be promoters of persecution. Thus the "fire" of division would come, and reveal who were the Lord's servants and who the enemies of truth. The truth is upheld, and the knowledge concerning it preserved, by those who know it preaching to others: this preaching tests both speaker and hearer, and by it strife is often engendered as is illustrated in the Lord's own life. Though at peace with God, and bringer of peace, the preacher finds, as Christ said would be, that division in households follows and the message of peace brings separation.

The fire was already kindled, and Jesus said he would not have it otherwise. He was the messenger proclaiming glad tidings on the mountains of the Lord's land, and he already knew what fires of bitterness and hatred were burning in the hearts of the rulers. So it must be; since the world loves its own and he was not of the world, the world would hate him. This subjection to hatred was continually a part of his experience, but he changed the figure as his thought turned to himself more particularly: "I have a baptism to be baptized with; and how am I straitened till it be accomplished" (verse 50). Jesus had already been baptized, but that baptism of John in Jordan was an immersion in water. This action of Jesus in being baptized was a symbolic fulfilling of all righteousness; it pointed forward to a "baptism" of blood when his voluntary death would, in Paul's words, be a "declaration of God's righteousness" (Rom. 3 : 21-25) in imposing death upon men as a punishment for sin. God offers forgiveness of sins to all who make the crucified one their representative by being "buried *with* him by baptism into death", for in doing so they endorse the declaration of God's righteousness which Jesus made in the voluntary laying down of his life.

Although Jesus spoke calmly of the cross, he was not indifferent to its shame, its horror and its suffering—the "baptism" with which he had yet to be baptized. The agony in Gethsemane, however, was not an isolated experience but a climax—the prospect had been a continual Gethsemane. He was straitened—afflicted, oppressed—until the mission was accomplished. He spoke of a cup and a baptism when Zebedee's sons and their mother would have bespoken chief places in Messiah's kingdom (Mark 10 : 38-

40). Could they drink of his cup of sorrows and be baptized into his sufferings and death, he asked them. He did not spare them, for he told them that they would share his sufferings: but he could not promise the privileged places in his kingdom, for those places were at the Father's disposal.

These figures of fire and of baptism were not lightly used. With steady vision, made known in vivid yet measured words, he contemplated going through "fire and water", from which by faith he would emerge tried and perfected.

67-70
TABLE TALK PARABLES

THE four parables: Ass or Ox in Pit (Luke 14 : 5); the Lowest Place (verses 7-11); Rules for Hosts (verse 12-14); and, the Great Supper (verses 16-24) are closely connected both in origin and in their meaning. They were all spoken on the same occasion and all the circumstances associated with them must be kept in mind.

The fourteenth chapter of Luke contains a very interesting record of a visit Jesus paid to the house of one of the chief Pharisees. This ruler invited Jesus to a meal, and the circumstances produced some of the most interesting table talk ever spoken. It was a Sabbath party, very common among the Jews of the first century, and often marked by luxury which became proverbial.

The attitude of the Pharisees to Jesus is surprising. He so frequently had denounced their hypocrisy, and they had manifested such a bitter hatred for his exposures of their follies, that we might have expected they would avoid any close association with him. Doubtless they varied as individuals, and after all, the interest aroused by Jesus was of a compelling character; his enemies could not ignore him. Many would be sure to seek some first-hand contact with Jesus, while yet not willing to extend an open friendship towards him. Luke says that at this meal "they watched him". There is "watching" in order to learn, and a malevolent watching that springs from sinister feelings. The latter ruled here.

A man suffering from dropsy was present. Admission was easily gained to a house in Palestine, and uninvited people could follow Jesus into the house. We are not told anything which points to the man's presence being a trap planned by the Pharisees; but seeing him there, they quickly wondered what Jesus would do. It was the sabbath—would he again break the sabbath laws by healing the man? Jesus answered their unspoken musings with a question, "Is it lawful to heal on the sabbath day?" Jesus submitted himself to questioning; but he also asked questions, generally very disconcerting questions for his opponents. The question being answered, criticism was silenced in advance; and Jesus healed the man.

67: Ass or Ox in Pit (Luke 14 : 5)

Another question followed which was a challenge to his hearers on the ground of their own attitude to the Sabbath, and at the same time a justification of what he had done. "Which of you shall have an ass or an ox fallen into a pit, and will not straightway pull him out on the sabbath day?" (verse 5). They knew what they would do under such circumstances. Self-interest on their part would lead to action: but Jesus was not moved by self-interest, but by consideration for the needs of the sick and troubled. The question is a parable; the sick, the diseased, the sinners, were so many sheep that had fallen into pits. Jesus, the Shepherd, for their sakes lifted them out. Another lesson based on attention to the needs of animals is recorded in 13 : 15; the words are illustrations, but they also have a parabolic significance. See for explanation of the underlying significance the Sheep in Pit (Matt. 12 : 11).

68 : The Lowest Place (Luke 14 : 7-11)

While the rulers present were watching Jesus, he observed the behaviour of their guests. Solomon had laid down a wise rule of etiquette at a feast when he said: "Put not forth thyself in the presence of the king, and stand not in the presence of great men: for it is better that it be said unto thee, Come up hither; than that thou shouldest be put lower in the presence of the prince whom thine eyes have seen" (Prov. 25 : 6, 7). The guests forgot this, and an unseemly scramble took place to get the seats of honour. Jesus had a word for the guests, which taught them a better way, and embodied a deeper spiritual lesson. The "parable" Jesus "put forth" counselled one bidden at a feast not to take the most important seat. Were he required to move to one less important it would be a shame to him; but if he took the lower seat and was then invited by the host to move upwards, he would be honoured by all present.

Jesus puts the "moral" in a form of words he must have used several times. "Whosoever exalteth himself shall be abased; and he that humbleth himself shall be exalted". The words occur in Matt. 23 : 12, Luke 18 : 14, and in both these passages the import is that God will exalt those who are lowly. This application in these other references suggests that when used in Luke 14 : 11 the words must not be limited to the changes that men make. In fact, apart from considerations of social standing, men in general are not at all concerned about exalting the humble. Self-confidence and "getting on" are held in too high esteem by men generally for Christ's rule to be observed by them.

The comment of Jesus leads us to look deeper. Did he see in the assertion of place by the guests any significance other than the pride and pushfulness of human nature? The deeper meaning of the ox in a pit of verse 5, and the obvious significance of the parable of the Great Supper that formed the next item of table talk, suggest that something more must be seen in the action of the guests than bad table manners.

The political situation then existing in Israel provides a national application of the parable. The rulers were political schemers; the Pharisees were fervent patriots. All the nation were animated by spiritual pride; they regarded themselves as the special favourites of providence, while the Gentiles were the "uncircumcised", "dogs", and unclean. Instead of regarding their subjection to Gentiles, as a well deserved chastisement and seeking to amend their ways in a humble walk before God, doing justly in their dealings one with another, the Jews resented the discipline and strove to be rid of foreign rule. In their opposition to the Romans the crisis was not long delayed. They sought by their own arrogant thrusting efforts to secure the place they thought belonged to them. Little service was paid to the idea that God was the disposer of nations—even of His own nation. He was lord of the feast—better were it, said Jesus, for them to wait God's good pleasure and in His exaltation of the nation they would have praise of all. In view of the deeper meanings that attach to so many of his lessons, we can well imagine that there would be many discussions for days among those who heard him concerning what he meant. Did his rebuke of petty social rudeness provoke anyone to wonder what ideas underlying it were in the mind of the Teacher, whose sayings seemed so simple but meant so much?

69 : Rules for Hosts (Luke 14 : 12-14)

After speaking to the unmannered guests, Jesus addressed the host in words that test the motives in hospitality. The words are not parabolic, but some of them form a text for the parable of the Great Supper that follows, in which Jesus repeats them. Since the parable of the supper reveals God's ways and purposes, the repetition of the language suggests that hosts who are concerned to please God should be moved by the same motives as God.

"When thou makest a dinner or a supper", says Jesus, "call not thy friends, nor thy brethren, neither thy kinsmen, nor thy rich neighbours; lest they also bid thee again, and a recompense be made thee. But when thou makest a feast, call the poor, the maimed, the lame, the blind: and thou shalt be blessed; for they cannot recompense thee: for thou shalt be recompensed at the resurrection of the just" (14 : 12-14).

While the language must be understood literally the idiom used must be recognized. While the words seem absolute—"call not these but call these others"—this absolute form was used idiomatically for emphasis: more exactly we should say. "Do not so much call these, as the others". A passage which might serve as a good illustration was the saying of Hosea quoted many times by Jesus—"I will have mercy and not sacrifice". The saying was not a prohibition of sacrifice but the inculcation of mercy as of greater importance.

Jesus touches the springs of action that may move men in asking rich friends. There is delicate irony in the way Jesus states it—"lest they also bid thee again". They are able to "ask back" and, says Jesus, there is a danger they might do it. Of course, Jesus means that the return visit was the real object in the first invitation being given. If, however, "poor, maimed, lame and blind" are invited, the sincerity of the motive is unquestionable. The poor have not the means, and the others lack the physical ability to provide an entertainment. But the action, as Jesus shows, does not go unrewarded; God will recompense at the resurrection. In both halves of this saying of Jesus, reward is mentioned. In the first it is sought of men and the motive is unworthy. In the second any reward expected is based upon faith in God, and that of itself cleanses the motive. Jesus does not eliminate reward from his teaching as enthusiastic altruists try to exclude it from their philosophies. Jesus has a much better understanding of both human nature and of God's purpose. God will recompense; and even in the Lord's own case, "for the joy set before him, he endured the cross" (Heb. 12 : 2). Who "set before" the Lord such an incentive of joy? Was it not the Father Himself? The same God has invited the poor and the crippled to His feast.

70 : The Great Supper (Luke 14 : 16-24)

A pious remark provided the link between the counsel to the host and this parable. "Thou shalt be blessed in the resurrection", Jesus had said. A fellow guest echoes the words: "Blessed is he that shall eat bread in the kingdom of God" (verse 15). The remark has been variously interpreted: some regard it as sincere and discerning; others as merely an unctuous comment. From the context preceding and the lesson involved in the parable following, it would appear to be the most reasonable interpretation to regard the speaker as a self-satisfied guest who complacently thought he would be among the guests God would invite to His kingdom. His words are merely a pious platitude. The reply of Jesus is really a parable about guests, although generally described, from words used in the parable itself, as the Great Supper.

A man made a supper and invited many guests. When it was ready he sent his servants with the customary second summons. Then the invited guests began to make excuses; whereupon in annoyance the host sent out into the lanes of the city for "the poor and the maimed, and the halt and the blind". Even then there was room for others. The servants were then sent into the highways to gather in others—that the house might be filled: at the same time he declares that those first bidden shall not be allowed to partake of the supper.

The meaning is clear, particularly in the light of New Testament history after the Lord's ascension. This parable, of course, closely resembles the parable of the marriage feast (Matt. 22 : 1-14) which some writers persist in regarding as a "double", the variations being mistakes of the gospel writers. But it has been truly said, "Like all good preachers Jesus repeated himself; and like all good preachers he never merely repeated himself".

The Kingdom is like a feast—a banquet (Isa. 25 : 6)—and God had invited the Jews as His guests in the proclamation of His purpose through the prophets. The second invitation of the story conformed to current practice, but its mention reveals that the invited guests not only lacked good manners, but had contempt of the host. Tristram says that to omit the second summons would be "a grievous breach of etiquette, equivalent to cancelling the previous more general notification. To refuse the second summons would be an insult, which is equivalent among the Arab tribes to a declaration of war". The pretence of having accepted the invitation was therefore an aggravation of the offence. The excuses which were made were frivolous—transparently silly. One had bought a field and must see it—but when did a man buy a field without first seeing it? The next had bought oxen and must try them—he was in fact on the way to do so. What a confession of incompetence, to buy and then try! But how slighting to advance so lame an excuse! The third man had what seemed a better case; the law did give certain liberties for a year when a man married (Deut. 24 : 5), but the liberties did not annul social customs.

The host was not, by such trumpery excuses, to be changed from his purpose. The men were unworthy—others should be invited. The streets and lanes of the city were to be searched for poor and crippled. In the application, the first invitations were to the rulers: the second, still within the confines of the city, referred to the "publicans and sinners" who responded to the invitation. The counterpart of the extension of the invitation to the men of the highways is manifestly the offer of salvation to Gentiles, as Paul said to the Jews of Antioch in Pisidia: "It was necessary that the word of God should first have been spoken to you: but seeing ye put it from you, and judge yourselves unworthy of everlasting life, lo, we turn to the Gentiles" (Acts 13 : 46).

The saying in the parable that the people of the highways should be compelled to come to the feast has been given a strangely perverse application. It has been used to justify persecution of heretics and compulsion to join a church. How manifestly inappropriate as the meaning of the words of Jesus is clear; no such "compulsion" would be needed to bring starving people to a free dinner: besides which, a single servant would not be sent to bring in a company by physical force. The compulsion of the gospel is that which springs from conviction based on reasoning out of the scriptures.

The parable is part of the indictment of the Jewish nation, and is also an additional rebuke to the Pharisee who had invited Jesus. The nation was full of excuses for not responding to God's invitations. They were to be therefore excluded, while the invitation would be passed on to others. The Gentiles have heard the word of the gospel and have believed.

71

A TOWER BUILDER AND A WARRING KING

(Luke 14 : 28-32)

THESE two parables, spoken at the same time, are so closely connected that they are considered together with their context.

During the last year of his ministry, Jesus on several occasions repulsed the crowds whose enthusiasm to make him a king was embarrassing to him and harmful to his disciples. About midway in this year great multitudes were following him, and it was evident that their enthusiasm needed some check. Jesus knew well that a crowd is not dependable, being swayed first one way and then another. Discipleship is individual, and calls for qualities never seen in the multitude. As Jesus had declared in the parable of the Great Supper, God "bids" men to share in His Kingdom, yet to be a disciple was difficult and called for rigorous self-discipline. The claims of home were second to his demands; natural affection must not interfere with loyalty to him (verse 26). He enforces this by repeating the saying that bearing the cross (with the implied readiness to sacrifice self) was a condition of discipleship. Note the repeated "cannot be my disciple" in verses 26 and 27.

He then enforces this exclusiveness by the two short parables, at the end of the second telling them for the third time that a man cannot be his disciple unless he renounces all that he has.

The parable of the Builder was spoken first: "For which of you, intending to build a tower, sitteth not down first, and counteth the cost, whether he have sufficient to finish it? Lest haply, after he hath laid the foundation, and is not able to finish it, all that behold it begin to mock him, saying, This man began to build and was not able to finish".

It was an age of ostentatious building, and many instances would probably be known of rash builders attempting more than they were able to complete. A wise man weighs up what resources he has and plans accordingly. Discipleship is building work; as Jesus said at the end of the Sermon on the Mount, the wise man was the one who built his character upon the foundation of his sayings.

Some have reasoned from the parable of the Tower Builder that a person coming to a knowledge of the truth may decline obedience if he desires, if on counting the cost he feels unable to become a disciple and to keep the commandments. He therefore may refuse to enter the service of Christ. Such an application was not intended by Jesus; the parable enjoins before embarking upon what is a costly enterprise, full consideration be given to the task. Jesus is not here teaching that it is better never to begin than to fail to complete the work, although that may be true. The fact is, men who hear the gospel and understand it, receive an invitation which is also a command calling for obedience. As a free agent a man can obey or refuse to obey, but the latter choice puts a man in opposition to God, and to him Jesus speaks the second parable. He has warned the enthusiastic would-be associate that men must count the cost of discipleship; he adds a parable requiring men to count the cost of refusal.

"Or what king, going to make war aginst another king, sitteth not down first, and consulteth whether he be able with ten thousand to meet him that cometh against him with twenty thousand? Or else, while the other is yet a great way off, he sendeth an ambassage, and desireth conditions of peace."

"So likewise, whosoever he be of you that forsaketh not all that he hath, he cannot be my disciple" (verse 31-33).

A man who refuses to obey God's command is a rebel. "As a king ready to battle he stretcheth out his hand against God and strengtheneth himself against the Almighty" (Job 15 : 24-25). Sin, like leviathan, is "a king over all the children of pride" (42 : 34).

A man who essays to fight against God should remember that with all his resources (ten thousand), he cannot meet "him that cometh against him with twenty thousand". Jesus does not set God's resources as only double that of man: by a change of preposition he indicates that while man has called upon all his resources in the ten thousand, God with twenty thousand has come against him with "only as many as He pleases to bring with Him" out of vastly more that could be brought. (Alford draws out the distinction in the prepositions.) It is vain to fight against God: all rebels against Him will be destroyed.

The lesson remains beyond the initial step to discipleship; it continues as long as life lasts. There are occasions in life when we may avoid making a decision, but we cannot escape the responsibility. When the Truth demands that we boldly avow our allegiance, whether in ecclesial difficulties or before men, and we do not act, the words of Jesus apply: "He that is not with me is against me". We may avoid undertaking a duty to be free from the responsibility and anxiety connected with an office, but such a decision carries the responsibility of not using the talents we have because of love of ease or freedom. The one talent man may say that his one talent is not much use, but his Master will expect an account of what has been done with it. There are no reasons which the Judge will accept for the talent having been hid in a napkin.

We have not the resources to fight against God. The wise course is to seek conditions of peace, and use our forces in His service. The one who ventures to oppose God is more rash than the foolish builder.

72
THE LOST SHEEP
(Luke 15 : 3-7)

LUKE records three parables together having one theme—in fact, they may be one parable in three phases, if we may understand Luke's words, "and he spake *this parable* unto them", as referring to the three stories of the lost sheep, lost coin and lost son. They are closely related and were doubtless given together by Jesus. They are the first section of a larger series. A connected theme can be traced through the sayings recorded in Luke 15 : 1—17 : 10.

The circumstances are described by Luke: "Then drew near unto him all the publicans and sinners for to hear him, and the Pharisees and scribes murmured, saying, This man receiveth sinners, and eateth with them" (15 : 1, 2). The series of parables that follows is concerned in one aspect or another with this conflict between Jesus and the Pharisees. They found fault with him for mixing with classes of people which they thought unfit for their company.

They showed a narrow spirit of complacent self-righteousness and self-satisfaction which is a danger of religious life founded on a ceremonial and legalistic basis. The publicans and sinners were men and women who were treated with disdain by the Pharisees. Some of them were sinners indeed by any standard of right living—"women of the city", thieves and other wrong doers; but the term "sinners" covered those who were outcasts, because their work produced ceremonial defilement, and those who, for one reason or another, did not follow the religious celebrations at the Temple. "This people are accursed", was a contemptuous description of men who failed in the observance of accumulated human rules which were pressed upon men as having divine sanction. Publicans were hated for selling their services for Roman pay, in collecting taxes which maintained Roman rule. But many of these were morally neither better nor worse than those who treated them with contempt. By mixing with such people, Jesus failed in the eyes of the religious leaders to be socially correct. A Rabbi, they thought, should not associate with the people in whose company Jesus was so often to be found.

But Jesus saw these people in an altogether different light. Poor they were—abjectly poor; religious outcasts in the eyes of the rulers; suffering from a sense of moral inferiority; but children of the stock of Abraham, lost sheep of the house of Israel. The gospel had a message for them to which many responded. If Christ's association with the poor was a ground of complaint to the rulers, it was also an evidence of his Messiahship to others: "to the poor the gospel is preached". It was a part of his work to "exalt them of low degree".

The group of parables beginning in Luke 15 contains first a defence of Christ's preaching to the "publicans and sinners" and passes on to include an indictment of his critics in the character of the "elder brother" of the third parable. Jesus then turns to his disciples and speaks to them the parable of the Unjust Steward, in which the conduct of the rulers is condemned (16 : 1-12). Further charges are made in plain direct language (verses 13-18), and then the parable of the Rich Man and Lazarus predicts a complete reversal in the day of awards of the two classes—Pharisees and the "sinners" who listened to Jesus. There follows the teaching on "offences" (17 : 1-6), and the series concludes with the stern call to discipleship contained in the parable of the Unprofitable Servant.

The lines of the three stories of "the lost" are exquisitely drawn. Jesus appeals to the well known experience of a shepherd, who finding one of the sheep is lost, immediately sets off to find it. He leaves the ninety and nine in the wilderness pasturage in the care of some fellow-shepherds—he was not foolish enough to risk having a hundred sheep lost. But his whole interest for the moment is on the one that is lost. He searches hill and crag until he finds it. He lays it across his shoulders, tired though he himself might be, and trudges back with light heart to call his neighbours to share his joy.

Jesus was "the shepherd"—foretold in many Old Testament prophecies. God was Israel's shepherd, and all the rulers of Israel were also so designated. Whereas many of the rulers were hireling shepherds and were often denounced as such, Jesus as a shepherd was like the Holy One of Israel. To him the neglected people of his day were sheep without a shepherd (Matt. 9 : 36). His duty was to care for the sheep and lay down his life for them. Isaiah, in the wonderful prediction of the arm of the Lord, declares on behalf of the nation: "All we like sheep have gone astray", but adds, "the Lord hath laid on him the iniquity of us all" (Isa. 53 : 6). He also testified that the Lord God would feed his flock like a shepherd (40 : 11).

The people were "lost sheep". We must guard against thinking of "lost" as expressing the point of view of the sheep. The "loss" is the experience of the shepherd, as the "coin" was lost to the woman. The counterpart is the "loss" which God knows when men stray from His ways. In Jesus God was seeking—this is the primary lesson indicated by the parables of "lost sheep" and "lost coin". The human reactions to God's search find a place in the parable of the prodigal.

In solemn yet forceful contrast to the "murmuring" of the Pharisees, Jesus says God rejoices over one sinner that repenteth. With the confidence that belongs to assured knowledge he prefaces the statement with: "I say unto you"; and while his critics grumble and sneer, God rejoices, and he is on the side of God and rejoices with Him.

The joy over the repentant sinner is greater "than over ninety and nine just persons who need no repentance". What does this mean? When we remember that there are no "just persons who need no repentance", but that there were men among the murmurers before Jesus who thought they were just and did not need repentance, we then can see that Jesus is using gentle irony. The repentant publican gave joy to angels; but there was no joy over the Pharisees.

73
THE LOST COIN
(Luke 15 : 8-10)

THE essential lesson of the Lost Coin is the same as that of the Lost Sheep. Something lost is found, and there is joy in the recovery. It is difficult, however, to think that this story is merely repeating the instruction of the previous one. There are other pairs of parables—the Mustard Seed and Leaven; the Hid Treasure and the Pearl Merchant—each pair having the same primary purpose but with different aspects emphasized.

The obvious differences in details in the form of the two parables of the lost sheep and lost coin are these: in the one the shepherd is the seeker, in the other the woman; the sheep goes astray—it has volition, silly or stupid though it be; the coin is lost by the owner: being inanimate it contributes nothing to the state of being lost; in the sequel to the recovery of the sheep there is joy in heaven, that is, God Himself rejoices: in the parable of the lost coin the angels of God share the joy.

Both illustrations were from homely everyday incidents. Sheep and shepherds were everywhere in the land; and in all the towns and villages were the poor of the land dwelling in small hovels of mud or baked clay, windowless to keep out the sun's heat and glare. The only light entering through the door, the inside was therefore dark and gloomy. To search the floor for the coin the women must light a lamp—usually a small piece of wick floating in a saucer-like vessel full of oil. The floor would be of trodden earth. The best way to find the small coin was to sweep together the dust and anything on the floor, and examine the small pile of sweepings carefully with the light of the lamp.

Why did Jesus choose a man—the shepherd—in the one case, and woman in the other? Was it to complete the picture and by the double figure make the appeal universal? The first hearers may not have seen more in it than that; but we must not deny, therefore, the possibility that more might be intended. The prophets searched their own messages to understand what or what manner of time was signified by the spirit in them concerning the sufferings and glory of Christ. It was revealed to them, Peter says, that the meaning of the message would be understood by a later generation (1 Pet. 1 : 10-12). There may then be a meaning other than the simple and obvious one that was apparent to any sympathetic listeners when Jesus spoke.

The shepherd as a figure points to God and to Jesus. In their co-operative labour the sheep were sought and found. In the use of the woman in the second parable, does Jesus look forward to the church? If so, it is a part of her anxiety, as of the woman in the parable, to recover the lost. "If any man be overtaken in a fault, restore such an one in the spirit of meekness", is the apostolic rule (Gal. 6

The sequel—a joy shared by the "women" and the angels—supports the view.

At creation the sons of God did shout for joy—so God declares: "The morning stars sang together, and all the sons of God shouted for joy" (Job 38 : 7).

"The sons of God did rejoice at creation.
The Morning Stars together sang."

The same "sons of God" are actively engaged in the new creation. The revelation to Daniel concerning Messiah the prince, came to him through Michael; the angels "desire to look into" the purpose declared by the prophets; they are ministering spirits sent forth to minister on behalf of the heirs of salvation. When the heirs of salvation enter into the life promised, is it not reasonable to think that the angels who have played a part in the providential care of God's sons of Adam's race will find pleasure in the triumph? May we not expect them to rejoice? Jesus says that they will.

There is great uncertainty as to the precise value of the coin to the woman. Valued at something under a shilling, in the extreme poverty of that time, it meant a serious loss. Some have thought that as one of ten, it was part of a bridal ornament for neck or head, and support is found for this in the claim that the Greek coin named by Jesus was not in circulation at the time. It may be so; but in the absence of certainty it is wise not to build upon the idea. Less wise is it to theorize upon a meaning, and then assert that to be fact which is only invented as a basis for the desired meaning.

The woman—the church—has a duty and a responsibility for the lost—a responsibility shared by the Lord himself. In that sharing in the work of God is its greatest honour. The community of believers in Christ enter into the labour of Christ in order that in a future day they may enter into the joy of their Lord.

74
THE LOST SON
(Luke 15 : 11-32)

THE three characters in this story all play so essential a part for the instruction Jesus had in mind that the parable could equally well be entitled, the Lost Son, the Elder Brother or the Good Father. The parable touches the emotions—the theme and the way it is told combine to make it one of the most moving of the parables. There are, however, important lessons which are overlooked by those who, influenced by the very human features of the prodigal and the father, restrict the application to sinners who repent and turn to God.

The parable introduces personal factors which were not possible in "the lost sheep" and "the lost coin". A coin is not aware that it is lost; a sheep might realize it is lost—it finds itself away from its fellows and is alarmed—but it cannot rise to any sense of folly in having strayed. The parable of the son who left home and returned, gives opportunity for presenting a number of aspects which are vital to a right understanding of the relationship to God of the men whom Jesus was addressing. It is important to keep in mind that the parable deals with the situation immediately before Jesus: it is not designed, as some have thought, to provide a philosophy of the atonement.

A man has two sons. The younger asks for the portion of the family wealth that would fall to him. Since the first son, according to the law, has a double portion, the younger of two receives a third. He very quickly realizes his inheritance and goes away to have a gay life, "wasting his substance with riotous living", as Jesus says in the narrative, but as appears from the angry resentful words of the elder brother at his return, in much more abandoned ways also. The story follows the lines of the history of men who come into the possession of money but who have no guiding principles and self-control. The young son spends all, having many companions so long as he has money, but finding himself at last with neither money nor friends. Reduced to farm labouring, he is set the task, particularly degrading for a Jew, of looking after pigs. He becomes so destitute that he is ready to eat the carob beans which he feeds to the swine. Then, when he has lost everything, he finds himself: "he came to himself". When living in sin he was a stranger to sanity; for sin is folly; "the thought of foolishness is sin".

With returning sense he reflected on the degradation of his position and his reflections, which we must regard as sincere, embody the spirit of true repentance. When David had sinned, he expressed in his penitential psalm what constitutes the real evil of sin. It affects our fellows; it affects ourselves; but most of all it affects our relationship to God. "Against thee, thee only, have I sinned", exclaimed David (Psa. 51 : 4). In a Jewish home the two sons had grown up familiar with the instruction of the law with its emphasis upon sin and trespass and transgression. The thoughts of the prodigal, then, take the form that reflects his early training. "I will arise and go to my father, and will say to him, Father, I have sinned against heaven, and before thee, and am no more worthy to be called thy son: make me as one of thy hired servants" (verses 18, 19).

The sketch of the father is psychologically sound. He is watching for the son's return; he has eagerly looked down the road many times; and now seeing him afar off he runs to meet and welcome him. Before the son has time to complete his confession, the father is giving orders for the festival to celebrate the return. The robe and the ring are put on the son: the fatted calf is killed. In rhythmic language the father exclaims: "This my son was dead, and is alive again; he was lost, and is found". The joy of the shepherd and the joy of the woman find a parallel in the joy of the father. "They began to be merry."

The elder son returns from the field, hears the festivities and enquires of a servant the reason. Informed that his brother has returned, he is angry at the reception given to him and refuses to go into the house. The father who had gone to meet the younger son now comes out to the elder to intreat him. He is met with angry expostulations full of self-revelation. The elder son declares that he had slaved for his father; he had not transgressed his commandments: yet his father had never given him so much as a kid that he might make merry with his friends; but when the wastrel comes back the fatted calf has been killed. "This thy son" —thus contemptuously he describes his brother! "Son thou art ever with me", the father answers; and the words fall softly and quietly, yet not without a pathetic note: "all I have is thine. It was meet that we should make merry, and be glad: for this thy brother was dead, and is alive again; and was lost, and is found" (verses 31, 32).

The application of the parable is evident. The "publicans and sinners" who were responding to the teaching of Jesus were the prodigals. Sinners truly; lost and straying, but now coming back to God, recognizing the folly and evil of sin, and confessing their sins. It was right that Jesus should rejoice at their reformation, that like the father in the parable, he should be glad. Mark how by that practical identification of himself with the father in the parable there is implied that Jesus, in some way not defined in the parable, is identified with God. While the prodigal represents the publicans and sinners, the elder son, angry and sullen, portrays the group of murmuring Pharisees who complained that Jesus received the outcasts.

The portraiture is subtle and masterly. The elder son had a slave-mind—he served. Complacently he claimed to have rendered a fulness of obedience that clearly is an over-statement. But the revelation of the true state of his heart comes in the complaint that he had not even been given a kid that *he* might have a good time. The complaint shows a secret sympathy with his brother's sinfulness; he had stayed at home, but his desire had been no different from his brother's. He too was "lost".

The two sons as depicted are intended to provide a contrast. The prodigal did wrong but recognized at last that he had sinned; the elder brother, while outwardly correct, was wrong in heart but did not know it. The one son had openly gone astray; but the other unconsciously admitted that in his secret desires he was no better, for he had friends that would not be welcome in his father's house—"my friends", he calls them, which in an oriental house indicates they were not friends of the family. The same alienation is shown in the complaint "thou never gavest me a kid"—he had wished for the kid so that he could go and make merry. Thus Jesus draws the character of the forbidding, unlovely, self-righteous, and unwittingly self-condemning professors of a legal religion. They claimed to be at home with God but really were strangers.

While the character of the elder son drawn by Jesus was a devastating revelation of the true state of his religious opponents, the father's attitude was displayed by Jesus himself. He was even then inviting the Pharisees to come to share in the joy of friendship with God: his message was for them as well as for the "sinners". Would they hear him?

The superb artistry of the story is seen finally in its abrupt ending. The story was incomplete; it required a decision on the part of the Pharisees to complete it. But as the sequel shows as a class they remained outside, for they would not go in, in spite of the Father's entreaty.

75
THE UNJUST STEWARD
(Luke 16 : 1-12)

THIS parable has been the subject of many ingenious and various interpretations. The steward has been regarded as signifying the Jewish priesthood, Pilate, Judas, Paul; and even Jesus himself; the tax collectors and penitents as counterparts of the steward have also found advocates. The rich owner has been thought to represent God, Satan, the Romans, and Mammon. The devil is certainly in the story but it is as the steward's "accuser" (the verb from the word *diabolos*). It can be imagined from the mere catalogue of these various applications of the owner and the steward that many different interpretations have been given to the details of the story.

Any interpretation given to the parable must take account of Christ's references to serving Mammon; of the Pharisees' evident application of the story to themselves since they derided Jesus, being as Luke narrates "covetous"; also of verses 16-18 which follow and which at first sight seem so unconnected.

The story concerns the steward of a rich man. The full management of his master's estate was in his hands— the letting of the farms, and the trading of the produce. He was accused of wasting his master's goods, and was thereupon called to present an account of his stewardship. The precise circumstances and duties of a steward and why he was called to account have been variously explained. Probably the account demanded by the lord was intended to substantiate or disprove the accusations which had been made against the steward; and the steward, knowing that his conduct would not bear investigation, recognized that the enquiry would lead to dismissal. He therefore began to think how he could meet the new situation. He ruled out digging and begging as possible solutions, and then bethought himself of a way by which he would have some claim on the debtors of his master. He called them to him and reduced their debts. It is possible, but far from certain, that the amount of reduction represented the overcharge he had made, his roguery extending to both master and tenant. In this case, by his action he rectified in measure some of his defalcations and also laid the debtors under an obligation.

His master heard of his astute, resourceful handling of the situation, and commended him for his prudence and shrewdness. The man was a rogue; his master was a man of the world, and understood the clever effort to make the best of the position. The morality of it does not appear to have interested him.

The system in operation at that time of farming out tax-collecting provided many opportunities for extortion. The tax gatherers as a class grew rich by extortion. Zacchaeus recognized his sin and made restitution. The people who heard Jesus would thus be familiar with circumstances which correspond with the story.

Jesus did not commend the man's conduct. On the contrary he emphasized the necessity for faithfulness (verse 11).

The parable ends in the middle of verse 9; the second half is the beginning of Christ's comment, which is based on the commendation of the lord of the steward for his shrewdness. "For", says Jesus, "the children of this world are in their generation wiser than the children of light." The sentence has to be completed: "than the children of light are with reference to their generation".

The men of the world "who have their portion in this life" are quick to discern what will be of advantage to them. The steward knew the men he was dealing with; they saw the advantage he offered; all were concerned with a benefit for themselves. The children of light do not show a corresponding resourcefulness concerning the spiritual things to which their enlightenment has related them. They are "sons of light" because the light of the knowledge of God's purpose has shone into their hearts. They are thus related to far more important things than are "the children of darkness". But while knowing the greater value of the future good compared with any present possession, few act consistently with such knowledge. Most men are limited to the horizon of present things, but make the best of the present with acumen and enterprise. The light of the gospel extends the horizon to the future, but without, in many cases, bringing an extension of outlook or of the enterprise that belong to the wider view. The present circumscribes action and motive.

Bullinger suggests that verse 9 should be a question: "And say I unto you, Make to yourselves friends of the mammon of unrighteousness; that, when ye fail, they may receive you into everlasting habitations? No. He that is faithful in that which is least is faithful also in much: and he that is unjust in the least is unjust also in much" (verse 10). This makes such excellent sense that it is a strong temptation to adopt it. The general sense of the A.V. is supported, however, by other translations, and this also yields sense in keeping with other testimonies. Following the A.V., the words of Jesus are counsel which contrasts with the steward's action. The man used money unscrupulously for present advantage. Jesus says that money must be so used that friends are gained, that in this way a man may secure that future which is known to children of light. The account of the judgment in Matt. 25 : 31-46 illustrates the meaning; and Paul's words also are relevant when he says: "Charge them that are rich in this world, that they be not highminded, nor trust in uncertain riches, but in the living God, who giveth us richly all things to enjoy" (1 Tim. 6 : 17).

On the latter interpretation verse 10 becomes a qualifying rule. In all the use of money faithfulness must be firmly observed: the present is the training for the future, and the quality of faithfulness shown now will secure the greater opportunities and responsibilities of the future age.

The present is represented by "unrighteous mammon" and the future by "true riches" (verse 9), with the further definitions as "that which is another man's" and that "which is your own". Unrighteous mammon is wealth—called the mammon of unrighteousness not because wealth is in itself wrong, but because it has such a power of corrupting men and leading them into unrighteousness. "True riches" are the future possessions of the people of God of which even the hope is likened to "a treasure" in earthen vessels. Mammon is "another man's" in the sense that no man has a permanent title to present possessions, whereas the future true riches are the inheritance for ever of those who attain to that future age.

Jesus adds warning to these lessons: a warning, the force of which we miss if we fail to remember that by service Jesus is thinking of the bondservice of the slave. "No bondslave can serve two masters." In the nature of the case it is impossible. A man today might serve two masters at different periods of the day, but a bondslave was at the full disposal of his owner. Any effort on the part of a slave to serve two masters would lead to a divided loyalty. Jesus says, "You cannot serve God and mammon". Wealth easily enslaves; for great possessions soon provoke a desire for still more, and avarice is a vice which holds a man fast. If a rich man would acceptably serve God he must be master and not slave to his possessions.

So far the application has been made to riches—it is so made by Jesus. But men are stewards not only of material wealth but of the mysteries of God's grace. "It is required of stewards", Paul affirms, "that a man be found faithful." From this angle the application by some expositors of the steward to the Jewish priesthood should be considered. This interpretation will be found to have a real connection with the story; it also gives it a parabolic meaning, instead of making it merely an illustration by contrast, concerning duty towards human wealth.

The Pharisees were covetous, as Luke says. The chief priests were also men of great wealth which they used to maintain relations of mutual toleration with the Roman rulers. Caiaphas managed to retain his office for eighteen years. The priestly party were not only wealthy but were also oppressive and arrogant, besides being favourable to Roman over-rule so long as the Romans kept them in office. The Talmud preserves some of the woes which the people pronounced upon "the house of Annas" "for their club", and "for their fist";

"For they are the high priests;
Their sons are the treasurers;
Their sons-in-law are temple officers,
And their servants beat the people with their staves".

In the parable the steward reduced the bills of his master's debtors for present advantage. The priests of Israel lowered the obligations to God, altering the standards of righteousness. A good illustration may be seen in the Corban law. By a legal fiction they "gave" to God anything which they ought to have used for the benefit of their parents, and so escaped the duty of honouring father and mother. Jesus very severely reprimanded this as teaching for doctrines the commandments of men, and making void the word of God (Matt. 15 : 1-9). The priests were stewards—but they acted in a worldly-wise way which was unfaithful to God's appointment. They served Mammon, not God—and in this larger interpretation of the parable Mammon must stand for all the desires which the flesh lusts after. They served self. The parable, though spoken "to the disciples", follows immediately after the indictment of the Pharisees drawn in the character of the elder brother of the parable in chapter 15. While then cast in the form of ordinary stewardship, the parable reflects the unfaithful selfish shrewdness of some of those who were listening to Jesus.

How does this view fit in with the words that follow? "They derided him (turned up their noses at him)"; and Jesus responded, "Ye are they which justify yourselves before men; but God knoweth your hearts". They thought to put themselves right with their fellows, to be well thought of, to be highly esteemed. But their standard of judgment was wrong, and God would judge their hearts. As they were stewards an account was required. The religious service they sought to maintain, for which they were even ready to sacrifice a righteous man (John 19 : 4-6), had become an abomination to God and would pass away. When Jesus was speaking the transition period had indeed come, for the "law and the prophets" were until John—that is, that dispensation when God's will declared by "law and prophets" was operative. But a new message with new conditions was being proclaimed—the kingdom was preached and men were pressing into it (verse 16). This did not mean that because the law was superseded, it was not authentic or authoritative. This is shown by the word "but", R.V.: "But it is easier for heaven and earth to pass, than one tittle of the law to fail" (verse 17). Even the little horns, the serifs, of the letters would not fail. The next verse with reference to divorce as so commonly practised by even the scribes and rabbis, is in the nature of a counterthrust. The teaching of Jesus, the sayings of which so often appear disconnected, many times presents a logical sequence of reasoning when the thought links are supplied. In this case, in effect he says, "I am not destroying the law but fulfilling it; but you have widened the conditions of divorce so much that many, while nominally married, are really no better than adulterers". This verse thus understood is also an illustration of the writing down of the debt men owe.

The story of the unjust steward and the comments that follow are thus an indictment of a priesthood which had betrayed a trust for their own selfish ends. The very method of selling sacrificial animals and changing money in the temple court, revealed an unfaithfulness in financial matters: what right had they to deal with spiritual matters, the true riches? God had set apart a court for Gentiles; they had taken it for dishonest uses. How could they claim to serve God?

The parable of the rich man and Lazarus that follows then becomes a sentence of judgment which is irrevocable.

Further lessons become apparent when we consider that the knowledge of God's salvation imposes a stewardship. The truth is bartered for present advantage when the light is obscured because faithful testimony would be followed by some financial loss. A man sells his soul who lowers the ethical standards of Christ's teachings for more business. Better less wealth and faithfulness, than riches and rejection by Christ. The early Christians became unfaithful when, for present gain, they adopted pagan practices; when idolatry was involved in attending a guild dinner when festivals were held in idol temples, a Christian accepted invitations to these gatherings only by lowering the values of his service to Christ. "Worship Caesar" was a test of loyalty to Christ which might cost life when losing life was the only way of gaining life. The formula "Jesus is lord" was a challenge to the "lords many" of the pagan world: it was also a test of faith for a first century Christian. The time came when "saints and angels" and the souls of dead men were worshipped, and the truth of God was betrayed. Are we today in no danger of copying the unjust steward by lowering the demands the Lord has made—in commercial dealings, in moral life, in the stewardship of God's grace?

76

THE RICH MAN AND LAZARUS

(Luke 16 : 19-31)

THE parable of the Rich Man and Lazarus is usually discussed as a contribution to the teaching of scripture on the death state. That Jesus used a common belief as the basis for his parable is generally accepted, but there is no reason for thinking that the use of such a belief in this way committed Jesus to endorsing it. The teaching of the parable in relation to the death state is considered in *The Christadelphian Shield.** We concern ourselves here with the lesson that Jesus intended to convey by the story.

There is an easily traced sequence in the context. In 15 : 1-2 Luke says that the publicans and sinners drew around Jesus to hear him. This led to the murmuring of the Scribes and Pharisees who said: "This man receiveth sinners and eateth with them". Jesus therefore addressed to the murmurers the three parables of the Lost Sheep, Lost Coin, and the Prodigal. The last of these left the elder son outside the house, angry and churlishly refusing to go in. That was the position of the Pharisees and scribes.

Turning to the disciples, Jesus told them the parable of the Unjust Steward, drawing the lesson of the faithful use of riches, warning them that it was impossible to serve God and mammon, and pointing to a still greater stewardship in which faithfulness was equally necessary.

The parable of the Steward and the comments of Jesus stung the Pharisees. They were "lovers of money", says Luke; and since a man cannot love money and love God, as Jesus had just said, they could not be lovers of God. Instead of receiving the admonition of Jesus they hardened their hearts and "derided" him. Jesus replied: "Ye are they which justify yourselves in the sight of men; but God knoweth your hearts: for that which is highly esteemed among men is an abomination in the sight of God". This

*Obtainable from the Christadelphian Publishing Office.

tore away their rags of self-righteousness. They performed their prayers and their alms that men might see them. They sought the esteem of men and received a receipt in full, as Jesus many times told them. There was nothing owing to them from God for anything they had done. But God was not indifferent: He did not esteem them, but regarded them as an abomination. Jesus adds three sayings, the connection of which is not at first obvious but which is traced out more fully in the consideration of the parable of the Unjust Steward. Really these sayings are an indictment of unfaithfulness on the part of those scribes and Pharisees. The law and the prophets were until John: they had not kept the law. Since John the kingdom was preached, but they did not seek to enter (verse 16). Yet not the least detail of God's law would fail (verse 17). In one respect (perhaps particularly so as rich men) they flagrantly set aside the law by the rules which had made divorce easy and common (verse 18).

Against this background of tense feeling of the rulers, and plain speaking on the part of Jesus, he adds the parable. "There was a rich man", obviously the rich money-loving rulers. How were they using their wealth? The unjust steward had shown wisdom even in his use of it, but the rich man did nothing but gratify his own desires. Opportunity was at his gate, but he ignored it. The poor and sick Lazarus would have welcomed even the crumbs from his table.

Then the scene changes to the future, and the positions of Dives and Lazarus are reversed. Too late the rich man was ready to recognize Lazarus, but now it is he who seeks the ministrations. Too late also the request that warning be given to others. There were "the law and the prophets", the divine testimony, and nothing could add to their authority, though one rose from the dead; if the opportunities provided by the knowledge of the law were neglected, there could be no purpose served by further revelation.

By a divine coincidence the request of the rich man in the parable was granted in the resurrection of another Lazarus, and the words of Jesus proved only too true. Instead of repenting they sought more determinedly to get Jesus put to death (John 11 : 47-57).

Primarily the parable shows that the Pharisees had lives centred in the present. Observe Abraham's answer, "thy good things"; the possessiveness of present things and the blindness to any future good, is clearly indicated. They might gain the world, but their lives were forfeit. The future was not theirs. The despised outcasts, pressing into the kingdom in response to the teaching of Jesus, would inherit the Abrahamic blessings.

We cannot miss a further application from a national point of view. Israel was rich as a nation: they had advantages "much every way", as Paul said. But the wealth was not for themselves. They were appointed a priestly kingdom, and they should have let the light of God's law and revelation shine to others. They were advantageously placed for so doing. They were not pushed away in some obscure corner, hidden under "bed or bushel", but set on the candlestick of the hills of Palestine, where all could see them and learn from them. Solomon had this aspect of their work in mind when he prayed that the stranger, coming from a far country for "thy name's sake", should be heard, "that all peoples of the earth may know thy name, to fear thee, as doth thy people Israel" (1 Kings 8 : 41-43). But Israel became self-centred and proud, and despised the Gentiles at their gates. But a change came. The Jewish nation was cast off, and has been through the fires of persecution, while the stranger at the gate has been introduced into the covenants of promise and has rejoiced in the hope of Israel.

When the change of heart is given to Israel (not included in the parable as it does not come within its purpose), they will recognize that Moses and the prophets testified that their redeemer would be raised from the dead, and they will then find that Jesus of Nazareth is he. Meanwhile, continuing in unbelief, there is no respite from the torment and the suffering the nation undergoes. Whilst possessing "Moses and the prophets" the vail is on their hearts when those Scriptures are read, as Paul declared 2 Cor. 3), but when they turn to the Lord the vail will be taken away.

77
UNPROFITABLE SERVANTS
(Luke 17 : 7-10)

To understand many of the sayings of Jesus, it is necessary to remember the social customs and the conditions of life in his day. The "servant" of this parable must not be thought of as a modern farm labourer, but as a bondslave of the first century. Applying the arrangements, so general today, of fixed hours and pay, to the situation of the parable puts the employer therein described in an unfavourable light. The parable is a transcript from life in Christ's day. Jesus said: "But which of you, having a servant plowing or feeding cattle, will say unto him by and by, when he is come from the field, Go and sit down to meat? and will not rather say unto him, Make ready wherewith I may sup, and gird thyself, and serve me, till I have eaten and drunken; and afterward thou shalt eat and drink? Doth he thank that servant because he did the things that were commanded him? I trow not. So likewise ye, when ye shall have done all those things which are commanded you, say, We are unprofitable servants: we have done that which was our duty to do".

"By and by" like most words and phrases in the English tongue which once described immediateness, has lost its note of urgency. Once signifying "immediately" it now denotes after an interval. Restore the idea that the servant, coming from the field is, without any break, told to prepare the master's meal, and we realize how completely the time and energy of a bondslave was at his master's disposal, When the man had done all required he had only done his duty; he had given no overtime labour, no extra service to which the master was not entitled.

The aim of the parable concerns the servant's duty; to see in the master a picture of an exactor and then to find in him a representation of God, is to read into the parable something not intended and to create needless difficulty. "So likewise ye"—in these words Jesus fixes the lesson; the theme of the parable is a bondslave's labour. This application is also indicated by the opening word "but" which relates the parable to the preceding discourse which concerned the duty of disciples.

The connection of the parable with the conversation of Jesus which it follows, appears to be this: Jesus had spoken of the grave responsibility of men who put stumbling-blocks in the way of their brethren (verses 1-2). He then points out the duty towards an offender that devolves upon the one offended. Since he knows, and possibly he alone, of the trespass, it is his duty to seek his brother's recovery by showing him his sin. If this brings forth repentance, forgiveness must follow. The Lord lays down a hard task; it is so much easier for human nature to bear malice and to nurse a grievance than to seek for peace in Christ's way. Christ's law is good for both the offended and offender. An offence grows bigger as it feeds on injured pride. To seek out a brother and tell him his faults with a view to their rectification calls for a sober constraint, which prevents exaggeration on the one hand and which fosters an understanding spirit on the other.

The disciples felt the difficulty of the instruction, and said, "Lord, increase our faith". Jesus in answer spoke of the faith as a grain of mustard seed by which a tree could be moved from one place to another. Then comes the parable of the Servant commencing with "but". Jesus had enjoined a difficult task; he had told them it was possible by faith. The parable declared the task to be a duty of the bondslave of God.

The service in the parable is truly exacting—a day's toil in the field extended to service in the house when rest would not only be welcome but might be reasonably expected. But the demands of the service of Christ are exacting too; they extend beyond the day to the evening hours. In his service fixed hours of work are unknown; and the simple duty of each servant is to perform, willingly and efficiently, all duties at all times.

Jesus never minimizes the task of discipleship. His sayings in many ways illustrated his own attitude to life and that which he called for in those who would follow him. Seeking the kingdom first; "hating" father and mother; taking up the cross; letting the dead bury their dead; never "looking back" when hand has been put to plough—all these sayings illustrate the fulness of his demands.

In making these calls for effort, for undivided loyalty, for lifelong service, for all powers to be used in the discharge of discipleship, Jesus shows himself to be a great leader. We have in recent years all observed the power of the call to heroic service when forcefully, fearlessly and unsparingly expressed. When the war-time Prime Minister of England took office, he called on his countrymen to a supreme service. He offered only blood, toil, tears and sweat: and the nation responded to a severe demand, made without any hiding of its rigours, when honeyed words would have failed. The same high quality of leadership in a great crisis was exhibited when at Dunkirk the nation only saved its army by a tremendous effort, and then at the loss of all equipment. Then the call was made and the challenge uttered: "We shall go on to the end, we shall fight in France, we shall fight on the seas and oceans, we shall fight with growing confidence and growing strength in the air, we shall defend our island, whatever the cost may be, we shall fight on the beaches, we shall fight on the landing grounds, we shall fight in the fields and in the streets, we shall fight in the hills; we shall never surrender, and even if, which I do not for a moment believe, this island or a large part of it were subjugated and starving, then our Empire beyond the seas, armed and guarded by the British Fleet, would carry on the struggle, until, in God's good time, the new world, with all its power and might, steps forth to the rescue and the liberation of the old."

This graphic and vigorous language demanded the united effort in which the last ounce of reserve would be called up to win. On another occasion he said: "This is no time for ease and comfort. It is the time to dare and endure".

If we can understand a human call which exacts a full response, which demands all, we may then understand the meaning of Jesus when, in relation to higher things, he tells us that the toil of the day may be followed by further duty at night, and that even then *all* is only what the service requires. When all is done there is no profit to the owner—no excess has been given beyond what is due.

The parable depicts the required spirit of the Lord's bondslaves. All who are bought by his death are his slaves (1 Cor. 7 : 21-23). Paul felt the designation of bondslave of Christ an honour as well as a mark of duty to be done: and Paul uses the figure of others who also have become "servants" of righteousness (Rom. 6 : 16-22).

The parable is a corrective to pride as well as a call to work. It calls for the recognition that in a real sense there is nothing we can give to God, and therefore all idea of merit is excluded. From this point of view the parable served to show to the disciples that the Pharisaic hope of creating a title to God's favour by personal merit was vain.

A strange use has been given to the parable by Roman Catholic interpreters. By a division of duties into grades, some for the common man, and higher duties for the fuller consecrate, the teaching of the parable was classed as a "counsel of perfection" for the observance of those devoted wholly to the religious life. Certain positive commandments were for all—but the demands for a fuller renunciation concerned the "perfect" who practise celibacy, renounce property, and enter monastic life. Such a division was designed to make Christianity easy for the multitude, while the "extra service" was given in the voluntary poverty and celibacy of the monastic orders. Such a view is far removed from the teaching of Christ. Jesus recognized no such grades of holiness—before all his followers he put the one high standard: "Be ye perfect as your Father in heaven is perfect."

The whole emphasis of this parable is put on the servant's duty. The use of such an emphasis is at times an essential part of a teacher's work, but a wise teacher also finds a place at the right time for other aspects of the relationship of master and servant. This Jesus did in the parable of the master who serves (Luke 12 : 35-38), which should be read in conjunction with the one considered in this section.

78
THE UNJUST JUDGE
(Luke 18 : 1-8)

If we may take verse 1 as a summary in Luke's report of what Jesus said, then we have the meaning of the parable provided by the Lord himself. Even if verse 1 should be Luke's own words, they are not therefore without authority for our guidance. They are still part of an inspired record. The authoritative key to the parable, then, is "that men ought always to pray, and not to faint".

The parable was spoken to disciples—appropriately in view of the subject. "He spake . . . unto them" takes us back to 17 : 22 for the antecedent of the pronoun: "And he said *unto the disciples,* The days will come when ye shall desire to see one of the days of the Son of man, and ye shall not see it". Jesus then warns them of the dangers of being deceived by false alarms that he has come; he speaks of his own sufferings and death, and of the conditions that will prevail in the day when he suddenly appears (see parable of Vultures for suggestions on the theme in Luke 17 : 21-37). The background of the parable is the idea of a time of waiting, of apparent delay, which would be perplexing to men of faith in every age. The conditions of the world would be conducive to disappointment and despair, when disciples might lose hope in his coming again.

Jesus therefore prescribes the antidote to counteract the effects upon the disciples of the conditions prevailing around them. Men must pray—must keep in touch with God, must be as Isaiah said, the Lord's remembrancers, who keep not silent and give Him no rest until He make Jerusalem a praise in the earth (Isa. 62 : 6, 7 margin). Prayer, earnest and continual "in faith expressed", keeps the mind fixed on divine things, and although judging by outward signs there is no proof that God has heard, yet faith, based on the word of God, assures us that He has. This parable is one of the places in the Scriptures where it is affirmed.

Men must pray—and not faint. The very juxtaposition of the two things shows that prayer is designed to prevent fainting. Men pray and do not faint: the converse is true—men faint because they do not pray. "We perish if we cease from prayer."

Jesus tells the parable of a judge who was unjust, without fear of God or regard of men. What is more—while most men hide their misdeeds from themselves and "rationalize" their conduct, this man knew his own character, and was so depraved that he took a kind of satisfaction in the fact. When the widow persisted in her demands he acknowledged to himself that he cared not for God or man: "though I fear not God nor regard man". Such a man was utterly unfit for the office of judge. Men of this character, however, have held office at one time or another in all countries, but the type of judge depicted in the parable has been more common in near eastern lands, both in the past and more recently under Turkish rule.

The widow was a pathetic figure in the east. Generally without friend or helper, she suffered injustice and wrong. The law of Moses has many warnings against oppression of the widow—a fact which shows how common it must have been. Jesus himself denounced the Pharisees because they devoured widows' houses.

The widow in the parable evidently suffered some oppression and sought redress. Her appeal fell for a time on deaf ears: but her persistence prevailed. She persevered in her complaint until the nuisance of her demands stirred the judge. With a sardonic pleasantry he said that while he was indifferent to God and men, the woman was an annoyance, and she might get violent and strike him. He had better be rid of her. The defenceless woman, who could neither bully nor bribe, yet bothered him into yielding. The word rendered "weary" is literally "give me a black eye"—hence in a general sense bruise, or strike. So Paul, using the same word, speaks of "buffeting" his body and bringing it into subjection (1 Cor. 9 : 27).

As Jesus had indicated the purpose before giving the parable, so at the end he draws the lesson intended by it. "Hear", he said, "what the *unjust* judge saith." It is necessary to stress the word "unjust"—for the character of the man provides a contrast. An unjust judge responded to the persistent petition of a helpless woman; what will a just God do for His own chosen ones? "Shall not God avenge his own elect, which cry day and night unto him, though he bear long with them?" The text upon which the R.V. is based in the last clause is generally considered to be more accurate than the A.V.—"and he is longsuffering over them". It may be doubted whether even this yields a very clear idea: but the general sense is that God may be longsuffering and seem to delay His response to the prayers of His people, yet the answer is sure to come. In the words of a quaint old commentator: "We prevail with men by importunity because they are displeased with it, but with God because He is pleased with it". God will answer, is the assertion of Jesus in the lesson of the parable: "I tell you", he declares, "that God will avenge them speedily". This does not mean God would do it immediately—the facts are against such an interpretation. What Jesus means is that God hears, but bears long, for He has His own time, but when the time comes His action will be swift and decisive.

Jesus ends his comment on a sad note: "Nevertheless, when the Son of man cometh, shall he find faith on the earth?" In spite of the fact that prayer prevails, and of the certainty that God will intervene, men do not believe in God's purpose. Jesus had said just before in the same discourse, that in the day of his coming men would be given over to eating and drinking as in the days of Noah and of Lot (17 : 26-29). Nowhere in the teaching of Jesus or of the apostles is the effect of the preaching of the gospel declared to be other than the saving of a remnant. God is *taking out of* the Gentiles a people for His name (Acts 15 : 14). The bearers of God's name, being instructed in the whole counsel of God, find in the deplorable indifference to divine things a confirmation of the divine message and an encouragement to persevere themselves.

While the parable is a lesson by contrast—how much more will God hear men—there is a certain appropriateness in the choice of a widow as the petitioner. The figure of the bride and the bridegroom in the parable of the Bridegroom (Matt. 9 : 15) is based on Old Testament references. In the Old Testament the figure of widowhood is also found, being used of Zion. During the present time, bereaved of her children under the law, Zion endures "the reproach of widowhood" (Isa. 54 : 4). This, however, will pass, for she will be restored to favour—her Maker is her husband, "the God of all the earth shall he be called" (Isa. 54 : 5). Jeremiah also lamented that the city of Jerusalem had become as a widow (Lam. 1 : 1). Widowhood in relation to God's people is the time when God's favour is not visibly manifested; when His people are apparently without defence and a protector. From this point of view the present time of Gentile ascendancy when God's saints have for centuries been downtrodden and persecuted might be compared to a state of widowhood for the church of Christ. When the times of Israel again come, like Ruth, the bride of Christ will find in her Bridegroom the redeemer of the inheritance and also a husband.

79
THE PHARISEE AND THE PUBLICAN
(Luke 18 : 9-14)

THE Lord Jesus made powerful use of contrast in several parables, notably when with a few clear strokes he gave a picture of two men who represent different classes in relation to himself or to God. A good illustration of this lesson by contrast is in the parable of the two men who prayed, found in Luke 18 : 9-14.

"And he spake this parable unto certain which trusted in themselves that they were righteous, and despised others:

"Two men went up into the temple to pray; the one a Pharisee, and the other a publican. The Pharisee stood and prayed thus with himself: God, I thank thee, that I am not as other men are, extortioners, unjust, adulterers, or even as this publican. I fast twice in the week, I give tithes of all that I possess.

"And the publican, standing afar off, would not lift up so much as his eyes unto heaven, but smote upon his breast, saying, God be merciful to me a sinner.

"I tell you, this man went down to his house justified rather than the other: for every one that exalteth himself shall be abased; and he that humbleth himself shall be exalted."

"The one a Pharisee": to all who heard the words it was a daring indictment of a class of men held in high esteem, who were very religious, and among whom were to be found some very sincere individuals. "A Pharisee as regards the law" Paul could claim for himself without shame. But there were a great many Pharisees whose life was only outward show—profession but not practice.

Pretence can invade all departments of life, even, as Jesus shows, influencing the attitude in prayer, when the thought that God sees the heart should strip sway the covering put on for men to see. But, as Jesus again makes clear, in that case a man is not praying to God. Although in his uttered words the Pharisee was addressing God, in reality he "prayed with himself". He was posturing, finding satisfaction in his own reflections. He stands apart, feeling assured and satisfied that he is a man apart from others; he is better than other men. He is not guilty of their vices; and on the positive side he fasts, and tithes his income even to the garden herbs, but all the positive things he boasted in concerned external rites. He does not search his heart and his motives; "to do justly, love mercy, and walk humbly with God" does not enter his mind.

In contrast, the publican, despised by his fellow Jews, despises himself as he stands before God. There is no pose, but a stricken sense of sinfulness, as with downcast eyes he smites his breast in his grief. But he appeals to God: "God be merciful to me a sinner"; or as the R.V. margin, "be propitiated"—a hint that the publican had in mind the mercy of the propitiatory—the mercy seat of God in the Holiest. The man must have had some discernment of the significance of the type of the day of atonement, when the High Priest sprinkled the blood of the sin-offering on the cover-lid of the ark of the covenant. He felt the need of mercy, but believed also that the throne of God was one of mercy when the sovereign rights of the Great King were acknowledged in the way He had appointed.

The publican, said Jesus, went away justified—accounted righteous—rather than the Pharisee.

One fundamental difference between the two men is in their realization of their need. Both come to God: both are sinners, but one knows it, the other does not. His failure springs from the very religiousness of his life, with its emphasis on rites. It turns his thoughts from conduct to ceremony, and emphasizing the form he loses sight of the meaning.

Are there no danger signals for us in the Pharisee's attitude? To "do" the "daily readings" from the Scriptures, to attend the meetings—are these actions a means to an end, or an end in itself? It is possible to repeat the offensiveness of the Pharisee, and like him to be blind to the fault.

The self-exalted was abased: he put himself high, but God esteemed him not; but the humble was exalted. In this conclusion Jesus again uses the words of the parable of the feast (Luke 14 : 7-11). There the men who strove for highest place were given the lowest.

Is it without purpose that Luke tells us next of the rich young ruler, who went away sorrowful; and in the following chapter (19) we read of the publican Zacchaeus, to whose house salvation came? Are they the living counterparts of the two men of the parable?

80

THE POUNDS

(Luke 19 : 12-27)

THIS parable closely resembles the parable of the talents recorded by Matthew, considered earlier in this study. In point of time the parable of the pounds was spoken before that of the talents. Luke records the place and circumstances under which the parable of the pounds was spoken, and from these we get a background of local conditions which doubtless suggested the parable. Jesus was near Jericho, or perhaps in Jericho at the house of Zacchaeus (Luke 19 : 1-10), and he was journeying to Jerusalem—less than twenty miles away. It seemed to the crowd, excited about the words and works of Jesus, that Jesus was about to assert his claim to be the Messiah, and to set up his kingdom (verse 11).

Two incidents of contemporary history, one of which had a local interest, may have suggested the parable. Herod the Great, who was first appointed procurator of Galilee by Julius Caesar, and then tetrarch by Anthony, went to Rome in 40 B.C., to oppose the claims of another, and was made king of Judea by the senate of Rome. Archelaus, son of Herod, inheriting the kingdom by his father's will, went to Rome to receive official confirmation of his title. The Jews sent an embassage to Rome to resist his claims but without success; Archelaus was confirmed in the office but without the title of king. Archelaus had enriched Jericho with buildings and owned a splendid palace there. The details of the parable, particularly the feature of Jewish opposition, make the reference to Archelaus practically certain.

The differences in details between the parables of pounds and talents are many. In the talents the leading figure is a householder; in the pounds a nobleman seeking a throne. The talents are distributed unequally, ten, five and one; but all equally receive one pound. Whereas a talent was worth about £250, the pound was only worth about £5. The rewards in the talents are the same; in the pounds they are proportionate to the gains. The talents was spoken to the disciples, but the pounds to a larger company—"a multitude".

In this last fact we may find a starting point for finding the reason for the differences. To disciples Jesus gives talents of varying value, for particular purposes; but in presenting the gospel to the multitude, the gift bestowed is one. The pound then is the one gift shared by all in Christ—the gift of God's salvation.

The large value of the talents denotes that the householder was concerned with the faithful use of the wealth for increase. The small value of the pounds, and the fact that it is given by a nobleman who would be less interested in commerce, suggests that the commission was not so much for the increase of wealth as to test the servants. So it is with the gift of God's grace to all: it is given for testing and for the formation of their character. The knowledge of the gospel is an individual responsibility for each one who receives it: but stewardship within the household varies in degree.

The rewards in the two parables differ: in the talents equal diligence receives equal reward—rulership and a sharing in the joy of the Lord: in the pounds where the endowments are the same but the diligence varies, so the rewards vary. Since the talents are the divinely endowed abilities, their energetic use enables each possessor to enter into the joy of the Master. The service rendered on the basis of the knowledge of the truth—the pound—brings rewards corresponding to increase.

The truth is a deposit, the "good deposit", Paul calls it. By active preaching of the gospel others receive the same "good deposit" as "a treasure" in the "earthen vessels" of mortal flesh; and as more come to know the truth it can be said by metonymy, "The word of God grew and multiplied" (Acts 12 : 24). It is written in the Old Testament that "they that turn many to righteousness shall shine as the brightness of the firmament" (Dan. 12 : 3). Paul gives a more direct application of this idea when he told the Thessalonians that their approval in the presence of the Lord would be his "joy" and "crown of rejoicing" (1 Thess. 2 : 19). Such converts, under another figure, are material gathered for God's house. All this material will be tested: "Every man's work shall be made manifest—if any man's work abide which he hath built thereupon, he shall receive a reward" (1 Cor. 3 : 13, 14). The thought of Paul in this third chapter of the first letter to the Corinthians might be regarded as a comment on the use of the "pounds".

The "inferiority complex" of the man who did not use the talent or the pound is shown in the same language in both parables. In Luke, however, he hid the pound in a napkin—a sweat cloth. Being lazy, he did not need this: he avoided the "sweat" of toil of the curse (Gen. 3 : 17-19); with an appropriate delicate irony the parable says he used the sweat cloth to hide his pound. He avoided the toil and he lost his pound, for the nobleman commanded that it be taken from him. This was right: the knowledge of the gospel has saving power; if it is not used as intended, the possessor having neglected the one means of a future has no title to reward. Take away the gospel from him, and he dies.

Verses 25 and 26 are best regarded as an interjection by the crowd and the Lord's reply. The people demur to the sentence that the pound shall be taken away and that the man with ten should receive one more, oblivious of the fact that his one "pound" having by his labour increased to ten is evidence of his fitness for further commissions. Jesus replies in the paradox which he used more than once. To the one who had increased his portion more is given; but he who had not used his portion loses the portion itself.

An important feature of the parable of the pounds not included in the parable of the talents is the citizens' embassage and its sequel. This feature would not be appropriate to a householder's journey; it belongs to the quest of a throne by a nobleman. The citizens sent an embassage after the nobleman. This actually happened when Archelaus went to Rome; it actually happened after Jesus had gone to the Father. The citizens of the kingdom, who in the parable are distinguished from the servants, are the Jews. After the ascension of Jesus, the apostles preached to the nation of Israel that Jesus was

Christ and Lord, but their message was rejected by the majority. This was equivalent to sending "a message after" Jesus, repudiating his kingship. Such a repudiation on their part was also a rejection of the gospel: and the sequel to that rejection occurs when the Lord returns. After taking account of his servants the nobleman in the parable says: "But those mine enemies, which would not that I should reign over them, bring hither, and slay them before me".

What other counterpart to this can there be than the destruction in the day of judgment, by Christ's command, of the rejecters of the apostles' invitation? The parable shows that they have a responsibility which will bring them from the sleep of death to judgment and destruction. The people were ready to accept his kingship on their own terms at the time when he spoke the parable: when the kingship upon the divinely appointed basis of his sacrifice was proclaimed to them it was rejected. The forecast of this in the parable was therefore a solemn warning that those who rejected him as Saviour and King, will yet meet him as judge to receive condemnation.

The Lord's servants too may find counsel and warning from the parable. The pounds are the Lord's property: while he is away the servants trade with the Lord's "pounds" until he comes: so doing they are engaged in the Lord's work. At times it may be wearying and difficult, but if it is remembered that the use of the pound is service for the Lord, the task becomes easier. Where personal feeling and discouraging obstacles would unite to induce one to desist from a merely human undertaking, nothing permits the Lord's work to cease. To "down tools" leads to loss of everything: to persevere will qualify for fuller service in a future day.

A POSTSCRIPT ON THE SYMBOLIC LANGUAGE IN THE GOSPEL OF JOHN

When we pass from the Synoptic Gospels to John's gospel we find a different range of topics presented for the most part in a different way. There is no parable like the Sower, no emphasis upon the kingdom of God; instead, the emphasis is on the person of Jesus Christ, his relationship to God, his work as the Saviour from death and hence his identity with the Messiah—for the Messiah of the prophets is a righteous man, redeemed and redeeming. The difference between the fourth gospel and the Synoptic gospels arises out of the particular purpose of that gospel. John wrote that men "might believe that Jesus is the Christ, the Son of God, and that believing they might have life through his name" (20 : 31). John's choice of incident and of the discourses of Jesus was made to illustrate his theme. How well he did it is clear to all who have given time and thought to his writings.

None of the parables we have previously looked at fits into John's scheme; Jesus did not speak his parables to illustrate the particular points upon which John focuses attention. John, however, introduces those discourses of Jesus in which his sonship to God and his relationship to men are the principal themes. These subjects were matters of Old Testament prediction, often not in spoken word, but in typical incident.

We have seen that the figures which are the basis of Christ's parables are rooted in Old Testament statements, in using which Jesus implicitly made a claim to be the Messiah. In the discourses in John's gospel, Jesus turns to events in the history of Israel and unfolds their meaning in relation to himself. In this respect John's record is to the gospels what the letter to the Hebrews is to the other epistles. Paul expounds in the letter to the Hebrews what he calls the "parable" (Heb. 9 : 9) of the Tabernacle, its furniture and the offerings; and the typical work of Aaron as priest; Moses, Joshua and Melchisedec are cited as types of Jesus. In the discourses in John's gospel Jesus himself expounds the "parable" of a number of incidents. In like manner in his prologue John touches on the experience of Moses, who saw God's glory while not permitted to "see God", and contrasts the fading glory, which on Moses' face reflected the glory in which for a little time he had been enveloped, with the abiding glory embodied in Jesus. John handles the theme with allusive reference to the events, expecting from his readers a sympathetic knowledge of the Old Testament. In this respect he reflects his Master's method in the addresses he records.

In chapter 1, the episode in which Nathanael finds the Messiah reflects Jacob's quest for the blessing of God. Jesus showed a knowledge of Nathanael's thought when he called him "an Israelite indeed, in whom there was no guile". The reference to Jacob, who prevailed to become a prince with God is clear, but it is confirmed by the reference by Jesus to the dream of Jacob's ladder and his assertion that the dream would be fulfilled in himself (1 : 51).

In chapter 2 Jesus speaks of the temple to be destroyed by the Jews but to be reared up in three days (verse 19). John explains that he spake of the temple of his body. Behind the figure is the history of God's dwelling place in Israel, first in the tabernacle and then in the temple built by Solomon. Jesus was the word made flesh *tabernacling* among us, as John affirmed (1 : 14). Related to this thought is the reference at the end of the ministry to the Father's house in which are many abiding places (14 : 1). We know from Luke that after his resurrection the Lord expounded out of the law and the prophets the things concerning himself—an experience which led his disciples to exclaim, "Did not our hearts burn within us while he talked with us by the way?" What might not the Lord have said had he extended his exposition of God's dwelling places!

Moses lifting up the serpent in the wilderness that serpent-bitten disobedient Israelites might find healing was no legend in the estimate of Jesus but history written with a divine purpose, and particularly with himself in view. The incident in Numbers 21 : 9 was amplified by Jesus as a type of himself; it was part of the volume of the book written concerning him, and being so written it expressed his Father's will which he must accomplish. This application carries with it an authentication of the part played by the serpent in Gen. 3—for only if that record is history can men be regarded as serpent-bitten, and in need of the healing which gives life through the crucified Son of God.

The living water of which Jesus spoke to the woman of Samaria turns the thought to Old Testament references to God the fountain of living waters, and to the covenants of life which God has made (Isa. 55 :1).

The manna in the wilderness is seen with Christ's guidance to foreshadow Jesus as the Son of God provided that men who would otherwise perish might have life (John 6 : 33). When, however, they "strove among themselves" about his claims to be the "living bread", he perplexed them further by taking up the other Old Testament use of the "bread of God". The offerings on the altar were so described in the Law (Lev. 21 : 6, etc.); and Jesus refers to his own offering of himself in sacrifice in the allusion to "eating his flesh and drinking his blood".

In Exodus 16 and 17 the provision of manna and of the water from the smitten rock are recorded in close connection. In John's gospel the Lord's application of the type of the smitten rock to himself as the giver of water of life follows the discourse on the manna (see John 6 and 7).

Another wilderness experience of Israel is behind the saying of Jesus that he was the light of the world. The custom of lighting lamps in Jerusalem at the feast of Tabernacles celebrated God's guidance of Israel by the pillar of fire (8 : 12).

The shepherd allegory of chapter 10 is based upon the shepherd references to God in the Old Testament, e.g., Psa. 23, Ezek. 34 : 12. The vine allegory of chapter 15 takes up the Old Testament allusions to Israel as the vine of God.

There are other more casual allusions—"the grain of wheat" and "the travail of a woman" and a few others—which catch up the thought of Old Testament references and carry them forward to their particular fulfilment.

This brief review shows how the figures of John's gospel both in origin and form are different from those of the other gospels. The fuller exposition of these figures belongs to the study of types and not of parables. They are considered in their context in the *Exposition of the Gospel of John*.

INDEX

(Parables are marked with an asterisk)

Genesis
1 : ... 16
3 : ... 264
3 : 17-19 ... 260
4 : 3, 4 ... 60
4 : 24 ... 129
15 : 6 ... 157
18 : 6 ... 104
18 : 14 ... 134
46 : 4 ... 199

Exodus
2 : 14 ... 209
16, 17 ... 264
20 : 8-12 ... 76
30 : 12, 13 ... 204
31 : 12-17 ... 76

Leviticus
2 : 13 ... 11
11 : 12 ... 40
19 : 18 ... 202
21 : 6 ... 264
27 : 30 ... 159

Numbers
15 : 9 ... 104
21 : 9 ... 264
29 : 12-34 ... 197

Deuteronomy
6 : 5 ... 202
14 : 22 ... 159
15 : 9 ... 25
18 : 21, 22 ... 145
24 : 5 ... 223
28 : 49 ... 163
30 : 11, 13, 19 ... 42

Joshua
6 : 26 ... 203

Judges
6 : 19 ... 104

1 Samuel
1 : 24 ... 104
25 : 11 ... 210

2 Samuel
21 : 17 ... 19
22 : 2, 32, 47 ... 53
22 : 29 ... 19

1 Kings
8 : 41-43 ... 246
12 : 4 ... 73

2 Kings
8 : 13 ... 38
21 : 1 ... 154

2 Chronicles
36 : 15, 16 ... 148

Job
2 : 10 ... 181
15 : 24, 25 ... 226
38 : 7 ... 232
39 : 40 ... 168
42 : 34 ... 226

Psalms
1 : 3, 5, 6 ... 42
9 : 8, 13, 14 ... 122
16 : 11 ... 183
18 : 25-27 ... 137
19 : ... 58
21 : 1 ... 183
22 : 2 ... 189
23 : ... 265
27 : 14 ... 193
28 : 1 ... 53
31 : 2 ... 53
32 : 6 ... 21
35 : 7 ... 79
40 : 2 ... 79
45 : ... 58
51 : 4 ... 234
61 : 2 ... 53
68 : ... 82
72 : 1 ... 155
80 : 8-16 ... 147
88 : 3, 4 ... 79
107 : 18 ... 122
118 : 22, 23 ... 151
118 : 26 ... 164
119 : 105 ... 19
132 : 17 ... 19
146 : 8 ... 115

Proverbs
1 : 32 ... 211
12 : 7 ... 52
14 : 11 ... 52
20 : 4 ... 200
23 : 6, 7 ... 25
25 : 6, 7 ... 219
26 : 14 ... 18
28 : 22 ... 25
30 : 17 ... 168

Ecclesiastes
11 : 4 ... 200

Song
5 : 1 ... 214

Isaiah
2 : 3, 4 ... 105
5 : 1-7 ... 147
5 : 2, 4 ... 148
8 : 14, 15 151, 152
9 : 2 ... 16
9 : 4 ... 73
14 : 9 ... 188
22 : 23 ... 186
25 : 6 63, 223
25 : 6-8 ... 214
26 : 4 ... 53
26 : 21 ... 190
28 : 16 ... 122
28 : 16, 17 ... 151
35 : 5 ... 115
38 : 18 ... 122
40 : 11 ... 229
42 : 7, 16, 18 ... 115
43 : 8 ... 116
44 : 8 ... 53
49 : 6 ... 215
49 : 9 ... 82
49 : 18 ... 61
49 : 24, 25 ... 82
50 : 4 ... 75
50 : 10 ... 15
50 : 10, 11 ... 215
52 : 1 ... 61
53 : 3 ... 198
53 : 6 ... 229
53 : 11 ... 56
54 : 4, 5 ... 254
54 : 5, 6 ... 58
55 : 1 ... 264
55 : 1-3 63, 178, 204
55 : 10 ... 92
55 : 10, 11 90, 193
58 : 6 ... 73
59 : 1-10 ... 116
59 : 5, 6 ... 61
59 : 20 ... 14
60 : 1 ... 14
60 : 2 ... 16
60 : 19, 20 ... 14
61 : 1, 2 ... 154
61 : 1, 10 ... 60
61 : 3, 10 ... 61
61 : 10 ... 154
62 : 1 ... 154
62 : 6, 7 ... 252
63 : 10 ... 20
64 : 6 ... 61
65 : 8-9 ... 63

Jeremiah
2 : 20 ... 73
2 : 21 ... 147
5 : 6 ... 45
6 : 16 ... 75
21 : 8 ... 42
24 : 1-3 ... 142
28 : ... 73
31 : 27 ... 92
32 : 17 ... 134
32 : 27 ... 135

Lamentations
1 : 1 ... 255
3 : 27 ... 73

Ezekiel
12 : 5 ... 172
15 : 1-16 ... 147
17 : 22-24 ... 142
19 : 10-14 ... 147
22 : 27 ... 45
33 : ... 101
34 : 5, 23 ... 65
34 : 12 ... 265

Daniel
2 : 44 ... 152
4 : 12 ... 101
9 : 26 153, 156
12 : 3 ... 259

Hosea
2 : 19, 20 ... 155
2 : 21-23 ... 92
5 : 13 ... 56
5 : 15 ... 56
6 : ... 78
6 : 1 ... 56
6 : 6 ... 55
7 : 1 ... 56
9 : 10 ... 142
10 : 1 ... 147
13 : 9 ... 56

Joel
1 : 7 ... 142
3 : 11, 12 ... 186

Zephaniah
1 : 17 ... 116
3 : 3 ... 45

Haggai
1 : 8 ... 45

Zechariah
9 : 9 141, 144
14 : 4 ... 143

Malachi
4 : 2 ... 14

Matthew
1 : ... 53
2 : 15 ... 53
3 : 17 ... 53
4 : 1-11 ... 53
4 : 16 ... 116
4 : 17-22 ... 109
4 : 23 ... 53
5 : 7 ... 113
*5 : 13 ... 9
5 : 16 ... 177
*5 : 14 ... 14
5 : 14-16 ... 16
*5 : 15, 16 ... 17
*5 : 25 ... 20
*6 : 19, 21 ... 23
6 : 22 ... 19
*6 : 22, 23 ... 25
6 : 23 ... 41
6 : 24 ... 27
*6 : 25-34 ... 29
6 : 26-30 ... 39
6 : 33 ... 32
7 : 1, 2 ... 35
*7 : 2 ... 32
*7 : 3-5 ... 35
*7 : 6 ... 37
7 : 7 ... 207
7 : 7-12 ... 208
7 : 9 ... 39
*7 : 9, 10 ... 39
7 : 11 39, 41
*7 : 13, 14 ... 41
*7 : 15 ... 44
*7 : 16-20 ... 46
7 : 21-27 ... 178
*7 : 24-27 ... 48
7 : 24-28 ... 122
8 : 6-8 ... 54
8 : 14 ... 54
8 : 17 ... 54
*8 : 19-22 ... 196
8 : 37 ... 53
9 : 1-8 ... 167
*9 : 12 ... 54
9 : 13 ... 78
9 : 14 ... 57
*9 : 15 ... 56
9 : 15 155, 254
*9 : 16 ... 59
*9 : 17 ... 62
9 : 35, 36 ... 64
9 : 35, 37, 38 65
9 : 36 ... 229
*9 : 36-38 ... 64
10 : 6 65, 116
*10 : 16 ... 44
10 : 16 ... 198
*10 : 38 ... 67
*11 : 7-19 ... 69
11 : 7, 8 ... 70
11 : 12 ... 71
11 : 15 ... 72
*11 : 29 ... 73
12 : 10 ... 78
*12 : 11, 12 ... 76
12 : 11 ... 218
12 : 14-21 ... 71
*12 : 22-30 ... 80
*12 : 43-45 ... 83
*13 : 3-9 ... 86
13 : 11-17 ... 87
13 : 14 ... 198
13 : 19 ... 88
*13 : 24-30
36-43 ... 92
13 : 24, 31, 33
44, 45, 47 88
*13 : 31, 32 ... 99
*13 : 33 ... 103
*13 : 34 ... 105
13 : 36 ... 105
*13 : 45, 46 ... 108
*13 : 47, 50 109
*13 : 52 ... 110
15 : 1-9 ... 241
*15 : 14 ... 113
*15 : 22-28 ... 116
*16 : 13-19 ... 118
16 : 18 ... 119
16 : 21, 25, 26 68
*16 : 24 ... 67
16 : 27 69, 138
*17 : 20 ... 123
18 : 1-13 ... 128
*18 : 7-13 ... 125
18 : 17 ... 93
*18 : 23-35 ... 128
*19 : 16-30 ... 131
19 : 30 135, 158
*20 : 1-16 ... 135
20 : 16 ... 158
20 : 18, 19 ... 69
*21 : 18-22 ... 140
21 : 21 ... 124
21 : 23 ... 141
*21 : 28-32 ... 144
*21 : 33-41 ... 147
*21 : 42 ... 150
*22 : 1-14 ... 153
*23 : ... 113
23 : 6, 7 ... 198
23 : 12 ... 219
*23 : 23, 24 ... 158
*23 : 25, 26 ... 160
*23 : 27, 28 ... 161
*23 : 37 ... 162
*24 : 27 ... 165
24 : 27 ... 168
*24 : 28 ... 168
*24 : 32-35 ... 140
24 : 34-58 ... 170
*24 : 42-44 ... 171
24 : 42-44 ... 173
24 : 42-51 ... 212
*24 : 45-51 ... 173
24 : 45 ... 175
*25 : 1-13 ... 175
*25 : 14-30 ... 180
*25 : 31-46 ... 185
25 : 31-46 ... 239

Mark
*2 : 17 ... 54
2 : 18 ... 57
*2 : 19 ... 56
*2 : 21 ... 59
*2 : 22 ... 62
3 : 4 ... 78
*3 : 22-30 ... 80
*4 : 1-20 ... 86
*4 : 21-25 ... 17
*4 : 24 ... 32
*4 : 26-29 ... 190
*4 : 30-32 ... 99
4 : 33-34 ... 99
6 : 34 ... 187
*7 : 24-30 ... 116
7 : 28 ... 127
*8 : 34 ... 67
*9 : 41-48 ... 125
*9 : 49, 50 ... 9
*10 : 17-22 ... 131
10 : 38-40 ... 216
12 : 1-9 .. 147
12 : 10, 11 ... 150

Luke
1 : 37 ... 135
2 : 34 ... 152
3 : 24 ... 205
4 : 18 ... 154
5 : 7 ... 109
5 : 16 ... 205
*5 : 31 ... 54
*5 : 33, 34 56, 57
*5 : 36 ... 59
*5 : 37-39 ... 62
6 : 12 ... 205
*6 : 38 ... 32
*6 : 39-41 ... 113
*6 : 41, 42 ... 35
*6 : 43, 44 ... 46
*6 : 46-49 ... 48
*7 : 18-33 ... 69
*7 : 41-43 ... 194
*8 : 1-14 ... 86
*8 : 16 ... 17
9 : 1 ... 65
9 : 1-6 ... 197
9 : 18 ... 205
9 : 22 ... 198
*9 : 23 ... 67
9 : 23 ... 197
9 : 29 ... 205
9 : 44 ... 198
9 : 53 ... 198
*9 : 57-62 ... 196
10 : 1 65, 197
*10 : 2 ... 64
10 : 2, 3 ... 199
10 : 3 ... 198
10 : 4 198, 200
10 : 8 ... 198
10 : 10 ... 198
10 : 16 ... 198
*10 : 18 ... 165
*10 : 25-37 ... 201
11 : 1 ... 205
*11 : 5-13 ... 205
*11 : 11 ... 39
*11 : 14-23 ... 80
*11 : 24-26 ... 83
*11 : 33 ... 17
*11 : 34-36 ... 25
*11 : 39, 40 ... 160
*11 : 44 ... 161
11 : 49 ... 73
11 : 52 ... 123
12 : 15 ... 210
*12 : 16-21 ... 209
*12 : 22-31 ... 29
*12 : 33, 34 ... 23
*12 : 35-38 ... 212
12 : 35-38 ... 251
*12 : 39, 40 ... 171
*12 : 41-48 ... 173
*12 : 49 ... 215
12 : 49 ... 22
*12 : 58, 59 ... 20
13 : 1-21 ... 102
13 : 15 ... 218
*13 : 18, 19 ... 99
*13 : 20, 21 ... 103
*13 : 23-24 ... 41
13 : 32, 33 ... 163
*13 : 34 ... 162
*14 : 5 ... 218
14 : 5-24 ... 217
*14 : 7-11 ... 219
14 : 7-11 ... 257
*14 : 12-14 ... 220
14 : 15 ... 222
*14 : 16-24 ... 222
14 : 26, 27 ... 225
14 : 26, 27, 33 13
*14 : 27 ... 67
*14 : 28-32 ... 224
*14 : 34, 35 ... 9
15 : ... 241
15 : 1-17 : 10 227
15 : 1, 2 227, 244
*15 : 3, 7 ... 227
*15 : 8-10 ... 230
15 : 11-32 ... 223
*16 : 1-12 ... 237
16 : 1-12 ... 229
16 : 13-18 ... 229

16 : 16, 17 ... 224
16 : 16-18 237, 245
*16 : 19-31 ... 244
17 : 1, 2 ... 248
17 : 1-6 ... 229
*17 : 6 ... 123
17 : 7 ... 124
*17 : 7-10 ... 247
17 : 7-10 ... 214
17 : 20 ... 170
17 : 20, 21 ... 165
17 : 21-37 ... 252
17 : 22 ... 251
17 : 22-24, 25 166
*17 : 24 ... 165
17 : 26-29 ... 254
*17 : 37 ... 168
*18 : 1-8 ... 251
*18 : 9-14 ... 255
18 : 14 ... 219
*18 : 18-23 ... 131
19 : ... 257
19 : 1-10, 11 ... 258
*19 : 12-27 ... 257
19 : 12-27 ... 180
*20 : 9-16 ... 147
*20 : 17 ... 150
21 : 29 ... 143
21 : 34 ... 173
23 : 46 ... 206

John

1 : 3 ... 14
1 : 14 ... 263
1 : 51 ... 263
2 : ... 64
3 : 20, 21 ... 177
3 : 29 56, 57, 155
4 : 35-38, 39 66
5 : 9 ... 76
5 : 25 ... 199
6 : 7 ... 264
6 : 26-29 ... 189
6 : 33 ... 264
7 : 22, 23 ... 79
8 : 12 15, 264
8 : 33 ... 74
9 : 5 ... 15
9 : 29-40 ... 115
11 : 9 ... 15
11 : 47-57 ... 246
12 : 35, 36 ... 15
12 : 46-48 ... 15
13 : 5-17 ... 213
14 : 1 ... 263
14 : 29 ... 181
15 : ... 265
19 : 4-6 ... 242
20 : 31 ... 262
21 : 17 ... 119

Acts

4 : 11 ... 153
4 : 11, 12 ... 121
7 : 51-53 ... 148
8 : ... 66
12 : 24 ... 259
13 : 46 38, 224
13 : 46, 47 ... 156
15 : 10 ... 74
15 : 14 156, 254
20 : 28, 29 ... 45

Romans

3 : 21-25 ... 216
4 : 3-8 ... 157
6 : 8 ... 204
6 : 16-22 ... 250
7 : 14 ... 74
8 : 1-3 ... 135
8 : 6 ... 26
9 : 23, 33 ... 153
10 : 42, 58
12 : 2 ... 192
12 : 8 ... 26

1 Corinthians

1 : 23 ... 153
2 : 11 ... 122
5 : 6 ... 47
5 : 11 ... 93
7 : 21-23 ... 250
9 : 27 ... 253
10 : 4 ... 121
12 : 4-11 ... 181

2 Corinthians

3 : ... 247
3 : 13, 14 ... 260
4 : 4 ... 16
8 : 1, 2 ... 26
9 : 6 ... 138
9 : 8, 11, 13 ... 26

Galatians

1 : 9 ... 32
5 : 9 ... 47
6 : 1 ... 231

Ephesians

2 : 20-22 ... 153
4 : 8 82, 181
4 : 29 ... 12
4 : 31, 32 ... 131
5 : 8 ... 16
6 : 5, 6 ... 26

Philippians

2 : 14-16 ... 17
3 : 2 ... 38
3 : 15, 16 ... 177
4 : 13 ... 135

Colossians

2 : 6, 7 ... 54
3 : 22 ... 26
4 : 6 ... 12

1 Thessalonians

2 : 16 ... 155
2 : 19 ... 259
5 : 1-3 ... 172
5 : 3 ... 173

2 Thessalonians

3 : 6 ... 93

1 Timothy

6 : 3-5 ... 93
6 : 17 ... 239

2 Timothy

2 : 15 112, 114

Titus

3 : 10 ... 93

Hebrews

2 : 11 ... 189
4 : 9 ... 78
6 : 7, 8 ... 48
8 : 2 ... 78
9 : 9 ... 262
12 : 2 183, 222

James

2 : 20-26 ... 157
3 : 1 ... 114
5 : 7 ... 191

1 Peter

1 : 10-12 ... 231
1 : 23 ... 90
2 : 4, 5, 6 ... 121
2 : 6-8 ... 153
2 : 7 ... 24
5 : 5 ... 213

2 Peter

1 : 19 ... 14

1 John

2 : 4 ... 47
4 : 2, 3 ... 47

2 John

8-10 ... 93
10, 11 ... 32

Jude

23 ... 62

Revelation

1 : 18 ... 122
2 : ... 47
2 : 7, 17, 26 ... 183
3 : ... 47
3 : 5, 12, 21 ... 183
3 : 20, 21 ... 213
11 : 18 ... 190
12 : 9 ... 189
13 : 1-11 ... 18[illegible]
14 : 15, 16 ... 19[illegible]
19 : 7, 8 ... 15[illegible]
19 : 8, 9 ... 21[illegible]
19 : 20 189, 19[illegible]
20 : 2 ... 8[illegible]
20 : 2, 10 ... 18[illegible]
21 : 7, 8 ... 18[illegible]
21 : 14 ... 11[illegible]
21 : 23 ... 1[illegible]
22 : 12 ... 13[illegible]
22 : 14, 15 ... 18[illegible]
22 : 15 ... 3[illegible]